Regaining Educational Leadership

Regaining Educational Leadership:

Critical Essays On PBTE/CBTE, Behavioral Objectives and Accountability

Ralph A. Smith, *Editor*
Bureau of Educational Research
and Department of Educational Policy Studies
University of Illinois at Urbana-Champaign

John Wiley & Sons, Inc.
New York / London / Sydney / Toronto

Library of Congress Cataloging in Publication Data
Smith, Ralph Alexander, comp.
    Regaining educational leadership.

    Includes bibliographical references and index.
    CONTENTS: Smith, R. A.   Introduction: educational criticism and the PPBS movement in education.—
Atkin, J. M. Professional leadership and PBTE.— ,
Broudy, H. S. CBTE/PBTE—[etc.]
    1.   Teachers, Training of—United States—Addresses, essays, lectures.   I.   Title.

LB1715.S4843   370'.732   74-22249
ISBN 0-471-80362-6
ISBN 0-471-80363-4 (pbk.)

Printed in the United States of America

10 9 8 7 6 5 4 3 2 1

To the College of Education of
the University of Illinois
at Urbana-Champaign

Preface

As I was assembling this collection of essays, efforts to promote efficiency in schooling were advancing and retreating: advancing where political bodies have been successful in enforcing various forms of accountability and retreating where opposition has flared up from individual teachers, teachers' unions, lay groups, and the educational profession. California and Florida are, no doubt, leading in attempts to achieve educational efficiency but, along with Texas, Michigan, and other states, are beginning to experience the consequences that follow from any attempt to impose a technical solution on educational affairs. Although much has been made of the purported ineffectiveness of the schools and of the so-called mindlessness of educationists, the essays here attest to the vitality of educational analysis and criticism, and they point up (in some instances with apologies for stating the obvious) that teachers and schools cannot be held solely responsible for the damage caused by massive upheavals in society at large. The essays speak eloquently for themselves, and the Introduction provides a context in which aspects of the efficiency movement may be more clearly perceived. Therefore, nothing needs to be said about the essays here, except a few words about their potential audiences.

In one respect the audience for this book is almost unlimited, since practically all levels of teaching, administration, and policy making have been affected in one way or another by the efficiency syndrome—by PPBS, PBTE/CBTE, behavioral objectives, accountability, and cost benefit analysis. Still, certain contexts come immediately to mind, such as undergraduate and graduate courses in educational administration, educational psychology, curriculum, and theoretical foundations (that is, the history and philosophy of education, educational policy studies, and cultural foundations). Educational workers in state departments of education will find the volume helpful in unraveling the political, economic, and distinctively educational issues that inevitably become blurred in government. And educational workers in the national government, in HEW and other units, may discover, if they do not already know, why resistance is often the reaction to national priorities, programs, and strategies in the area of education. If nothing else, this book says that legislative enforcement of efficiency has gone far enough and that it is time for a proper division of labor to be accepted. The government must learn to give professionals and lay groups the responsibility for educational decision-making that rightfully belongs to them. If this is done, then the inherently manipulative actions of government in policy matters will be neutralized. Indeed, educational leadership and diplomacy have no more urgent task in the years ahead than to articulate the nature of the complex polity that makes educational decisions in a democratic mass society. When this is done, we will be in a better position to understand the role of government and technique in the area of educational policy-making.

Ralph A. Smith

Acknowledgments

Gratitude is expressed first of all to the authors who either wrote original essays for this volume (J. Myron Atkin, Hugh Petrie, Frederick Rodgers, Philip Smith, Mauritz Johnson, Donald Arnstine, Arthur Wirth, Maxine Greene, and Walter Clark, Jr.) or gave their kind permission to reprint their work. Thanks are also extended to publishers and the staff of John Wiley with whom it has been a pleasure to work. I am especially indebted to Paul Nash of Boston University who suggested Wiley as a potential publisher. Any book involves attention to numerous details, and for conscientiousness in such matters, Mrs. Glenda Rhoads has been invaluable. Finally, I wish to mention the College of Education at the University of Illinois at Urbana-Champaign from which I have received continuous intellectual stimulation and support for the past ten years.

R.A.S.

Contents

1. Introduction: Educational Criticism and the PPBS Movement in Education
   Ralph A. Smith, Editor   1

2. Professional Leadership and PBTE
   J. Myron Atkin   15

3. CBTE/PBTE—Do They Mean What They Say?
   Harry S. Broudy   24

4. Performance-Based Teaching: A New Orthodoxy?
   Frederick C. Neff   36

5. Conceptual Confusion and Premature Policies
   Mauritz Johnson   46

6. Can Education Find Its Lost Objectives Under the Street Lamp of Behaviorism?
   Hugh G. Petrie   64

7. Instructional Objectives and Observable Behavior
   Philip G. Smith   75

8. Educational Objectives and Existential Heroes
   Leonard J. Waks   87

9. The Adequacy of Systems Management Procedures in Education
   Michael W. Apple   104

10. The Ideology of Accountability in Schooling
    Martin Levit   122

11. The Dominion of Economic Accountability
    Ernest R. House   135

12. Accountability: What Does Not Go Without Saying
    Harry S. Broudy   149

13. PBTE and Measurement: A Program Based on a Mistake
    Donald Arnstine   165

14. Minority Groups and PBTE
    Frederick A. Rodgers   176

15. *A Humanistic Approach to Performance-Based*   186
    Teacher Education
    Paul Nash
16. *Choice versus Performance: An Existential Look*   202
    at PBTE
    Maxine Greene
17. *PBTE: A Question of Values*   212
    Arthur G. Wirth
18. *Performance-Based Teacher Education and the*   224
    Teaching of English
    Walter H. Clark, Jr.
19. *Do Behavioral Objectives and Accountability*   235
    Have a Place in Art Education?
    Elliot W. Eisner
    Editor   247
    Contributors   249
    Index   253

Introduction:
Educational Criticism and the PPBS Movement in Education

The general purpose of this volume is to provide critical perspectives on selected aspects of the efficiency movement in contemporary education, especially on what is known as performance-based and competency-based teacher education. The discussions are intended primarily for policy-makers, administrators, teachers, students, and the concerned public. My principal objective is to restrain the momentum of what I call the PPBS movement in education. Although this movement is rife with conceptual confusion and poses fundamental ethical issues, these facts have not prevented educational policies based on questionable premises from being prematurely enacted. Indeed, given the ways in which the situation has evolved, the task is nothing less than that of regaining educational leadership from those who have committed themselves, the schools, and teacher preparation to a technical ideology that fails to do justice to the complexity of educational enterprise. The technocratic mode of mind—that is, a mode of mind that fastens on instrumentalities at the expense of substantive considerations—must be relegated to its proper place in the theory and practice of education. This is a necessity lest the tragic consequences of educational history be visited upon present and future generations.

It will be recalled that in his account of the cult of efficiency in American education from 1910 to 1929, Raymond Callahan acknowledged that resisting the business-managerial conception of administration would have been difficult for schoolmen—business ideology was after all pervasive in the society. But some leadership, he believed, could have been expected from the universities where superintendents and principals were receiving their training. University professors, however, chose to move with the tide, as many are choosing to do today and, instead of exerting a restrain-

1

ing influence on the efficiency movement, professors of education contributed to the movement's momentum. The educational tragedy that resulted, claims Callahan, was fourfold. It came to be

> . . . that educational questions were subordinated to business considerations; that administrators were produced who were not, in any true sense, educators; that a scientific label was put on some very unscientific and dubious methods and practices; and that an anti-intellectual climate, already prevalent, was strengthened. As the business-industrial values and procedures spread into the thinking and acting of educators, countless educational decisions were made on economic or on non-educational grounds.[1]

The lessons of history are seldom learned, and it is not surprising that many of the practices noted by Callahan are being repeated today, although, one is tempted to add, with a vengeance. What is different today, however, is that many educators in higher education are not moving with the tide and are insisting that before enacting new policies, decision-makers should at least confront relevant educational, conceptual, and ethical issues. I refer of course to the contributors to this volume and many others. These educators are thus attempting to exert the kind of restraining influence on educational technocracy which Callahan lamented was absent in the period he studied. Such educators are not, it should be emphasized, necessarily anti-technology or anti-technique, or for that matter merely negative in their criticism. Indeed several of them have written wisely on the role of technology in a system of democratic mass education. And alternatives to typical P/CBTE schemes are suggested in many of their writings. What they are providing are critical analyses of misleading or erroneous ideas either tacitly assumed or explicitly stated by advocates of efficiency in contemporary education, and in so doing they are rendering the public and the educational profession a valuable service. Before discussing some of the dimensions of the contemporary efficiency movement, a few words are in order about the meaning of the expression "the PPBS movement in education" and how it tends to involve performance-based and competency-based conceptions of teacher preparation, as well as related notions such as behavioral objectives and accountability. For although a great deal of educational criticism addresses itself to the concepts of performance-based and competency-based teacher education, referred to here as P/CBTE, and associated notions, it is within the context of a PPBS approach to education that I think such notions assume their full significance. I underline this point because contributors to this volume do not

---

[1] Raymond E. Callahan, *Education and the Cult of Efficiency* (Chicago: University of Chicago Press, 1962), pp. 246-47.

in large explicitly discuss PPBS (Planning, Programming, Budgeting, Systems).

The PPBS Movement in Education

The history of the PPBS movement in education is yet to be written for the obvious reason that it is still evolving. Some of its roots, however, can be located in the history of curriculum reform in American education, in behavioral psychological theory, and in recent theories of management science and systems analysis design. Many of the essential elements of PPBS were fashioned by the Rand Corporation while studying Air Force deterrence strategies and were later incorporated into Defense Department planning under Robert MacNamara, and then by executive order of President Johnson into all governmental agencies, including Health, Education, and Welfare. Leo Ruth has written that state and local implementation of PPBS procedures follows closely the procedures described in President Johnson's Bureau of the Budget Bulletin No. 66-3, dated October 12, 1965, titled "Planning-Programming-Budgeting."[2]

In education, PPBS has thus come to imply procedures for educational planning, preparing budgets, evaluating performance, and allocating resources. Although performance-based and competency-based conceptions of teaching and learning and new methods of teacher certification are not logically entailed by a PPBS approach, they are compatible with it. In other words, once a school system decides to plan in the manner of PPBS a sequence of events tends to follow. And whether or not the same sequence is replicated in each instance, the character of PPBS and associated activities is such as to raise a number of important questions about procedure. For example, in the first issue of the *PPBS Users Newsletter*,[3] the director of evaluation and research for a Pennsylvania school district described how they got started in PPBS, and I am assuming that this is characteristic of PPBS's educational style.

The PPBS activity of this district involved first of all the development of a program structure, a program budget, and a program analysis in a selected curricular area, in this case second-grade reading (called reading at the third level primary team). Second-grade reading was the program level (i.e., the elementary level) of a program (in reading) that was included in a program group (e.g., basic instruction in contrast to business affairs), that was part of a program area (instructional programs in contrast to instructional support and community services). After the development of the program structure a new program budget showing cost data

---

[2] Leo Ruth, "Dangers of Systemthink in Education," in H. B. Maloney, ed., *Accountability and the Teaching of English* (Urbana, Ill.: National Council of Teachers of English, 1972), pp. 67-74.

[3] *PPBS Users Newsletter*, 1 (January 1972), pp. 9-12. The newsletter is now defunct.

was prepared. As the author of the article states, in "a PPB System, the program budget requires not only new forms and procedures, but involves instructions and guidance on the use of the document for policy formulation, long-range planning, evaluating programs and allocating resources."

The next step consisted of a program analysis, which was defined as "the identification and utilization of specific elements within a program," such elements being necessary preconditions for program evaluation and further planning. The elements of the analysis consisted of (1) the title of the program, (2) a description of the program and its processes, (3) program goals, (4) program objectives, (5) program constraints, (6) a program budget, and (7) program accomplishments. The program in reading ultimately involved 24 teachers in eight elementary schools who were responsible for about 550 pupils.

Central to the program analysis undertaken was the careful specification of objectives, where an objective was defined as "a desired result that can be measured within a given time and under specific conditions. It satisfies all the criteria for a behavioral objective."

Accordingly, second-grade reading objectives were formulated in precise behavioral terms. An initial list of 109 objectives was pared down to 20 "crucial" objectives deemed "most essential for achievement" by second-grade pupils in reading. Agreement was also reached on the kinds of tests to be used. The formal process of measuring pupil achievement then began. At the end of the instructional period, 539 pupil progress forms from the eight elementary schools were submitted to the district office for statistical compilation and analysis, and then later presented to the various schools. The achievement data included (1) the percentage of achievement on a district-wide basis of the twenty objectives arranged in rank order, (2) the acceptable level of performance for each objective by both school and district, (3) the percentage of achievement for each objective by both school and district, (4) the highest and lowest achieved objectives by both school and district, and (5) the percentage of achievement by broad reading skill areas by both school and district.

No mention is made in the description in question that reading achievement scores were actually increased, but it is claimed that there were nonetheless "benefits." The first benefit, purportedly, was a more efficient allocation of resources, especially of the teacher's time. "If the teacher," it is said, "is able to allocate her time, as well as other resources . . . to meet the needs of the pupils in the most beneficial and economical manner, then a positive cost-benefit correlation can be achieved. To this end the teacher needs to define exactly what she is trying to accomplish (desired outputs), to measure performance of individual students toward the achievement of the objectives (actual outputs), and to allocate her resources in such a way as to close the gap between the two before the end of the year." Other benefits that were claimed for this approach to reading were more purposeful instruction, more effective student evaluation, and progress toward comprehensive planning. At one point, it is said that because "a great deal of the measurement has to be done on an individual (teacher-pupil) basis, the project tended to humanize the instructional program."

Here then is an image of the sequence of activities involved in a PPBS approach, a sample of the language, and a sense of the PPBS style. Now what does this approach have to do with P/CBTE, that is, with performance-based and competency-based modes of teacher education, accountability, behavioral objectives, systems analysis, and other topics discussed by authors in this volume? The links can be discerned in the following ways. Performance-based and competency-based programs of teacher preparation, and teacher certification based on such programs, can be construed as one way to prepare teachers for the reading program just described. Graduates of such teacher preparation programs would presumably (a) be able to write behavioral objectives for reading, (b) be willing to be held accountable for achieving specified outcomes, (c) be capable of recasting their teaching in light of test data, and (d) be willing to adopt a cost-benefit attitude toward instruction and education, to adopt, for example, a technocratic mode of thinking and acting. Again, it is not that a PPBS approach to education *requires* the use of behavioral objectives, commitments to P/CBTE schemes of teacher preparation, and the management of schooling by measurable results. It is simply, if I am right, that these things tend to get associated and lumped together.

What is wrong with this way of teaching reading, or of preparing teachers in P/CBTE programs who will teach this way? Shouldn't professional institutions graduate competent pedagogical performers? First of all, it should be noted that the Pennsylvania school district in question intends to specify and measure "outputs" in *all* program areas "so that teaching and administrative decisions regarding resource allocation can be made." Therefore, it is not simply a matter of teaching reading. The PPBS approach is to be used in planning and evaluating the whole curriculum. Again, the effort, if successful, would have the effect of making all teachers, including teachers of the arts and humanities, into cost-benefit experts in the allocation of their time and resources.

The questions that critics have raised about such educational assumptions and procedures can be subsumed under four considerations: the policy-making dimension, the conceptual dimension, the empirical dimension, and the humanistic dimension.

The Policy-Making Dimension

The first reservation that educational critics have about a technocratic approach to education involves concern about the ways educational policy is being made in this country, a purportedly open society committed to democratic procedures of uncoerced decision-making. A number of different groups and agencies, of course, contribute to the process of formulating educational policy, foremost among which are federal and state government, the community of educational researchers, local communities with their numerous interest groups, the guild of professional educators, educational critics and, more recently, foundations, businesses, and teachers' unions. Given the different assumptions and aims of these various groups, it is not surprising that educational debate in this country not only assumes a variety of forms but also generates considerable conflict. Certain groups, however, will emerge with more power than others and will use this power to try to influence policy. Where is the locus of the greatest educational power today? It is clear that government, at both national and state levels, is influencing the direction of American education more than any other sector in the society. This power derives primarily from the prestige of government and its control over monetary resources. It is important, therefore, to try to understand how the government thinks about education.

There may not be consensus on this interpretation, but it has been convincingly argued that the federal government, given its distinctive structure, is committed to supporting only those educational policies and ventures that promise in one way or another to help maximize the economic growth of the country.[4] The government, for example, is inherently disposed to think about education in terms of economic assumptions about the efficient allocation of resources within the context of certain national priorities. The model that economic theory has devised for thinking about such matters is essentially a model of productive functions, in which an attempt is made to increase productivity by calculating as precisely as possible a variety of input-output ratios. An economist and leading practitioner of PPBS in education thus writes that "we can relate education to a production function. A production function represents the relationship between inputs of productive factors and outputs per unit of time, subject to certain constraints. Ideally, a production function shows what each set of physical inputs, service conditions, and technologies will produce in terms of specified outputs—for example, education."[5] Again, a PPBS approach offers a model of efficient production as a paradigm for the planning, managing, and evaluating of education, and it derives its image, inspiration, language, and methodology primarily from economic and organization theory, computer science, and military and space technological

---

[4] James E. McClellan, *Toward an Effective Critique of American Education* (New York: J. B. Lippincott, 1968), Chap. IV, esp. p. 48.

[5] Werner Z. Hirsch, et al., *Program Budgeting for Primary and Secondary Public Education: Current Status and Prospects in Los Angeles* (New York: Praeger, 1972), p. 12.

delivery systems. "Systems management" is a shorthand term for much of the methodology involved.

Now, the fundamental question is whether an industrial model of efficient production is an appropriate one for thinking about the complex enterprise of education—of helping persons to discover and cultivate their distinctive humanity. Are the complex states of mind and disciplined forms of thought and action which we designate as "educated" adequately captured in such abstract notions as "specified output"? Once more, many critics think not. It is pointed out that the industrial model, when applied to education, oversimplifies highly complex situations. In essence, it reduces educational enterprise to what in the factory is called "piecework," that is, a situation in which each person works on a precisely defined task as his contribution to the ultimate product. This approach is efficient for producing Mustangs in Detroit and for sending capsules into space. But, even if it were defensible to divide up educational activity into precise tasks, the analogy with industrial processes would not hold. The social system, the immediate milieu, as well as human recalcitrance and indifference, affect teaching contexts much more than they do manufacturing situations. The general goal of education, moreover, is not to increase productivity (by either increasing output or decreasing expenditures) but to cultivate certain qualities of mind, namely the intellectual, moral, and aesthetic virtues. And it is erroneous to believe that education, which is notorious for its lack of consensus regarding uniform goals, can be envisioned as an activity for which it is possible to gain consensus as a precondition for determining the most efficient means for achieving objectives.[6] Indeed, the equating of "specified output" with "education" reflects a state of mind that misunderstands the nature of education.

Furthermore, cost-benefit analyses have not always proved to be that helpful in the military and business where cost overruns and manufacturing malfunctions have become commonplace, and there is criticism within government that many systems techniques are time-consuming, overly expensive, and often useless.[7]

---

[6] These points are set out in somewhat more detail in R. A. Smith, "An Educator's View of Industrial and Educational Growth," *The Educational Forum*, Vol. 35, No. 1 (November 1970).

[7] Leo Ruth, op. cit. And Charles Frankel, writing of his experience during the Johnson administration as Assistant Secretary of State for Educational and Cultural Affairs, records: "The byword . . . was 'cost-benefit analysis.' It was hoped that this method of carefully weighing alternatives by measuring their costs against their projected benefits might introduce more rationality not only into the planning of military weaponry but into decision-making throughout the government. Yet this was the Administration that made decisions, not once but repeatedly, that took the country ever more deeply into a war that had mounting costs and indiscernible benefits." In *High on Foggy Bottom* (New York: Harper & Row, 1968), p. 232.

What we are witnessing then is a complex of economists, social scientists, systems analysis engineers, government officials, finance experts, and educational administrators who favor an industrial model of education bidding to become the new "power élite" in education. And it is because the model of efficient production is inappropriate for such a human enterprise as education that critics are moved to express concern about the role this complex is playing in shaping educational policy.

The Conceptual Dimension

There are further misgivings by educational critics about excessive reliance on the use of behavioral objectives in P/CBTE schemes. Now, to be sure, it is not always clear exactly what the proponents of P/CBTE are assuming when they use the terms "behavior" or "behavioral objectives." But it would appear that the use of such language implies a commitment to external methods of intersubjective evaluation, usually by means of objective achievement tests, of instructional objectives stated in precise behavioral terms. Strictly speaking, in behavioral theory only publicly observable movements and utterances can be used as indicators of learning. Internal or mental events are believed to be either nonexistent or irrelevant. When there is talk about accountability it is usually with regard to holding teachers responsible for achieving prespecified behavioral objectives. Recall that in the school district mentioned earlier the teaching of all subjects was ultimately to be evaluated in this manner. However, again it might be asked, what's wrong with that? Critics have found a number of problems in the behavioral objectives approach to instruction.

First, no one denies that teachers are responsible in some sense for their actions. This is an obvious ethical obligation. It is something else, however, and much more controversial, to say that for a teacher, a program, or a school to be responsible (to be held accountable) means producing specific measures of learning achievement, that things must be counted up and quantified. As several writers have pointed out, this is not the only way to be held accountable, although it may be expedient for a variety of political and practical reasons. It is further held that the evaluation of teacher performance cannot rely exclusively, or even mainly, on achievement results for the following rather obvious reasons—at least they become obvious when entertained.

A teacher, obviously, does not control all the variables that influence learning. The universe cannot always be counted on to cooperate. Again, consider social class, milieu, intelligence, disposition and capacity to learn, and school organization—all may conspire to frustrate successful teaching and learning. Worthwhile teaching efforts do not logically imply successful learning. Conversely, successful learning may occur in conjunction with poor teaching. Dedicated teachers who work under nearly impossible conditions are thus not likely to embrace a "results only" approach to an evaluation of their teaching.

Second, it is generally assumed by performance-oriented educationists that objective measurement by means of achievement tests, often not designed by teachers themselves, is desirable because such measurement is more reliable than individual, subjective judgments that are supposed to be notoriously biased and unreliable. But, as Hugh Petrie points out in this volume, this need not be the case. Individual judgments can also be reliable and unbiased, as any teacher knows who has made an individual, subjective judgment that a learner is in fact beginning to display critical understanding or aesthetic sensitivity. Teachers are much more likely to trust their own judgment in many pedagogical matters than they are the results from a raft of objective tests.. Teachers who have spent any time with a group of students know how little objective tests reveal about a student's overall development. It is clear, however, that P/CBTE is opening the gates to a flood of objective tests and measurements simply because they are a convenient way to get information on purported achievement, this notwithstanding the fact that currently available achievement tests are said to be quite crude when used as indicators of significant learning. They simply do not plumb the depth or intensity of a learner's knowledge, understanding, or sensitivity. Available tests are nonetheless being used and, instead of the goals of teaching determining relevant types of assessment, available tests are all too often determining the goals of teaching.

Third, the preference for behavioral psychology, for taking into account only the publicly observable, is just that, a theoretical preference, and a highly controversial one. And public policy cannot justifiably enforce adherence to one highly controversial theory of behavior over another. It is commonplace knowledge that behaviorism as a theory of human behavior and method of evaluation has been soundly criticized.[8] But perhaps it is enough to note that important learnings and dispositions do not always surface "within a given time and under specific conditions." Harry S. Broudy has effectively used the writings of Michael Polanyi to underline the fact that we learn and forget selectively, and that things learned at one time or in a certain context often surface at unexpected times in unpredictable associations. Learnings, that is to say, often function in tacit, nonobservable ways. All we can do in schooling, Broudy suggests, is to build interpretive contexts for learning and try to develop basic concepts and tactics relevant to a variety of outcomes. Results cannot be

---

[8] See the critical essays by H. H. Price, Noam Chomsky, and H. S. Broudy, in H. S. Broudy, R. H. Ennis, and L. I. Krimerman, eds., *Philosophy of Educational Research* (New York: Wiley, 1973), Chap. 11.

guaranteed, at least not complex results that are nonetheless worth aiming at. In short, teaching should be relevant to learning, should bear on it in some way, but to repeat, teaching cannot be evaluated solely on the basis of behavioral results.

The Empirical Dimension

Little needs to be said about the empirical dimension of P/CBTE and related efforts. At the time of this writing it is nonexistent. There is no research that shows or even suggests that P/CBTE schemes are more effective modes of teacher education than present modes, yet the P/CBTE bandwagon rolls on. It is not only that performance contracting, which shares many features with P/CBTE, has proved to be unsuccessful; other research indicates that prespecification of desired outcomes does not necessarily improve learning.[9] This has led Ernest House to conclude that the improvement of teaching and learning is not really the aim of PPBS.[10] Rather it is control of education for the purpose of increasing efficiency, again if not by expanding educational output then by decreasing expenditures. If so, the humanistic rhetoric of P/CBTE is beside the point. Nor is it necessary to read critics of the movement to establish the absence of an empirical base. Arthur Wirth points out that P/CBTE advocates admit it themselves. For example, in a book called *The Power of Competency-Based Teacher Education* we can read that "the fact of the matter is that at this point in time there is no firm evidence as to the knowledge or skill base needed to effect desired educational outcomes."[11] If this is true, then from whence does the "power" of CBTE derive? Now, it is one thing to *suggest* to educators that a new approach to education be tried to judge its feasibility, or to argue persuasively that a specific approach might have potential for generating worthwhile research, but it is quite another to legislate, to enact into law, an approach that has not been thoroughly researched.[12] No other significant profession would tolerate such moves.

---

[9] P. Duchastel and P. Merrill, "The Effects of Behavioral Objectives on Learning: A Review of Empirical Studies," *Review of Educational Research*, Vol. 43, No. 1 (Winter 1973), pp. 53-69.

[10] Ernest House, "The Price of Productivity: Who Pays?" *Today's Education*, Vol. 62, No. 6 (September-October 1973), pp. 65-69.

[11] Benjamin Rosner, et al., *The Power of Competency-Based Teacher Education: A Report* (Boston: Allyn and Bacon, 1972), p. 122. An article by Rosner in the Spring 1973 issue of New York University's *Education Quarterly* uses the term "promise" instead of "power."

[12] In this connection, a recent decision by the Attorney General of Texas is noteworthy. In an opinon rendered January 4, 1974, it was ruled that the Texas State Board of Education does not have the authority to mandate competency-based teacher education programs, to which the Board has made a formal commitment. The opinion

The Humanistic Dimension

The new efficiency movement claims to have a humanistic dimension, but it is clear that its humanistic impulses are radically disjunctive with its highly technical procedures, indeed its alarmingly technical procedures. It is this infatuation with technique and the language of technique that has prompted critics of PPBS to say that it lacks a sufficiently humanistic dimension, that in opting for industrial, military, and space technologies of problem-solving and decision-making it ends up preferring the technical and the mechanical to the human and the complex, all the talk about the individualization and personalization of learning notwithstanding. After all, performance-based, behaviorally prespecified programs may be "individualized" merely by letting students move through them at their own paces, but this may do absolutely nothing to "humanize" students.

More than anything else, however, it is the language of P/CBTE that reveals its technical bias and mechanical conception of mind. The use of a technical terminology stemming from the preference for an industrial model of efficient production in education has already been remarked. Here is another sample. According to an Office of Education official, "The first step in applying a systems approach involves the rather specific definition of what outcomes or results are desired. It is against these specifications that the system, *whether space ship or educational program* is to be built. . . . With behavioral objectives, it should be possible to associate behavioral change with program cost."[13] The next step, of course, is to envision teacher education under the aspect of space travel such that professional educational preparation can be discussed, as two educational writers have discussed it, in terms of "thrust," "energy output," "management and delivery systems," "targets," "data-based feedback system," "internal control and predictability," "guidance and management support," and endless "inputs" and "outputs"—and all this from a relatively restrained description of CBTE.[14] Now it might be said that writers who use these terms do not really think that managing education is like monitoring space

---

commented on the vagueness, the exclusiveness, and the rigidity of the Board's standards. *Phi Delta Kappan*, Vol. 60, No. 7 (March 1974), p. 469. For the difficulties experienced in Michigan's accountability venture, See Jerome T. Murphy and David K. Cohen, "Accountability in Education—the Michigan Experience," *The Public Interest*, No. 36 (Summer 1974), pp. 53-81.

[13] Quoted by Sue M. Brett in "The Federal View of Behavioral Objectives," in John Maxwell and Anthony Tovatt, eds., *On Writing Behavioral Objectives for English* (Urbana, Ill.: National Council of Teachers of English, 1970), p. 46. Emphasis added.

[14] W. Robert Houston and Robert B. Howsam, eds., *Competency-Based Teacher Education* (Chicago: Science Research Associates, 1972), pp. 1-16.

travel or mass producing Vegas. But if so, why the penchant for techno-logical jargon? Why the predilection for a certain kind of imagery? Why the infatuation with technique and specification? Why the conceptual carelessness and casual analogizing? Why so little thought? One can only conclude, as Michael Apple stresses, that it is the scientific aura created by the use of such language that impresses, and not the substance of the notions implied by the expressions.

This does not mean that the new movement makes no claim to having a humanistic dimension; there is much talk about personalizing instruc-tion. It is rather to point out that the movement is an unhappy combina-tion of management science, behavioral psychology, computer technology, politics, and humanism. Technical rationality and humanism need not, of course, be mutually contradictory. Their conjoining, however, as Albert William Levi has pointed out so well, requires considerable finesse.[15] Ref-erences to humanistic psychologists on the one hand, for example, do not mesh with a fondness for flowcharts and technological jargon on the other. Nor ought one to speak of "maximizing sensitivity," as one P/CBTE proponent was heard to utter. Sensitivity may be refined or cultivated, but not "maximized." It is the failure, then, to handle the union of technique and humanism with a sense of fittingness and appropriateness that further makes P/CBTE schemes suspect. And it is not surprising that, captivated by modern technology, advocates of efficient education often reject the images of profession and pedagogy embodied in the cultural heritage, in the history of educational wisdom. Indeed, one would never know from some of the writings of the PPBS movement that there is such a literature.

To many, all of this goes without saying. But it is a peculiarity of the present situation that even teachers of the arts and humanities, who might intuitively be expected to be critical of prespecification and technical man-agement procedures, are beginning to endorse P/CBTE. Some music edu-cators have even suggested that music teachers must, if necessary, force their way into accountability schemes, must learn how "to cost out the music program," lest music be assigned to a low priority in the curriculum. And a group of English teachers apparently had no serious reservations about formulating and publishing over 200 pages of representative per-formance objectives for English education. One may call such scientism in the arts and humanities a betrayal of humanistic thinking, and it is part of the larger betrayal of intellect in the movement at large.[16]

---

[15] Albert William Levi, *Humanism and Politics* (Bloomington: Indiana University Press, 1969), esp. Chap. 7.

[16] Scientism in the arts and humanities is well exposed by Jacques Barzun in *Science: The Glorious Entertainment* (New York: Harper & Row, 1964), esp. Chaps. 9 and 10.

The basic issues are thus delineated, and the question is whether a large proportion of educators will be captivated by technique, or whether they will try to understand education and schooling in their proper complexity. If the former, that is, if schooling goes the way of technique, then its technocratic leaders must answer for the adoption of a questionable model of educational planning and operation (the industrial model), a questionable learning theory (behaviorist), and a questionable evaluation system (objective tests and measurements). If schooling goes this way, it will in effect have abandoned professional leadership to the technocrats.

There is an alternative. Educators need not submit to scientific management. Teachers of the humanities especially ought to act as the conscience of the educational profession, ought to oppose the infatuation with technique with the basic concepts of their disciplines—concepts that stress the importance of human variability, complexity, uniqueness, and originality. Above all, they should be vocal about rampant scientism in their own domains.

What are the prospects that educational leadership can be regained from the technocrats? It is difficult to say, although the growing number of critics is encouraging. At the same time, as I have indicated, technical efficiency in education is being endorsed by numerous educators if in some instances only out of a sense of futility in opposing it. Others, of course, those clutching the reins of the bandwagon, see nothing wrong. As for those who are critical of the technical bias in P/CBTE, they will doubtless continue in the tradition of intellectual and humanistic criticism. Humanism can mean different things, but one of its chief meanings is criticism; it uses criteria derived from history, literature, philosophy, religion, and the arts to judge events and actions; and it makes a special effort to be sensitive to the *spirit* of an event, decision, or policy.[17] Humanism is a never-ending quest for value, and it recalls persons to moral and aesthetic perception when the forces of dehumanization become pervasive. Humanism may also be said to have as one of its principal tasks the estimating of the consequences, in human terms, of values discarded or vulgarized. In asking what image of man a situation proposes, it constantly seeks to arrest the decline of the human estate and to set it once again on its proper course. Humanism, in other words, is locked in endless combat with the forces of the mechanical, the subhuman, and the antihuman. In criticizing the efficiency movement in education, it is thus performing one of its traditional functions.

Perhaps the important conclusion to be drawn from humanistic criticism of P/CBTE is that restrictions of manner must always be kept in the forefront of discussion. "Results" can be obtained in a number of ways,

---

[17] Humanism as criticism is persuasively demonstrated by Levi, op. cit.

as Stanley Kubrick's *Clockwork Orange* painfully shows, but not all ways are ethically acceptable. The passion for results may well produce undesirable side effects. Performance contracting undertaken by commercial firms provides a portent. All sorts of rewards, including consumer goods and money, have been used to reinforce learning. It is another instance of the end justifying the means, and if the demand for results gets tied to salary increments, promotion, and job retention, then efficiency advocates must answer for what will surely be an intolerable educational situation—a situation in which, as Ernest House has warned, suspicion, acrimony, inflexibility, cheating, and authoritarian control will be typical.[18]

P/CBTE, says J. Myron Atkin in this volume, represents the bankruptcy of professional leadership. Anyone who has thoughtfully considered the movement can only agree.

---

[18] House, op. cit.

2. *Professional Leadership and PBTE*

J. Myron Atkin

Performance-based teacher education is the most visible manifestation at the university level of the accountability pressures on the educational system that came to full flower in the late 1960s. As it became fashionable to describe schooling in terms of "inputs" and "outputs," and demands increased to guarantee that tax dollars produce certain familiar and well-accepted changes in students whose education was supported by public funds, influential spokesmen for the teacher education enterprise responded by advocating PBTE programs. Exactly what must teachers be able to do? Whatever the answer to this question the desired behaviors should be specified and aspiring teachers should be trained in each of the necessary skills. Furthermore, it often has been suggested that licensing be withheld until competency in these skills is certified.

What are the desired competencies? The ability to diagnose a six-year-old's word recognition problem stemming from reversal of the letter "b"? Teach it. The ability to accept a suggestion about teaching mathematics from the father of a third grader without antagonizing the parent? Teach this skill if possible and if it seems essential. The ability to comfort a five-year-old whose knee is skinned on the playground? Teach this skill. The ability to interpret a ten-year-old's manipulation of a balance board as sufficient evidence of his understanding of second-class levers? Teach it.

How long is the list? Five thousand competencies? Twenty thousand? Whatever the number, plan the teacher education program to ensure acquisition of the requisite behaviors. The less practical studies need not be dropped, but if there is little time for them, the first job is to prepare

This article was prepared especially for this volume.

teachers in the specified skills. If there isn't much time in the teacher preparation program to create the opportunity for prospective teachers to ponder the long-term effects or moral implications of teaching a child long division by awarding candy after each correct response, perhaps the opportunity to reflect on such a matter will come later. Do not worry about courses dealing with social and political factors affecting change in the educational system for prospective teachers if these studies do not relate to building identifiable teacher competencies. Let them be crowded out if necessary— though presumably with regret. And, if knowledge of ancient civilizations, foreign cultures, primitive peoples, economic principles, or even the purposes and history of education do not seem related directly and obviously to the teaching act, it is questionable whether it should occupy time in teacher education programs at the expense of the skills that lead to measurable and unambiguous pedagogic impact.

Whatever the merits of PBTE—and there are merits; many skills not commonly taught to prospective teachers should be—the movement crashed on the teacher-preparation scene with the crusade-like quality that seems to characterize American thinking about educational change during the postwar period. Furthermore, consistent with the mode of thought that considers the educational system infinitely tractable, the new visions were expected to be implemented quickly; government and foundation money was made available to help it happen. The PBTE bandwagon was boarded by most teacher education institutions, by the American Association of Colleges for Teacher Education, and by teacher certification authorities in most of the 50 states.

Visualize, if possible, the effects of a similar crusade to redesign the teaching of law, veterinary medicine, or engineering. In most professional fields, there would have been demands that evidence be provided that the new visions are wiser than the old and also result in better programs. Whatever the level of disenchantment with existing preparation programs, there would have been insistence that feasibility be demonstrated at the very least. There would have been considered caution about modifying a system that demonstrably had served most purposes well for decades. Perhaps it is because our thinking about teacher education is closely coupled to our thinking about elementary and secondary education that we have come to expect exhortations to institute dramatic modifications in the system, then take those exhortations as competent criticism whatever their source: legislatures, the media, budgeteers, and business interests.

Because the pressures for change in teacher education seem to come from the same sources that have demanded accountability from the elementary and secondary schools in the form of guaranteed changes in student behavior, it may be instructive to examine a few characteristics of recent thinking about the problems of change at all educational levels.

As is well known, the space age ushered in a new mode of thinking about education. To that point, the public seemed to take quiet pride in the schools. The educational system was viewed as a potent and beneficial force during the American melting-pot period and afterwards. Teachers and the schools were respected if not glorified; school people were appreciated and valued. True, there were rumblings of discontent. But they came most loudly from university-level academics who for decades denigrated the quality of education in the common schools. The progressive education movement particularly signaled a disturbing retreat from a formalism that professors knew and were determined to preserve. But professorial criticism of the schools was an old and relatively minor force for modification of teacher education programs until the late 1950s.

On October 4, 1957, the Soviet Union launched Sputnik I. The United States was not first in launching an artificial earth satellite, Americans were told, because of deficiencies in the educational system. Our schools were not rigorous enough, especially in educating talented youngsters. For patriotic reasons, private foundations and the federal government poured money into the schools and rhetoric into the media to demand certain changes. University-level academics were accorded leadership positions to improve the teaching of science, math, foreign languages, and other fields. Taken aback and a bit guilt-ridden, school people generally accepted the direction of the academic community, and they began developing and installing new programs that were invented in the universities.

By the early 1960s, however, the attention of the public turned dramatically away from problems of education of the talented and toward the problems of redressing racial inequality. Again the schools were singled out. Again they were expected to develop programs to ameliorate a severe social problem. As the 60s progressed, the media rapidly reported a succession of fresh priorities: joylessness, correction of environmental problems, and improvement of the status of native Americans, for example. Each time the schools were expected to reflect the apparent shift in public concerns. Each time the schools were seen as a front-line agent in modifying the society.

Although school people made earnest attempts to meet the new missions, they did not solve the old problems. Racism remained in America despite school integration. Poverty remained a problem as the country entered the 1970s, as it had been before, despite attempts to train the poor for gainful employment. In instances wherein the country clearly achieved new goals, the credit did not go to the schools. The United States did move ahead in the space race, but the achievement was attributed to American industrial know-how rather than to an improved educational system.

Much of the public saw teachers and school administrators as continually failing to meet the goals that were articulated as each new program was pressed on the schools. Rather than ask whether the goals were realistic—rather than assess seriously how powerful a force the schools might be in producing racial harmony for example—the inclination was to assume that school people were misguided, stupid, or poorly managed, else they would have produced the promised changes made possible by government grants. Hence the pressures for performance contracting and voucher plans. Adopt businesslike methods, and solve problems in businesslike ways.

During the 1960s, professionals in education also may have accustomed themselves to the fact that new directions for the educational system are determined by prestigious figures and organizations outside the system. A former Harvard president and chemist becomes the authority on schooling for the poor and on teacher education. An MIT professor and physicist becomes an authority on general school reform. A New York City mayor becomes an expert on school governance. These capable men, and others like them, often introduced important educational ideas. Their suggestions, however, usually were accorded awesome attention and influence, even within the education professions. At least there were few attempts by established educational leaders to temper the new program—either by presenting alternative plans or by providing information that might improve the wisdom of the new policies. Educational leaders might have been expected to help shape the evolving plans by introducing their own visions and experience—or at least try. Instead, they exhibited three types of general reactions: passivity, toadying acceptance of the new schemes, or mindless rejection of them.

On the part of those who hurried to fall in step with the developing trends, there was little attempt to point out that the American educational system consists of well over two million teachers employed by about seventeen thousand separate governing units. The individuals who staff the system have ideas of their own, and many of these ideas have enjoyed success for decades. Injections of new practices into such a system without full recognition of existing strengths is a strategy poorly designed to effect change or preserve quality; yet that is exactly how many tens of million dollars were spent during the 1960s to modify American schools.

Such a style of governmental policy formulation was not restricted to the educational system. The 1960s was a decade of brash optimism about our ability to modify fundamental elements in the social structure if only we were wise enough to identify barriers to progress and determined enough to remove them. We sought direction during that period (and still do) from a fascinating meld of electronics engineers, economists, business managers, and recent liberal arts graduates who found it congenial to deal with large and complex systems by identifying goals, assessing costs and benefits, specifying inputs, and charting throughputs. These energetic people turned their talents to housing problems, race relations, poverty, health care, transportation, environment, and crime—as well as to education. They created new programs for the poor, new medical care plans, and new housing developments.

Now we hear about expensive housing programs developed during that period that destroyed a sense of community; we hear about programs to improve health care that seem to do little more than raise the income of physicians; we hear about poverty programs that accorded new power to ruthless exploiters of the poor; and we hear about transportation programs that clogged the cities. Nevertheless, in the field of education, we do not seem to have diminished our enthusiasm for a wholesale change in the system based on the shiny plans of bright amateurs. Or so it seems, judging from the enthusiasm accorded the PBTE pressures by education deans, most public school administrators, and the American Association of Colleges for Teacher Education.

PBTE and most other well-publicized plans for social reform during the past decade reflect a view of change seen as *engineered* progress. We use many models and metaphors in our strategies for improving the educational system, and it may clarify our view of educational change to examine a few of them before looking at the model derived from engineering.

One model often invoked is based on strategies for change in agriculture. New practices to improve crop yield are developed in laboratory settings, often at universities. The new methods of combating pest infestation or reducing weeds are taken to the field by the agricultural extension agent, a key figure in a large network established to inform and convince the farmer to change his methods. The farmer, interested in increasing yields and profits, adopts the new practice when it is demonstrated to be effective.

A variation on the agricultural model stems from medical practice. New treatments are developed by pharmaceutical firms to combat various diseases. The pharmaceutical "detail man" carries the word of a new treatment to practicing physicians. The physician makes a match between symptoms he sees in the examining room and the information provided by the detail man, and then he prescribes accordingly.

When this model and the agricultural model are applied to the field of education, it is assumed that the teacher is awaiting results of research that point in the direction of more efficient practice, always ready to implement plans that suggest that children can learn more readily if the new methods are adopted. Underlying the assumption is the apparent conviction that teachers share the same goals and that these goals can be identified. If it then can be demonstrated how the goals can be achieved more effectively, practice will change.

The most prevalent metaphor used during the 1960s, when developing plans for educational change, stems from the field of engineering. The econometricians and systems analysts who speak of inputs, outputs, and throughputs are relying on the engineering metaphor; so, too, are the educational planners who speak of behavioral objectives, linkage agents, and interfaces. The engineering metaphor undergirds the thinking of all those who see the educational system as a mechanism to be redesigned to meet certain agreed upon and prespecified goals.

When a spacecraft is to be built, the performance specifications of the vehicle are determined in advance. How large a payload will it carry? What is the maximum size in view of the engine likely to be available? What are the acceptable costs?

When the metaphor is employed in the field of education, it becomes necessary to choose, from among the broad array of possible and desirable educational goals, a limited number that can be targeted and stressed. The goals that lend themselves to ready specification are those that are usually selected. Then the system is modified, in theory at least, to achieve these goals as efficiently as possible. Other contributors to this volume question in detail the mischievous practice of assuming that the readily identifiable objectives are those of highest general priority. My purpose here is to identify shortcomings associated with the engineering metaphor itself. Any device, any engineered system, produces effects in addition to those that are identified in advance as goals. Thus a vehicle can be designed to travel at 95 miles an hour, carry six passengers, become obsolete in three years, and cost less than $5000. But if it also pollutes the atmosphere to an unacceptable degree, causes slaughter on the highways in an unprecedented fashion, and consumes scarce fuel at an insatiable rate, perhaps the design goals were poorly selected. Or perhaps broader expectations for such vehicles have shifted during the period between drawing board and first production model.

The side effects of educational systems are as important as the main effects. The fact that children congregate in the schools and interact among themselves may be as important in producing changes in the child as the formal instructional programs we design. Social systems even more than mechanical systems are juggled at great risk. In our single-minded pursuit of a few desirable educational goals, we may be inattentive to the subtle and desirable outcomes the system already achieves and achieves well.

Furthermore, the engineering metaphor suggests that we look only at results. Thus schooling for its own sake is overlooked. Perhaps it has come to be accepted as an attribute of civilized society that children be accorded the opportunity to attend humane institutions that enable them to learn about the culture into which they have been born. Any simplistic view of the outcomes of the school experience that leads to drastic modifications of an institution that has evolved and proved adaptable over many decades may be socially unacceptable no matter how appealing the promised changes may seem on first glance. Thus electronic schemes to teach youngsters individually may indeed help them learn certain important skills more effectively than a teacher would, but if it limits the opportunity of socializing with other children and in the process handling subtle, complex, and unanticipated problems of human interaction, it may be depriving young people of important learning experiences.

The intent here is not to suggest that much of our instruction cannot be technologized effectively. It can. But let us institute new programs with appropriate caution, with minimum destructiveness, and with as full a recognition as possible of the softer and seldom-stated effects of the present system.

The most powerful influences of the educational system are attributable to three factors: (1) who chooses to teach, (2) the peer group relations among children, and (3) how the institution is organized, its rules and regulations. The impact of these factors overwhelms the effects of the formal instructional program. Therefore, if modifications in the curriculum cause different people to choose to teach, or establish new rules and regulations for the institution, these elements had best be considered carefully both for their positive and negative influences. For example, if changes in the role of the teacher suggest that the skills of a technician are predominant, then we had better anticipate that individuals who find it congenial to think of themselves as technicians will choose to teach, and others will not. PBTE suggests just such a move in our conception of the teaching role.

Teachers choose to teach for hundreds of reasons, and the purposes of one differ from the purposes of another. One teacher considers it important to provide a model for children that illustrates that adults are compassionate and reasoning, that they meet new problems rationally and sympathetically. Another teacher considers it important to toughen the children to the teacher's perceptions about life's realities; schedules are to be maintained; and punishments are to be meted out for lassitude or wrongheadedness. Another teacher considers his prime goal that of instilling an appreciation for the discipline in which he is steeped. Another teacher considers her main goal to become a companion to young people, providing a sympathetic and encouraging ear to accounts of their youthful struggles and joys. Motivations of teachers probably are as varied as teachers themselves.

Indeed, most teachers choose the profession because of their private perception of the type of adult the teaching field permits them to become and that they want to be. A teacher who chose the profession because of its opportunities to counsel young people rejects reflexively an approach that seems to liken the schools to an assembly-line facility in which the purpose is to produce certain agreed-upon products. All too often our strategies for educational change fit the personalities of those who propose the changes rather than those who are asked to implement them. This is hardly a blueprint for realism.

A less dramatic metaphor for educational change than the one stemming from engineering is suggested by the processes of biological evolution. An evolution metaphor suggests that those who are interested in educational change become sensitive to natural variation within a complex system. The strategic problem becomes one of identifying variations with adaptive and survival qualities, then developing plans to nurture these variations to enable them to spread where desirable. An obvious merit of the evolution metaphor is that strategies based on such an approach obviate the necessity of injecting new plans into a large and complex system, then running into unanticipated difficulties. In just about every elementary school in the United States, there is a powerful teacher who seems to be able to manipulate the social system of the school to blunt innovation. Educational change strategies that assume new practices will take root because they are obviously efficient fail to account for the social and political dynamics of a school and a school system. On the other hand, if an attractive variation already has surfaced, a number of pressures not only within the school but within the community and among the children have already been met successfully. The problem becomes one of understanding how these forces were accommodated, defeated, or capitalized upon in the establishment of the variation.

The evolution metaphor suggests that change is slow and may not seem profound over short periods of time, however realistic such a metaphor might be. For change strategies based on an evolution metaphor to represent even a gradual force for progress, however, there must be a reassertion of professional independence, particularly on the part of teachers and their administrators. For independence to be productive, there must also be a degree of self-confidence and professional pride. It is questionable whether the battered teaching profession, continually told of its ineffectiveness, can be helped to develop self-confidence by its present leaders. Quite the contrary, the most prestigious figures within the educational system often feel compelled, while establishing their own authority and influence, to berate teachers for their inadequate vision, their wastefulness, or their ineptitude. Such leaders staff key positions for education in the federal government, many colleges of education, a majority of state education departments, and a large number of superintendencies. Given their record, they do not seem to be the individuals who will help counter the excesses of voucher plans, performance contracting, PBTE, and other dramatic schemes for imposing new but sometimes short-sighted practices on the system.

Who are the educational leaders who can protect the public and the profession from destructive mischief if they are not in Washington, in state capitals, in colleges of education, or in the superintendent's office? Teachers seem to be learning that they will have to speak for themselves if they are to resist plans that seem damaging to children—or if they are to develop their own strategies for improving the educational system. Most of the influential voices so far who are questioning the wisdom of the new proposals for community control, behavioral objectives, performance contracting, or PBTE have come from the organized profession.

One of the least comprehensible features of the accountability pressures on the educational system—of which PBTE is an outstanding example— is the fact that of all social agencies the schools historically are closest to the people. The 17,000 separate governing units are responsible to the American electorate as is no other element of government. The people have frequent opportunities to make modifications within the educational system if they are not satisfied. In view of this fact, it is difficult to explain the frenzy with which the established educational leaders have often tried to conform to the latest visions of the opinion-makers.

My guess is that teachers gradually will strengthen their efforts to influence the profession by taking increasingly assertive collective action. Unless they receive help from people who have responsibilities for teacher education and for governmental policy formulation, they will build strategies for educational change, at least initially, in a fashion that may be attentive primarily to their own self-interest as a group. There are dangers in such a plan of action. Yet teachers hardly can be blamed as they begin to take matters into their own hands.

The PBTE episode illustrates the bankruptcy of American educational leadership insofar as educational policy formulation is concerned. Major directives consistently are formulated by figures outside of the profession. Part of the reason is that educational leaders from within the system have not managed in significant numbers to gain the respect of powerful figures in government and the foundations. This fact reflects partly a distrust of career educationists. But partly it reflects a lack of forcefulness, self-confidence, and independence on the part of educational leaders themselves. Ultimately, educational policy is wise if it is established by wise people. If wisdom is buttressed by experience, we stand to benefit the country and the educational system to the maximum. Unfortunately the educational system has not seemed to nurture leaders who have influential ideas. But there is no reason why a commitment to professionalism is inconsistent with imaginative planning for modifying the educational system. If reform is to reflect more of a grassroots impetus than heretofore —and to be effective change must have a strong grassroots component in a huge enterprise—we have to seek greater cooperation between governmental leaders and professional educators than has been reflected in interaction between the two groups during the past 20 years. And the cooperation must be fostered on an equal footing among the parties. We may be very far from such an accommodation in American education.

3. PBTE/CBTE—Do They Mean What They Say?

Harry S. Broudy

When first the talk about competence-based (CBTE) and performance-based teacher education (PBTE) programs was heard, most colleges of education faculty either ignored it or absentmindedly nodded approval. After all, who in his right mind would base a teacher education program on noncompetence or on nonperformance? Later, when the U. S. Office of Education, the American Association of Colleges for Teacher Education (AACTE), and other agencies threw their influence and funds behind the movement,[1] the professors reacted with a vague anxiety, puzzlement, and some, scenting a new source of grants and projects, began sniffing out ways of getting into the act. Now that many certification boards and state departments of instruction are threatening to withhold certification from programs that are not competence based or performance based, or at least do not use these terms lavishly, schools that did not get into the act either because they could not or would not are really worried.

Source. This essay was originally presented as an address to The Twenty-Second Annual Teacher Education Conference, sponsored by the Office of Teacher Education of The City University of New York, March 23, 1973, New York City. It was published in the proceedings of the conference, *Upheaval in Teacher Education: The Regents' Master Plan*, eds. G. B. Gottsegen and S. A. Milgrim.

[1] "Committed to the concept of systematic management by objectives, the Office of Education expects to give additional impetus to the development of performance-based teacher education programs through providing support for the establishment of a number of educational renewal sites," writes William L. Smith, Associate Commissioner, EPD, U.S.O.E. in "A Resume of Performance-Based Teacher Education" (Washington, D.C.: American Association of Colleges of Education PBTE Series: No. 1a, March 1972).

But should they be worried? If the exhortations and pressures in behalf of PBTE/CBTE are simply calls to improvement of existing programs of teacher education, they should arouse zeal, not anxiety. If, on the contrary, the rhetoric of PBTE/CBTE betokens fundamental changes in the role of the teachers college or college of education in the preparation of teachers, then the worry may be well founded.

It was clear by the middle 1960s that a two-pronged attack was being launched on the public schools, the teachers, and the teachers of teachers. One prong was the criticism from blacks, Chicanos, and the poor in general that they were not getting equal "quality" in their schools. "Quality" for these groups meant—as for most people—achievement in the three Rs and whatever else it took to continue schooling or to "make it" economically. This inferior schooling was blamed for their socioeconomic disadvantage.[2] The demand, therefore, was for changes in the public schools— decentralization, vouchers, performance-contracting—anything that would succeed where the public schools allegedly had failed. Teacher education was to aim at competence in the inner city school—ability to manage the classroom, provide effective instruction, and to "relate" to the psychological problems of minority groups. "Can this teacher operate competently in an inner city school?" "Is your program based on the conditions and demands of such schools?" These would be the criterial questions for teacher education and certification.

The other prong was propelled by what, for convenience, may be dubbed the counterculture, as was exemplified in the writings of Kozol, Friedenberg, Holt, and their coterie. It attacked the schools not so much for their lack of efficiency in teaching the standard skills and subjects, but rather because they put such outcomes ahead of sensitivity to "human" needs. The schools were accused of oppressing the young in general, but the children of the poor and the black in particular. The proper aim of the school, on this view, should be the liberation of the oppressed from the values and hangups of the middle-aged WASP teacher and parent. Teachers should be "selected"—not necessarily prepared formally—from among those who could "relate" to the young, who could individualize school experience to every need and to personalize it so that Charles Reich's Consciousness III would displace Consciousness II.

It was clear that these two camps of attackers did not agree on the nature of competence nor upon the performance that might constitute com-

---

[2] At first the term "cultural disadvantage" was also used, but later this was rejected as implying that black culture was inferior to the WASP variety. At this writing, a heavily financed Carnegie study is trying to convince the public that educational equality does not produce economic equality. Christopher Jencks et al., *A Reassessment of the Effect of Family and Schooling in America* (New York: Basic Books, 1972).

petence. But they did agree that existing programs were unsatisfactory. The liberation brigades proposed nothing more definite than free schools taught by liberated people, but they did provide political support to the efficiency lads who were and are the most vocal promoters of the PBTE and CBTE movements. The combined effects of both types of attack produced a general receptivity to alternatives—the more the better. PBTE and CBTE emerged as highly touted alternatives to the standard program of teacher education as found in most colleges of education.

The PBTE/CBTE promoters insist first that the tasks found in the *real* classroom, especially the difficult classroom, define the program; second, that the program specify these tasks in sufficient detail and in such a way that those who care to do so can tell whether they have been performed, or not, especially if they are not. The latter demand is firmly rooted in the doctrine that school objectives should be defined in behavioral terms, that is, in terms of observable behavior. The latter requirement, it is felt, will keep the institution honest and the faculty clear headed.[3]

The uneasiness inspired by these notions in some quarters of teacher education has been expressed in concern that PBTE programs would impoverish the goals of schooling by eliminating its less obvious effect on intellect, appreciation, and character. It was also attacked on the grounds that behaviorism is antihumanistic, witness B. F. Skinner's *Beyond Freedom and Dignity*.[4] Further, it was noted that predetermining educational objectives left little room for spontaneity and creativity in teaching or learning. Other educators were unhappy with the mechanistic image of the school as a factory turning out "products."

The PBTE defenders, for their part, denied that the program was anti-intellectualistic or antihumanistic. On the contrary, they avowed loyalty to humane values, but wanted to make sure they were achieved, not merely proclaimed. Forcing teachers to specify broad humane outcomes in terms of performances would do just that. Another response was that the educationist establishment was merely defending an existing program that was hopelessly irresponsible for the product so that its animadversions on PBTE were to be discounted as "defensive."

What then are we to think about CBTE and PBTE and their critics? If broad humane and intellectual outcomes are not excluded by PBTE, then they must be statable as "performances." Can the ordinary use of

---

[3] Hence the intimate relationship between PBTE, behavioral objectives, and the demands for accountability. Cf. Ernest R. House, "The Dominion of Economic Accountability," *The Educational Forum*, Vol. 37, No. 1 (November 1972), pp. 13-24. Reprinted in this volume.

[4] Cf. Maxine Greene, "Defying Determinism," *Teachers College Record*, Vol. 74, No. 2 (December 1972), pp. 148-54.

"performance" be stretched to cover such processes as critical thinking, creative imagination, aesthetic appreciation, and humanistic encounters? What shall count as a performance? If everything involved in teaching is a performance, then what is a nonperformance? Is the opposite of performance a promise or is it a covert mental state? Is performance the opposite of a credit, course, or degree?[5] Analogous questions could be raised about the meaning of competence. Is the controversy no more than a tempest in a semantic teapot, or is something more at stake?

Preparational versus Operational Competence

When we say that a prospective teacher T can do X, for example, design a lesson on bees, we ordinarily mean either that T has already done X, and therefore can be expected to do it again whenever it is appropriate to do so; or we mean that T has practiced making lesson plans and will be able to do one on bees. She or he may not have practiced the one on bees, X, but can be expected to adapt what has been practiced to a lesson on bees.

In other words, competence may be *operational* or it may be *preparational*—the first is actual doing; the second is putative doing. Both can be "demonstrated," but they are not necessarily equivalent. The difference is important because there is a type of teacher "training" that could claim to be based on operational competence. This is a form of apprentice training on the job in which T does X under guidance and continues doing X without guidance after the apprenticeship is over.

This is a venerable and effective form of occupational training, and if this is what PBTE/CBTE proponents have in mind, they should not be backward about saying so. The advantages of an apprenticeship program are not lightly dismissed. After all, the best proof that T can do X is that he is already doing it. Furthermore, at any given moment, the performance of the apprentice can be judged as successful or not; the judge does not have to infer operational competence from preparational competence. Why then, despite these advantages, did law, medicine, engineering, and education move from apprenticeship training to the establishment of formal institutions to prepare practitioners?

The usual reason given is that when large numbers of practitioners are needed, apprenticeship may be an inadequate form of training. Although this would account for the introduction of normal schools and schools of nursing, it does not account for the stubborn maintenance of apprentice

---

[5] "For too long, the emphasis in training programs has been on the mere accumulation of credits, courses, and degrees as evidence for readiness to undertake professional roles. Demonstrated competency, the real test of readiness, is the focal point for emphasis in performance-based training programs." William L. Smith, op. cit., p. 1.

training for plumbers and carpenters, on the one hand, or for the abandonment of apprenticeship in medicine, law, and engineering, on the other. However, the need to train large numbers of practitioners formally does necessitate the analysis of the practice into teachable form, that is, so that it can be methodized.

A more plausible hypothesis for the formalization of "professional" preparation is, I believe, the possibility of rationalizing at least some of the rules of practice by theory. Once a body of facts, principles, and theories is developed to guide and justify rules of practice, apprenticeship—learning by doing alone—is impossible. The existence of such a body of theory and theoretically-rationalized practice is the *raison d'être* of a professional school, and indeed of the university as a whole. However, the price paid for emphasizing theory is that the outcome of professional training tends to become preparational rather than operational competence.[6]

An apprenticeship program is direct and fairly simple. The learner is integrated with the activity of the master on the job, and when the master judges that the learner's performance matches his own or that of a standard workman, the apprentice becomes a journeyman and later a master on his own account.

If, however, we are asked to devise a program for *preparational* competence, the task is much more complicated. The prospective teacher does not simply imitate the performances of the master as he would if he were an apprentice. Instead, he is asked to address himself to a set of exercises that in various ways represent the *classes* of tasks to be encountered in the classrooms of real schools in a vast agglomerate of real communities. To devise these exercises, we become reflective about the teaching process, abstract common elements and phases from it, and make up a package of the knowledge, skills, and attitudes that plausibly will produce in the novice the accomplishments of the master.[7]

To say that a competence is *preparational*, therefore, is to say that it is not identical with any real operation, because every real situation is in some sense unique in content and context. On the contrary, *preparational*

---

[6] It is, therefore, *almost* a contradiction in terms for a university to serve as a site for apprenticeship. I say "almost" because advanced work in scholarship is virtually an apprenticeship in scholarly activity. Yet there is a difference, because the university is the place where scholarship is done, whereas it is not the place where professionals render service to their clients. Thus a Ph.D. candidate in history can sensibly be regarded as an apprentice of one or more professors of history; he is doing "their thing," but a person preparing to teach history in the public schools is not an apprentice of the Professor of the Teaching of History, who may or may not be teaching history in the public schools.

[7] The Sophists, among the earliest educationists, were doing this for the teaching of grammar and rhetoric more than 2000 years ago. Pedagogy emerges when people, especially young people, have to be taught formally what they do not learn "naturally."

competence merely means that there is good reason to believe that if T is preparationally competent, he will be able to adapt some general principles, rules, and techniques operationally to a wide variety of particular situations. In other words, operational competence does not rely on transfer of learning; preparational competence does. At times the PBTE/CBTE movement seems to be saying that teacher training should consist of developing operational competence directly; at other times it seems to be saying that preparational competence can be made more reliably transferable than the conventional program does.

Now, in the curriculum for preparational competence, several mixes are possible. It can be made up of:

1. Sample techniques only: the cookbook approach.
2. Sample techniques plus some generalized rules: a manual of procedures.
3. The above, plus principles that generate or justify the rules.
4. Rules and principles only.

I take it that CBTE and PBTE would reject number 4; indeed this seems to be the major ground of their animus against many conventional programs, viz., that they are merely verbal exercises. I do not know of any educationist who defends number 4; practice teaching of some sort is always included in the conventional program. So let us eliminate number 4 from further discussion.

What about number 1, techniques only? When accused of trying to reduce teacher education to techniques, the PBTE/CBTE people demur—with or without benefits of consistency—that this is a straw man.[8] However, let us concede the point and shift to number 2, techniques, plus some rules for using this or that technique. Or does one have to move to number 3, adding principles or theories to justify the rules?

Here it is not clear what the PBTE/CBTE advocates say or mean to say. For example, in one project[9] an "educational psychology objective" is stated as follows: "The intern can demonstrate skills in motivation

---

[8] In one study reporting the problems of first-year teachers, one finds 75 items, each beginning with "How to," although some of these problems turn out to require more than techniques for solution, for example, how to get along with administrators; how to make oneself understood by students; how to select content; how to establish rapport with a class; and how to apply evidence and test hypothesis with relevant data. Frank W. Broadbent and Donald R. Cruickshank, "The Identification and Analysis of Problems of First Year Teachers," Paper read at Annual Convocation on Educational Research, October 19, 1965.

[9] Ambrose A. Clegg and Anna Ochoa, "Evaluation of a Performance-Based Program in Teacher Evaluation: Recommendations for Implementation," Washington University, Seattle.

based on recognition of personality needs." Another: "The intern can demonstrate knowledge of the interests characteristic of elementary school children of both sexes at all grade levels."

Presumably, "skills in motivation" are techniques, but is "recognition of personality needs" also a technique? Or does the teacher have to have knowledge about personality needs in order to recognize them? Are there rules such as the following perhaps: "Whenever a pupil strikes another pupil more than once in a five-minute span, his personality needs require outlets for aggression. In all such cases use aggression motivation technique #5." If this sounds absurd, it is because the proponents of PBTE assume that there is a general agreement as to the knowledge and general procedures that correspond to "personality needs" and "motivational" devices, and no such silly rules are necessary. But if this assumption is correct, then translating them into explicit behavioral objectives is unnecessary; if the assumption is incorrect, then something very much like the rule stated above would be necessary.

What about the intern "demonstrating knowledge of the interests characteristic of elementary school children . . ."? Does this mean that during his stay in college he "studied" verbal materials that constituted this knowledge and can recite it on demand? Or is there another way of demonstrating this knowledge?

Suppose two teachers are demonstrating their knowledge of the interests of children by assigning reading materials calibrated to them. Teacher A has studied the interests and materials in a textbook, has passed a test on them, and can state them. Teacher B has not studied them at all. Instead, Teacher B has been provided with a table that tells her precisely what reading to assign for a child at a specific grade, age, and sex. Both teachers now assign reading #5 to a given pupil. Have both teachers "demonstrated" the same knowledge? If reciting on demand is an adequate demonstration of knowledge, then the conventional programs claim that their graduates do have this kind of competence. If, on the other hand, a demonstration requires a "correct" performance in the classroom, then the performances of teachers A and B ought to differ so as to indicate the differences in their knowledge.

The difficulty with the overt performance criterion is that a correct performance does not carry its own rationale on its face. T can do X without knowing why X is being done or how X achieves whatever effects are expected from it. Consequently, if the objective is to "demonstrate" knowledge, there is no one predetermined performance that constitutes an unquestionable "demonstration." If it is to demonstrate "understanding," "application," or "interpretation," the criterial performance becomes even more problematic.

If the passages quoted from Mr. Williams's statement of the official USOE-AACTE position are taken at face value, then courses, credits, and degrees are not reliable demonstrations of operational competence and therefore not reliable as preparational competence either. Now much of what is done in courses for which credits and degrees, for example, are granted is knowledge about educational problems and procedures, so we must infer that it is this component rather than practice teaching that destroys the reliability of credits and courses as predictors of real or operational competence. *Ergo*, such materials or courses should be eliminated from the program unless operational competence is demonstrated independently by correct performances in the classroom. Yet when the conclusion that the elimination of theoretical work should follow from the PBTE manifesto is drawn, PBTE advocates object that this was not their intention.[10] But to repeat, if a correct performance is possible without knowledge, then a program containing a theoretical component may not preclude operational competence, but it is not a necessary condition for it.

The issues, then, are of two sorts: one is whether knowledge, understanding, and appreciation of certain theoretical or noetic materials are needed at all for good teaching and, if they are, whether they can be demonstrated in publicly observable, predetermined, and predescribed performances.

If PBTE sticks to observable behavior as a necessary criterion for performance, then it faces the task of identifying the behaviors that are to be called explaining, understanding, appreciating, and the like. I am not aware of any successful effort to do this, any more than we have been able to describe purposive behavior in purely behavioral language. If, on the other hand, PBTE admits mentalistic, introspective data into its descriptions of "performance," then it must sacrifice its claims to complete definitiveness, observability, and novelty. It cannot, it seems to me, consistently incorporate into its own program the alleged weaknesses of the conventional programs it is attacking and convert them into virtues by the incantation of the magic words "performance" and "competence."

This is more than semantic hair splitting, because if knowledge and theory are crucial in justifying the existence of a professional school, including a college of education, then denigrating or diminishing the role of knowledge and theory in the preparation of educational personnel erodes the need for such a college. Of course, the study of education as a process or as an institution could warrant the continuance of such an institution, but its role in the preparation of classroom teachers might become otiose.

Specifiability and Observability

As one reads the PBTE/CBTE literature, its two major emphases at times seem to coalesce, at others to separate. At times the "new" program concentrates on making the outcomes expected of the program explicit, for

---

[10] "A Critique of PBTE," AACTE: PBTE Series: 4.

example, on naming or describing them in words. At other times it urges that the outcomes not only be made explicit, but also that they be described in language that has unambiguous, verifiable, behavioral reference. For example, to describe the steps T is to follow in making a lesson plan for the teaching of fractions is to specify it. Whether an observer can tell that T is or is not making a lesson plan for the teaching of fractions—if it is to go beyond recognizing the words—depends on whether or not what T is doing is observable. If I were merely to say, "I am now practicing transcendental meditation," I would be specifying something which only I can verify. Unless transcendental meditation can be translated into standardized body movements or incantations, nobody else can verify my claim that I am doing transcendental meditation.

In a teacher-education program one conceivably might find outcomes that are:

1. Specifiable and observable, for example, writing on chalkboard and reciting multiplication tables.
2. Specifiable but not observable, for example, understanding the binomial theorem.
3. Observable but not specifiable, for example, pupil is "at home" in group.
4. Neither observable nor specifiable, for example, some of the effects of general education or a good home.

I shall not defend my choice of examples for these four types of educational outcomes. The important points are whether types 2, 3, and 4 are or are not empty classes, and just which mix of these outcomes a PBTE/CBTE program proposes to implement.

For example, many conventional programs contain items of type 2 and are condemned on grounds of nonobservability—of being merely conceptual and verbal. However, many CBTE programs seem to be satisfied if all of the items are specified, even though not all are observable; for instance, "teacher can conduct a discussion of social issues" or "teacher can relate to pupils of varying cultural backgrounds" are closer to type 2 than to type 1.

Type 4 is certainly anathema to PBTE—the unobservable and ineffable are the very essence of what PBTE is trying to eliminate from teacher education. But what about liberal arts courses as part of the program? How are the "products" of such courses to be incorporated as observable elements?

For example, how would one justify the study of the history of education as a component of teacher education? A teacher might be hard put, when counting up the performances of a day, a week, or a year, to specify the effects of the course in history of education in these performances. It would be even more awkward to say in advance that a teacher will "use" such history in this or that performance. Yet the whole teaching style of X may be affected in unspecifiable ways by the layers of meanings that the study of history and many other subjects has built into his background. For, paradoxically, some studies function not because they are retained as learned, but rather because we forget selectively, so that only a framework of cognitive and evaluative categories remain to shape perception and feeling without themselves being perceived.[11]

Yet I do not find PBTE programs advocating the elimination of general education requirements because they do not meet the requirements of specifiability and observability. Some even would admit foundational courses in history and philosophy of education into the program, despite the alleged reports from teachers in service that only practice teaching and experience in the classroom have helped them.

Here again, we cannot have it both ways. Strict adherence to the observability criterion rules out many of the conceptual components of the teacher education curriculum. Even specifiability rules out some modes of functioning that intuitively, at least, we acknowledge as important.

What Do They Really Mean?

I am led to suspect that the effort to have it both ways explains much of the ambiguity of the whole movement. It may be that all PBTE devotees intend to say is something like this: "Teacher education programs contain as parts of the professional sequence components that *promise* operational competence. Traditionally these are theory courses and practice teaching. The methods courses in particular, but also cognate *courses* in curriculum, organization, and class management do not now produce operational competence. These 'courses' we propose to eliminate *as courses* and to substitute laboratory and clinical or even actual classroom experiences for them."

Stated in this way, CBTE makes a great deal of sense, because teacher education has always been weak on the laboratory and clinical phases of professional training. Partly this has been occasioned by the cost of good laboratory and clinical work (education programs are relatively inexpensive), and even more by the mistaken belief that student teaching somehow combines all the virtues of the laboratory, the clinic, and the internship.

However, so construed, CBTE is hardly a novel proposal and certainly not a radical one. It does not entail the slicing up of the teaching act

---

[11] Precisely because of this paradox, it has seemed to some of us that Michael Polanyi's notion of tacit knowing, that is, using the fruits of learning that we cannot make explicit deserves more attention than it has received.

into modules of minute segments called performances and reducing teacher education to practicing these segments. The radical import of PBTE/CBTE comes out only when it is construed as seeking to make a program *entirely* out of laboratory and clinical work of field experience *without the theory and knowledge that is presupposed by such work in other professional fields.*

Unfortunately, the rhetoric of PBTE/CBTE has been taken as justifying *any* alternative that can meet the performance criterion, as if anything would be better than the conventional program. Some of these alternatives are so devoid of theory that they constitute a death blow to the attempts to develop the college of education as a professional school on the models of colleges of law, engineering, medicine, and business administration. This model may be called technology. Technology is rationalized technique, the *logos* of method. Professional schools apply theory to their problems of practice. The push for PBTE need not be, but as promoted is compatible with a regression from technology to technique; from theory to rules of procedures; from professional education to paraprofessional training.

Institutionally, the regression would make it logical for the bulk of teacher preparation to be done in postsecondary institutions as one of the technician specialities. After all, this kind of training turns out acceptable electronic technicians, auto mechanics, and the like. There is no reason why it could not turn out good technical paraprofessionals in teaching as well. The two-year normal school operated on this pattern and, in many countries, it is still the standard way of training elementary teachers. There is something to be said in favor of the well-trained paraprofessional as against a poorly trained pseudo-professional.

Furthermore, the PBTE approach, interpreted strictly, could articulate well with an increased use of programed instruction, with or without sophisticated hardware. Indeed, any hope of increasing the productivity of school services lies in the use of standardized interchangeable procedures by relatively low-paid operators. PBTE programs could turn out such help much better than the existing programs. This is not to say that the existing programs make very impressive career demands on the prospective teacher, but being embedded in a four-year baccalaureate program they give the illusion of being professional. In fact, the four-year program merely selects college graduates for whom teaching is an inexpensive hedge against unemployment. However, being intelligent and having a college degree, they expect more from the job in money and prestige than it will afford them.[12]

---

[12] I have treated this problem at unconscionable length in Chap. 3 of *The Real World of the Public Schools* (New York: Harcourt Brace Jovanovich, 1972).

There are many other ramifications of the PBTE proposals—if they are stated clearly, taken seriously, and interpreted strictly. The uncritical acceptance accorded to these proposals by institutions preparing and certifying teachers makes one doubt whether they really understand what sort of sticks are hidden behind the golden carrots. Perhaps this is what one critic of education meant by the "mindlessness" of teacher educators, but I believe that, however belatedly, their minds are beginning to function again.

Being mindful would mean thinking critically about the following questions.

1. Are the current certification programs for beginning teachers really professional in their demands on the candidate?
2. Could paraprofessional training be done in institutions other than colleges of education?
3. Is it feasible to create a four-year, fully professional teacher education program that would be comparable to a four-year engineering program?
4. What sort of laboratory, clinical, and internship experience would a fully professional program require and cost?
5. Given such a program, what tests of preparational competence would be suitable and acceptable for initial certification?
6. What should be the role of the state and of the profession in constructing and monitoring such tests?

4. *Performance-Based Teaching: A New Orthodoxy?*

Frederick C. Neff

I.

It has been remarked that one of the reasons that John Dewey's educational views caught on and were so widely adopted was that he was so little understood. It might be added that one of the reasons that Progressive Education came under attack and eventually faltered was that its practitioners tended to identify it almost exclusively with method and either ignored or failed to understand its theoretical underpinnings and philosophic goals. We are now offered a method of teaching that singles out "performance" as the test of a learner's knowledge, skills, and attitudes, the assumption apparently being that whatever is learned has its behavioral counterpart. Whether the method called "performance-based teaching" will survive as a viable movement or whether, like Progressive Education, its founders for lack of purpose, will ultimately depend, not upon the efficiency of its methodology, but upon the extent to which it can be directed toward defensible ends. This is to say that classroom procedures and teaching devices have no inherent value. They can be assessed only in terms of the beliefs, outcomes, and habits of thought they are designed to foster.

Thomas Huxley once observed that it is the fate of every new truth to begin as a heresy and to end as a superstition. What sets this evolutionary process in motion is the unresisted temptation to capture new ideas and

Source. This article is published with permission of the author and the Macmillan Publishing Company and is part of a forthcoming work titled *Selected Readings in the Philosophy of Education,* Fourth Edition, edited by Joe Park.

to contain them within the confines of a method—to formalize, ritualize, and institutionalize them. As a result, method is initially enlisted in the realization of an idea, then is joined with the idea, then becomes indistinguishable from the idea, and, finally, replaces the idea. Reductionism in this sense represents the tendency to confound means with the ends they were originally designed to serve, culminating in some instances in an actual substitution of means for ends.

Aristotle, for example, was himself an empiricist and a champion of observation and testing, but it was not long before his outlook became reduced to and identified with the fruits of his own necessarily limited observations; "Aristotelianism" thus came to represent a circumscribed methodology that Aristotle himself would have disavowed. Jesus was a moral and humane teacher who preached tolerance and compassion, but soon tolerance and compassion became ritualized and reduced to the performance of specified acts at appointed times and places. The thrust of ideas represented in the thought of Hegel became, in both Marxism and fascism, reduced to politics and ideology. Among his interpreters, the imaginative and figurative creations of Freud often became reduced to ghostly demons and ancestral entities that were thought to enslave our feelings and proscribe our behavior. In the thought of John Dewey, the emphasis upon practicality was assumed by many to mean an exclusive attention to method and overt acts of performance, whereas it was Dewey who reminded us that "theory is . . . in the end the most practical of all things." The point is that when ends become reduced to means, when the performance of acts becomes a substitute for a thoughtful appraisal of purpose, performance behavior becomes an end in itself, and purpose and meaning become obscured. This is what has happened wherever science has been reduced to scientism, wherever religion has been reduced to ritual, and wherever education has been reduced to method. To the thoughtful educator, the attempt to reduce all education to acts of performance thus becomes a matter of serious concern.

II.

To say that because teaching is an activity it is therefore reducible to a kind of performance behavior is a grossly deceptive statement. The notion that, because man is an animal, he is therefore nothing but an animal, the late evolutionary naturalist Sir Julian Huxley called the "nothing-but fallacy." A similar sort of fallacy appears when it is argued that because teaching and learning occasionally involve, make use of, and are manifested in performance, education is therefore nothing but performance. When it is applied to areas of learning that are by nature or by definition nontheoretical—where specific knowledge or simple skills are involved—the performance argument is fairly adequate. The best way to evince the fact that one has learned how to swim is to demonstrate swimming ability through performance. If typing or shorthand skills are in question, performance is called for by way of demonstrating that one can typewrite or take dictation in shorthand. Reading and computation skills are likewise subject to measurement in terms of performance. Has one learned how to operate a lathe? Again, the test is performance.

When, however, we begin to move into historical, moral, and humanistic areas of learning—where attitudes, perspective, and judgment are called for—we begin to sense the inappropriateness of attempting to apply the criterion of "performance." Mastery of a knowledge of history—if we mean something vastly more than a mere ability to recite facts—is not reducible to a performance; rather, its significance resides in the extent to which judgments about and perspectives on the past, present, and future are modified by virtue of historical knowledge. What is meant by integrity or character is not mastery of a series of discrete acts, each of which is to be identified, categorized, and labeled a "performance of character." On the contrary, character represents an attitude whereby a high degree of moral consistency obtains in human conduct. Otherwise, we should be compelled to say that during the intervals between the performance of specific moral acts, a man had no character. It is the perdurable idea, moral principle, or attitude—not the performance of separate acts—that constitutes what is meant by character. This is to say that, although acts of behavior may from time to time be representative of character, character itself is neither reducible to nor confined within such acts. Historical knowledge or moral integrity is thus not itself a form of behavior; rather, it is knowledge and integrity that shape and give meaning to behavior.

The ability to distinguish between the gross and the subtle, between immediate objectives and long-range purposes, and between the appropriate and the inappropriate is what demarcates the classroom hack from the master educator. Whereas the hack conceives teaching as limited to ritual and performance, the educator views it is a means for the liberation of intelligence. Although both may engage in activities that may loosely be termed "performance behavior," the hack is a captive of his method, while the educator utilizes methods only as they are consonant with his goals. The former conceives "performance" in terms of drug-store prescriptions and cookbook recipes, the latter in light of the ends he seeks to accomplish. The hack resorts to coercive manipulation through rewards and punishments; the educator employs discussion, mutual understanding, and inquiry. The former uses the method of imposition; the latter is concerned with the refinement of choice-making abilities in the context of alternatives.

III.

It serves little purpose to argue that, because everything man does involves some sort of behavior, therefore behavior is all there is to thought and conduct. Such a truism is both specious and misleading. If all man's activities are behavioral, then the term "behavior" becomes either meaningless or superfluous; just as, if the only color in the universe were red, "red" would have no meaning. Terms assume meaning only as they can be distinguished from other terms.

Inclusion within the behavioral rubric of activities such as thinking, willing, pondering, judging, imagining, and the like calls for a careful and thoroughgoing reassessment of the concept of behavior itself. Just as moral controversies today are seldom resolvable in terms of an old-fashioned either-or, good-or-bad dichotomy, but, rather, involve different and competing conceptions of the good, so controversies concerning the nature of behavior are least fruitful when they center merely upon the question of what is and what is not behavioral. Our important concern is better phrased when questions are raised, not about whether thinking, for example, is or is not a form of behavior, but about how thoughtful behavior differs from thoughtless—and other—kinds of behavior. Simply to lump all human activities in a general catchall of behavior, as though to do so settled once and for all the whole matter of what constitutes thought, is both naive and deceptive. Acts of charity and acts of murder, it may be granted, both represent forms of behavior. But it scarcely follows that, because both kinds of acts are behavioral, there is no qualitative difference between them.

Nevertheless, there are people in education today whose enchantment with behavior is such that, in their zeal to reduce every aspect of life and thought to a "performance" level, they would ignore certain subtle yet highly significant distinctions within the gamut of human learnings and human activities. In the crass demand for "Performance! Performance!" there is danger of neglecting to account for the subtle nuances, the speculative hypotheses, the spiritual aspirations, and the philosophic thrusts that are characteristic of the nature and history of man and that defy captivation and classification within the confines of systems. In the words of the late Justice Felix Frankfurter, "Life, with its exuberance and irony, has a way of making mockery of such systems."[1] Man is, in the phase of Aldous Huxley, a "multiple amphibian," compelled to move and act in several incompatible realms—biological, spiritual, emotional, cerebral, and social. The infinite depth and complexity of human nature must make us wary

---

[1] Felix Frankfurter, "The Meaning of Dewey to Us All," in H. W. Laidler, ed., *John Dewey at Ninety* (New York: The League for Industrial Democracy, 1950), p. 11.

of the notion that its superficial aspects represent all the being there is and that every human quality is reducible to its quantitatively measurable counterpart. As Stanislav Andreski has stated it:

> When the psychologists refuse to study anything but the most mechanical forms of behaviour—often so mechanical that even rats have no chance to show their higher faculties—and then present their most trivial findings as the true picture of the human mind, they prompt people to regard themselves as automata, devoid of responsibility or worth, which can hardly remain without effect upon the tenor of social life.[2]

The behavioral argument is sometimes used to defend the notion that, since thought, reflection, and imagination are forms of behavior, then all forms of behavior must be thoughtful, reflective, and imaginative. Again, there is a parallel between this notion and the presumption of earlier "progressive" teachers that, since learning is an activity, then all activities must involve learning. The fact that many activities can be miseducative was rather conveniently overlooked. Yet, the connection between thought and activity needs to be preserved. In his *The Concept of Mind,*[3] Gilbert Ryle undertakes to destroy what he calls the myth of the dogma of the ghost in the machine—the Cartesian notion that an inner mind is separable from outward behavior. Descartes, it will be recalled, was an out-and-out dualist, believing that mind and body exist in two separate realms, each governed by its own, independent principles. The Cartesian myth, according to Ryle, is responsible for an indefensible dichotomy between mind and body, between thought and action.

Dewey, likewise, rejected Cartesianism, adhering to the view that thought is continuous with action; nevertheless, he retained a pointed distinction between the two. Ryle, however, argues that action is not simply an extension of thought but that thought is identical with action. Here, again, we are moved precariously close to equating the two, with the unfortunate result that action can easily be mistaken for thought, in which case we are in difficulty again. When, however, we qualify certain kinds of action as thoughtful and others as thoughtless, we are in effect recognizing a distinction which the mere equation of thought and action fails to account for.

That attitudes and feelings are themselves forms of behavior is likewise open to question. In the words of Stanley Elam:

> . . . while performance-based instruction eliminates waste in the learning process through clarity in definition of goals, it can be applied only to learning in which the objectives sought are susceptible of

---

[2] Stanislav Andreski, *Social Sciences as Sorcery* (London: Andre Deutsch, 1972).
[3] Gilbert Ryle, *The Concept of Mind* (New York: Barnes & Noble, 1949).

definition in advance in behavioral terms. Thus it is difficult to apply when the outcomes sought are complex and subtle, and particularly when they are affective or attitudinal in character.[4]

The poet Keats's insight that "heard melodies are sweet, but those unheard are sweeter," and Browning's reference to "all, the world's coarse thumb and finger failed to plumb" remind us that not every human thought and feeling rises to the surface level of perceptibility. Even the noted behaviorist B. F. Skinner concedes that "many feelings have inconspicuous behavioral manifestations."[5]

IV.

Whereas the Deweyan conception of the relationship between thought and action is holistic, the present emphasis in performance behavior appears to be merely analytic. It tends to isolate performance from thoughtful and long-range purposes, of which it is only a representation and to which it is properly subservient, thus dignifying the trivial and denigrating the important. It suggests the sort of analytic definition of education that Professor C. J. Ducasse formulated when he wrote:

> Education is activity of one or another particular kind A, by a person T (teacher); activity A being motivated my T's desire to cause in a person P (pupil)—who may or may not be the same person as T— a response of kind R, which T believes will immediately or eventually result in acquisition by P of some capacity C, which T desires P to acquire; activity A being shaped by T's belief (i) that the existing circumstances are of a certain kind S; and (ii) that, under circumstances of kind S, activity of kind A by T would more or less probably cause or contribute to cause directly or indirectly in P acquisition of the desiderated capacity C.[6]

Involved in such an analysis is an attempt to tease out the several ingredients of the teaching-learning process, presumably under the impression that the juxtaposition of these separate elements is all that is required for learning to take place. But no competent teacher guides learning in such terms. If he attempted to do so, his endeavors would be limited to a mechanical process of sheer indoctrination. What provisions, for example, is made for an exchange and interchange of ideas? How is the emergence

---

[4] Stanley Elam, *Performance-Based Teacher Education: What Is the State of the Art?* (Washington: American Association of Colleges for Teacher Education, 1972), p. 17.

[5] B. F. Skinner, *Beyond Freedom and Dignity* (New York: Knopf, 1971), p. 106.

[6] C. J. Ducasse, "On the Function and Nature of the Philosophy of Education," *Harvard Educational Review*, **XXVI** (Spring 1956), pp. 103-111.

of problem or novel situations provided for? What regard is taken of the interests, nature, or aptitudes of the learner? It is significant, also, to recognize that the only activity mentioned is lodged with the teacher, while the key words describing the role of the pupil are "response" and "acquisition."

Authoritarianism can present itself in many guises. What the indoctrination or conditioning thesis presumes is that there is no essential difference between the training of an animal and the education of a child. Because an animal is incapable of decision-making on the basis of principle, the outcomes of animal training must be predetermnied. The seeing-eye dog will halt at every curb, with the result that—*but not in order that*—its master is better able to avoid stumbling or walking into traffic. But there is no evidence to support the contention that it acts out of a sense of moral purpose; its behavior is strictly a matter of conditioning. As Professor Harry Broudy has remarked, "Skinner quite rightly doesn't worry about whether his pigeons understand what they are doing so long as they do it."[7] Because human beings are capable of formulating, altering, and abiding by principles, the outcomes of learning that is distinctively human must be open-ended. To say that education involves a continual reorganization of experience is another way of saying that education enables the learner continually to reconstruct himself, his outlooks, his ways of viewing himself and his world. Subtle attempts to blur over or to compromise the distinctions between training and education had best be viewed with suspicion. One of the most forthright attempts to bring in the conditioning technique under the guise of democracy is found in the following passage from the writings of the American educational sociologist, Ross L. Finney:

> Ours are the schools of a democracy, which *all* the children attend. At least half of them never had an original idea of any general nature, and never will. But they must behave as if they had *sound* ideas. Whether those ideas are original or not matters not in the least. It is better to be right than original. What the duller half of the population needs, therefore, is to have their reflexes conditioned into behavior that is socially suitable. And the wholesale memorizing of catchwords . . . is the only practical means of establishing bonds in the duller intellects between the findings of social scientists and the corresponding social behavior of the masses. Instead of trying to teach dullards to think for themselves, the intellectual leaders must think for them and drill the results . . . into their synapses.[8]

---

[7] Harry S. Broudy, *A Criticism of Performance-Based Teacher Education* (Washington, D.C.: American Association of Colleges for Teacher Education, 1972), p. 11.

[8] Ross L. Finney, *A Sociological Philosophy of Education* (New York: Macmillan, 1928), p. 395.

Mere employment of the Pavlovian technique—producing anything from the simple salivation of a dog to the complex moral and social dilemmas raised by Anthony Burgess's *A Clockwork Orange*—fails to meet head on the fact of the basic, irreconcilable cleavage between the democratic conception of man as a free, choice-making individual and the absolutist notion of man as an object of behavior manipulation and thought control.

V.

In our urgency to emphasize skills and knowledge, we have neglected to attend to a consideration of the ends toward which skills and knowledge are to be directed. We have failed to distinguish between what might be called the *necessary* and the *sufficient* conditions of education. Our attempts to achieve a scornful detachment have resulted in an obsession with manners and surfaces. In our concentration upon mere performance, we are likely to turn out teachers who—like one of those audio-animatronic robots at Disneyland—are perfect facsimiles of teaching until you get close and hear the gears whirling. Unaccompanied by a cultivation of taste, mere ability to read is no guarantee that what is read will not be limited to the pornographic, the trivial, and the useless. Mere ability to write can be used for the purpose of demanding a bank teller to hand over his money. Mere knowledge of chemistry, unrelated to a reflected-upon system of values, can result—indeed, has resulted—in the production of bombs, napalm, and other devices for the destruction of human lives. Unless we are willing to pay the price, mastery of the fundamental skills cannot be separated from the moral, ethical, and humane ends that education is ultimately designed to serve.

The current tendency to concentrate upon efficiency and methodology is apparently predicated on the notion that, once a method has been perfected, the use to which it will be put is of no great consequence. In the later years of his life, Albert Einstein remarked, "Perfection of means and confusion of goals seem—in my opinion—to characterize our age." The need to chart our course before embarking upon it has been pointed out by Boyd Bode, who wrote: "There is little comfort, when we don't know where we are going, in being assured that we are on our way and traveling fast." A similar observation has been voiced by Lewis Mumford, who has said that "If society is paralyzed today, it is not for lack of means but for lack of purpose." That education is inescapably a value-ridden undertaking has been pointed out by John L. Childs. In his words: ". . . anyone who is conducting the education of the young should realize that he is involved in that basic philosophic enterprise of trying to distinguish the better from the worse in modes of human living."[9]

---

[9] John L. Childs, Foreword to Frederick C. Neff, *Philosophy and American Education* (New York: The Center for Applied Research in Education, Inc., 1966), p. v.

Nor is the centrality of theoretical ends limited to education. The pleading of cases in a court of law is an activity that demands a kind of "performance" competency. But it hardly follows that prospective lawyers need have no prior understanding of theoretical concepts of individual rights, of equity, or of the basic values of human life. What distinguishes the shyster from the respected jurist is his philosophy of law. Although both have available to them the same legal techniques, it is the principles and values in terms of which techniques are directed that make the difference. Similarly, a physician may be ever so competent in diagnosing an illness, in prescribing medicine, or in administering an anesthetic. He may be ever so skilful in knowing how to perform an abortion, how to perform euthanasia, or how to perform a lobotomy. Yet, knowing how to perform such operations is obviously no substitute for a viable and reflectively formulated code of ethics, without which procedural decisions cannot responsibly be made.

Whether in law, in medicine, or in education, the ends to which an enterprise is geared determine the direction it takes and the basis for its evaluation. Ends without means are poor indeed; but means without ends are poorer still. The inspiration, the zest, and the excitement that are associated with education as a noble calling come not from methods and techniques but from the values it seeks to foster.[10] But we miss the whole purpose of education when, in the words of Santayana, we merely redouble our effort, having forgotten our aim. If success in education is not very different from success in life, we might do well to recall the words of Walter Pater:

The service of philosophy, of speculative culture, [of education,] toward the human spirit, is to rouse, to startle it to a life of constant and eager observation. . . . Not the fruit of experience, but experience itself, is the end. A counted number of pulses only is given to us of a variegated, dramatic life. How may we see in them all that is to be seen in them by the finest senses? How shall we pass most swiftly from point to point, and be present always at the focus, where the greatest number of vital forces unite in their purest energy? . . . To burn always with this hard, gemlike flame, to maintain this ecstasy, is success in life.[11]

---

[10] According to Lillian Weber, associate professor of early-childhood education at City College of New York: "Our view is that good learning is accompanied by zest and energy. But there can be no set pattern, because one child may need structured help while another needs utmost freedom to explore. In fact, we urge teachers to retain whatever of the old traditions they need. . . . The main thing is to try to restore the human dimension to education."

[11] Walter Horatio Pater, *The Renaissance* (New York: Mentor Books, 1959), pp. 157-158.

VI.

It is important to bear in mind that the performance-based approach to teaching and learning represents, after all, but one among many debatable theories of teaching and learning. Once instituted and "officialized," however, it—like a state religion—is likely to become a new orthodoxy, deviation from which will be viewed as heretical. Essentially a learning theory, it, ironically, lays claim to being nontheoretical. At present it can be assessed only in terms of its hypotheses and anticipated results, since it has yet to prove itself in regard to long-range effectiveness. To the extent that it is exclusively a learning theory, it cannot properly be construed as an educational theory. In so far as its methods can serve contrary and mutually incompatible ends, it has no built-in or self-corrective philosophy to guide it. Concerned primarily with skill and subject-matter proficiency, it is conceivably adaptable to a complete and successful mastery of the wrong things. It seems to be focused, not upon educational values, but exclusively upon specific teaching and learning objectives. One gathers the impression that occasional references to innovation and creativity represent attempts to placate critics more than they reflect a genuine ingredient of performance-based teaching itself.[12] What few references there are to theoretical aims, goals, and values appear to be "hitched on" as afterthoughts, not guidelines for procedure. Because performance-based teaching is primarily a technique, in no sense does it qualify as an educational philosophy. Finally, one cannot but raise the question whether such a method would not be as applicable and effective—perhaps more so— in a totalitarian setting as within the framework of democracy.[13]

The overriding task of education today relates to a revitalization of its service in the realization of humane ideals, a reformulation of its professional identity, and a recapturing of its sense of direction. It is precisely because methods of teaching and learning can be geared to questionable and conflicting ends that a reinstatement of the crucial role of principles, purposes, and values is our most urgent educational need.

---

[12] Albert Shanker, president of New York's United Federation of Teachers, says: "Actually, the creative teacher is the one who has the greatest chance of being fired by outsiders. Who will be the evaluators? What are their values? How do they propose to improve or dispose of teachers?" It might also be asked how a person with a strongly developed aesthetic sense, a passion for innovation, a desire for reflection, or a strongly marked independence could possibly be happy within the strictures of performance-based teaching.

[13] If, as many educators believe, "quality education" hinges upon the values of the nation as a whole, perhaps the American "success motif" is itself in need of reexamination. Says Harvard Sociologist Seymour Lipset: "In the United States the thing that matters is who wins, no matter how. There is more emphasis on accomplishing something, no matter what means are used."

5. *Conceptual Confusion and Premature Policies*

Mauritz Johnson

It would be difficult to find anyone who advocates ineffective teaching, favors the preparation of incompetent teachers, or believes that abstract pedagogical knowledge serves any useful purpose if it does not enlighten the performance of educational practitioners. A movement to certify teachers on the basis of demonstrated competence and to prepare them to perform their tasks effectively should, therefore, enlist the enthusiastic approval of everyone. Even one—*especially* one—who has for many years taught teachers and directed teacher education programs would readily acknowledge the shortcomings of current programs and welcome research and experimentation with alternative approaches. The trouble with movements, however, is that they are not subject to anyone's control. The responsible, intelligent initiators soon find themselves joined and then engulfed by a strange assortment of impatient zealots who ignore or fail to grasp subtle distinctions and inject a bewildering variety of contradictory and untenable ideas that subvert and dissipate the original purposes. Movements are stopped from within.

The literature associated with the PBTE movement is unusually voluminous, and every caution one would wish to urge is to be found in it somewhere. Every criticism, therefore, can be dismissed as a misinterpretation. Each proponent has his own selective view, which does not embrace all that has been written. He tends to agree with the criticisms, but protests that they are not applicable to PBTE as it should be understood. But how can one know what features are to be taken seriously?

Surely, official actions of certifying agencies must be accorded serious

---

Source. This article was prepared especially for this volume.

attention. These policy decisions are widely publicized and, indeed, a score card is maintained reporting the status of the movement in each of the states (Roth, 1972; Schmieder, 1973). Some states are passively watching and waiting, some are in the discussion stage, and others are experimenting and developing materials and instruments. Such activities merit applause. There is much to be done and much to be clarified before implementation can even be considered.

Yet some states have already officially committed themselves to certification on the basis of demonstrated competence with no assurance of either the soundness or the feasibility of their vague proposals. Since professional certification staffs must be fully aware of the ambiguities, uncertainties, and controversies associated with the movement, one can only conclude that they found themselves in a position where they could not resist political pressures for some ostensible token of guaranteed return on educational tax dollars. Nevertheless, these premature implementation decisions intensify the need for an examination of the confused rhetoric of the movement.

The case of New York State will serve as a starting point for the discussion that follows. The seriousness of the action taken there is, as elsewhere, compounded by its extension beyond certification to intrude upon teacher education. Because the meanings of "competency" and "performance" are far from clear, some of the sources of the confusion surrounding them will be briefly analyzed. However, even if this confusion did not exist, it would not follow that the selection and organization of the content of a teacher education program must rest, totally or even principally, on the same *basis* as certification. In the concluding sections of the chapter the multifaceted nature of teacher education will be illustrated.

A Policy on Performance

The New York State Education Department (1972, p. 2) has proclaimed it to be "an accepted fact" . . . "that teacher education, certification, and practice must be reformed" and has further announced its conviction that "pupil performance should be the underlying basis for judging teacher competence" and that "the basis for certification should be teacher competence rather than total reliance on college courses." Each of these three pronouncements has a built-in escape hatch. The first omits any such adverb as "universally" or "widely" and therefore leaves one to wonder just who it is that accepts the "fact" that reform is needed. In the second, the key word is "underlying"—no mention is made of the *manifest* basis for judgment. The saving term in the third statement is "total"—it implies that there ought still to be *partial* reliance on college courses.

That these statements could not have been meant to be taken seriously in any case is evident from three associated assertions. The brave prescription as to how teacher competence should be judged is accompanied by the parenthetical observation that this cannot now be done because "measures of pupil performance are inadequate . . . and teacher competences have not been identified." (In other words, if we had some ham, we could have ham and eggs, if we had some eggs.) Furthermore, it turns out that not only should competence be only a partial basis for certification, but "competence" will include ". . . competence in general background knowledge, subject matter knowledge, and teaching skill." Anyone who labored under the perfectly sensible but apparently mistaken assumption that "competence" was somehow restricted to "teaching skill" can now both ponder the meaning of "competence in knowledge" and rejoice that teachers will still be expected to possess it.

The third reassuring statement is one over which no one can cavil: ". . . no one has been able to state with assurance that the teachers who are certified can produce specified learning gains in the pupils they are to teach." Here is a fact that is indeed widely accepted, and to it might be added the corollary that no one ever will be able so to state, although the degree of assurance will be inversely proportional to the size of the specified gains.

If these statements appeared in a journal article, they would be relatively harmless. But they are backed up by a decision by the distinguished and powerful New York State Board of Regents "to establish a system of certification by which the State can assure the public that professional personnel in the schools possess and maintain demonstrated competence to enable children to learn." And, indeed, by September 1, 1980 there is to be ". . . a state-monitored system of performance assessment centers in which those desiring certification will have to demonstrate their competence to professionals." (N.Y.S. Education Department, 1972, p. 3, 7.) A variety of ways in which competence can be demonstrated is suggested. But conspicuously absent in the proposal is the "underlying basis" identified earlier, that is, pupil performance.

Any idea that promises to increase the effectiveness of teachers through preparation more relevant to their tasks deserves attention. But without careful thought, research, development, experimentation, and demonstration, it does not deserve to be implemented, much less mandated. This was the point that Shanker (1973) made in behalf of a united teaching profession in New York State. In doing so, he praised the Rosner report (1973), which, "unlike other reports on this problem and in apparent criticism of recent legislation in a number of states mandating that in the future teachers be certified on the basis of performance . . .," treated the idea as a hypothesis to be tested and insisted on "a proper period of research and development before the program becomes operative." What need to be developed are ". . . instruments (for teacher evaluation), instructional materials (for teacher education), laboratory facilities for training, and incentives for inservice teachers . . ." (Shanker, 1973, p. 3-4).

Preparation for Certification

In a narrow sense, it is of little concern to teacher education institutions how a state chooses to certify its teachers so long as the state does not tell the institutions how to educate them. Of course, under the "old" system, if the state decided that all teachers had to have a course in the history of teacher certification, then institutions that wanted their graduates to be certifiable in that state would have to offer such a course. And to some degree, certification authorities may have their own ideas of what should be included in a course in, for example, educational psychology, and may refuse to approve a program that includes a course with the right title but the wrong content. But, in the main, institutions have been conceded the right to devise their own programs within a broad pattern and to exceed minima whenever sound teacher education seemed to demand it.

In a broader professional sense, those who prepare teachers are properly very much concerned about the bases and standards used for certification. Therefore, a decision to base certificaton on a criterion-referenced competency evaluation may be applauded by some as a step toward stricter accountability and denounced by others for limiting the teacher's role to that of a technician or tactician. Regardless, however, of whether a group of teacher educators did or did not favor the approach, they should have little difficulty making whatever program adjustments might be required to assure that upon graduation the majority of their students could qualify for certification. But it is quite another matter to ground a criterion-referenced certification process on a teacher-education program that is "performanced-based."

Perhaps teacher educators who foresee a dangerous encroachment upon their domain are reading into the proposals and pronouncements something that is not there. As the saying goes, there may be less in them than meets the eye. To be sure, the New York State document softens the statement that for purposes of future program accreditation "performance-based and field-centered teacher education is recognized as a most promising approach" by adding that "variations or alternatives which demonstrate achievement of the Regents goal and also reflect the convictions underlying this goal, will also be carefully considered." This is reassuring, indeed, but what is one to make, then, of such other assertions as the following?

"These [current trial] projects . . . reduce the number of education courses in that they eliminate course-counting itself and concentrate attention on the prospective teacher's ability to bring about predictable accomplishment on the part of pupils."

"It is also imperative that the potential teacher's rate of progress through the [performance-based] teacher education program be determined by demonstrated competency. . . ."

" 'Field-centered' . . . means that most, but not necessarily all, teacher education be conducted in schools or other educational agencies in the community" (N.Y.S. Education Department, 1972, p. 4).

The fallacy that is implicit in this whole scheme is the assumption that if an agreement could be reached on the requisite competencies, then this set of competencies would serve as an appropriate basis for the organization of a teacher education program. Once this assumption is made, then the equally fallacious corollaries follow, that candidates should proceed through the list as rapidly as they can or wish and that the "field" is the most appropriate setting in which to acquire and demonstrate the competencies. To some extent these assumptions are probably valid for the training of technicians; they are valid for teacher education only to the extent that teachers are viewed as technicians.

Skill and Knowledge in Teaching

"Performance" is often associated with "skill," but not every performance requires skill. Most of the acts performed by teachers in the classroom could probably be performed by any intelligent adult and by some children, if they knew what should be done. Teachers probably vary little in their abilities to execute the performances called for in a detailed instructional plan. The improvement that is possible in the actual performance is limited primarily to the achievement of somewhat greater poise and efficiency of action.

Knowing what to put into the plan and in what respects and under what circumstances to depart from it is quite another matter. In this regard, teachers differ widely. But these functions demand knowledge more than ability to perform. Most teachers could perform quite satisfactorily if they knew what to do. To a greater extent teachers are employed for their knowledge and understanding than for their skill in performance. When teaching is poor, it is more likely due to the wrong things being done than to the right things being done poorly.

It is quite possible, of course, for a teacher to know perfectly well what to do and still not do it because he is irresponsible, has insufficient time or resources, or is prevented by some stupid regulation from doing it. But seldom does he fail to do what he knows to be appropriate because he lacks the ability to perform the action called for. Some teachers are inept at keeping records, distributing materials, forming subgroups, leading discussions, and the like, but this ineptness can be overlooked if they *know* which records to keep, which materials to distribute to whom at what time, what subgroups to form and for what purpose, and what topics to discuss and why. In teaching, it is indeed performance that counts, but what performance is forthcoming depends very much on the teacher's knowledge and motivation and relatively little on any particular performance capabilities, skills, or "competencies."

The Concern about Competence

If the foregoing analysis is essentially correct, there is something incongruous and potentially dangerous in any decision to organize an entire program of teacher education on the basis of a list of competencies. Likewise, it would be unsound to base the certification of teachers solely upon the demonstrated performance of a limited set of tasks associated with teaching. A credential for admission to what should be a learned profession cannot be treated like a Boy Scout merit badge, to be earned by checking off a series of tasks as soon as each has been demonstrated.

It is easy to see how a layman, disturbed by the failure of many children to learn to read adequately, might arrive at the conclusion that the solution to the problem lies in insisting that all new elementary teachers demonstrate possession of the "skills of teaching reading." It is doubtful, however, that many laymen would consider this necessary condition a sufficient one for certification.

According to most people, it would go without saying that the teacher also knew why reading is taught, was well-grounded in literature and the linguistics of the English language, was familiar with the several theoretical positions regarding the nature of the reading process and the research findings in support of each, and was to some degree an expert on how children develop and differ and why they behave as they do. Why then are so many presumably expert professional educators so willing to limit the preparation and licensure of teachers to the acquisition and demonstration of competencies?

To arrive at even a partial answer to this question, and simultaneously to enter a word of caution against such a restrictive view of teacher education, one must put the entire issue into a broader context. For what is being advocated with respect to the training of teachers is also being urged upon teachers everywhere, in whatever way they may have been educated. Instead of "performance" and "competency," code words that seem to be restricted to the teacher-preparation enterprise, the more widely used catch phrases are "behaviorally-stated objectives," "criterion-referenced evaluation," "mastery learning," and "accountability." Each of these expressions represents a perfectly valid concept, but in a few short years, they have been distorted beyond recognition and have been misapplied to a degree that is dangerous.

Conceptual Confusion

The six phrases to which reference has been made have several features in common. All emphasize *specificity* and all pertain to *outcomes* of instruction. Moreover, they are all essentially concerned with *evaluation* of those outcomes, yet several of them are very frequently infelicitously used in connection with the planning and organization of the instruction itself. The effect in these instances is that objectives become confused with evidence that they have been achieved.

Behaviorally-stated objectives. To state an instructional objective "behaviorally" is not in all cases to make it a "behavioral objective." There are objectives that might be called behavioral, but there are also many that cannot under any circumstances be so designated. If that which is to be learned is a behavior, such an objective can only be stated in behavioral terms. Objectives that are not behaviors can, if necessary for purposes of evaluation, be expressed in terms of behaviors that one is willing to take as indicative of their achievement, but since the desired outcomes are products, not processes, they cannot be equated with the behaviors that serve as tokens of their acquisition.

There are many possible indicators of the achievement of an objective such as "understanding the concept of prime number," and no one of them is an adequate synecdoche for the original objective. Nor would any responsible teacher of mathematics be satisfied to limit his instruction to such a trivial objective as the ability to recite the first 10 prime numbers or to tell whether 239 is prime. This is not to suggest, however, that there is any way for him to tell whether or not the concept has been learned other than by requiring some such behavioral manifestation of it. Moreover, he probably cannot manage to teach the concept without having his pupil engage in behaviors of a samilar nature as "learning activities."

All learning activities, then, as well as all evaluative indicators and some instructional objectives, are "behavioral." But with respect to objectives, "behavior" is used in two related but distinctly different senses. One sense pertains to the ability to do something, for example, a performance *capability*. The other sense pertains to a reliably predictable mode of responding, for example, a "habit" or "attitude." These are performance *tendencies*, and refer to what an individaul *will* do or at least is likely to do, not merely to what he *can* do. The distinction is that between potentiality and actuality, or more accurately, probability.

Precisely the same distinction can be made between the two terms that are often used synonymously in connection with teacher education. "Competency" implies potentiality, whereas "performance" suggests actuality, although most commonly, performance is used to denote "evaluative evidence" of competency.

Criterion-referenced evaluation. When the behavior that will be accepted as evidence that something has been learned is specified in advance of instruction, that performance becomes a "criterion behavior" for evaluative purposes. There is much insistence today that not only the nature of the performance, but the circumstances under which it is to be demonstrated and the standards of acceptability be specified. This permits the learner to prepare for the test, the whole test, and nothing but the test, without any distractions or uncertainties. And it encourages the teacher to be single-minded in "teaching for the test," heretofore a professional misdemeanor.

Now, it should be perfectly evident that "criterion referenced" evaluation is not distinctive by reason of requiring a performance, since all testing requires performance of some kind. The difference is that, in conventional testing, the performance to be required is not announced in advance, but is sampled from a wide range of possible appropriate performances without the learner's knowing beforehand which ones he will ultimately be called upon to display.

Criterion referencing is usually contrasted with "norm referencing," and indeed, the contrast is partially valid. Criterion referencing implies a predetermined standard that is ostensibly independent of any historical record of performance or the concurrent performance of peers, whereas in norm-referenced evaluation, a specific performance is evaluated by comparing it with the performances of some specified past or present group.

It seems doubtful that a standard could be set without some reference to what had already been shown to be possible, but it is an essential feature of criterion referencing that "good" and "poor" are unrelated to "above- and below-average." This, however, can also be the case when the specific behavior to be demanded is not specified in advance.

Many teachers who construct tests by sampling from a pool of relevant performances do not judge the results by comparison with those of any group, but instead specify standards in absolute terms pertaining to the quantity and quality of performance on the particular set of tasks constituting the test. The trouble with this is that the difficulty of the tasks may differ considerably from one testing situation to the next, but the point is that not all evaluation in which norm referencing is absent is necessarily criterion-referenced in the sense of advance specification of performance tasks.

Mastery learning. "Mastery" can mean either "perfect performance" or "performance to criterion." Perfection being so rare, it usually carries the latter, more realistic, connotation. This, of course, leaves open the decision as to what criterion shall be set equivalent to mastery. One man's mastery may be another man's incompetence. Indeed, a leading proponent of "mastery learning" has described an experimental program in which an "absolute standard" of mastery was in fact defined in a norm-referenced manner on the basis of the performance of a particular previous group (Bloom et al., 1971, p. 53).

But aside from the definitional problem, there is another, even more serious question regarding mastery, which has never been satisfactorily answered. Under what circumstances is mastery an appropriate goal? The implications are that mastery is curently not demanded at all and that it ought to be demanded of all students in all aspects of all programs. Neither of these conclusions is tenable. Some students are held to a standard that could qualify as mastery in some aspects of some programs. And that is probably exactly as it should be, but it does not say for which students or for which aspects of which programs mastery is appropriate.

Accountability. Holding students to mastery standards is one form of "accountability." Holding teachers responsible for the achievement of students is another, and one which has for a variety of motives captured the interest of some influential laymen and public officials. It underlies the proposals to certify teachers on the basis of demonstrated competency and to judge teacher education programs on the basis of their success in bringing about that competency. Keying accountability to program outcomes requires that intended outcomes be stated in advance in rather specific terms. It also requires reliable and valid means of measuring outcomes and some basis for attributing them to specific instructional personnel or program aspects.

On the surface the argument for outcome accountability is attractive. People like to think that they pay for services only on the basis of results. Yet, in whatever spheres of living this may be the case, it is not the customary practice with respect to professional services. Physicians are not held accountable for guaranteeing cures nor are lawyers held accountable for assuring favorable verdicts. If they are held accountable at all, it is for exercising sound judgment regarding which currently available procedures are most appropriate in a specific situation and for carrying them out correctly. For more than this they cannot be held accountable, since more than this no human being can do.

Unless one is prepared to deny that students bear any responsibility for their own learning and that some circumstances relevant to learning are beyond a teacher's control, one cannot properly hold a teacher accountable for the unsatisfactory achievement of students, unless he can be shown to have been guilty of ignorance, poor judgment, incompetence, or nonfeasance, with respect to correct practice in the situation at hand. Teacher certification can address itself only to the first three of these and, in view of the minimal significance of skillful performance in teaching, the two priorities for certification are knowledge and judgment. Furthermore, since "good judgment" rests primarily upon knowing what features of a situation are significant when a decision is required, the two priorities reduce to one. Again, the conclusion is reached that teachers are employed principally for their *knowledge*, general and specialized, scholarly and professional. It is to the possession of such knowledge that their credentials should, in the main, attest.

Implicit and Explicit Competence

The relationship between certification requirements and teacher education programs ought to be slight. An institution must of course assure that its program is such that an acceptable proportion of the candidates who complete it satisfactorily are certifiable, but credentialing necessarily deals with minimal acceptability, whereas program planning is concerned with maximal quality. Certification rules can indicate what must not be omitted from a program, not everything that should be included.

There was a time when certifying agencies reviewed each individual's application for evidence that certain specific courses had been satisfactorily completed. Then came a brief period of enlightenment during which they encouraged each institution to develop within broad guidelines the best program it could conceive and, when it was approved, they permitted the institution itself to attest to the certifiability of those who successfully completed it. In an uneasy truce, academics and educationists collaborated in institution-wide, and even inter-institutional, efforts to chart suitable programs for the education of teachers. Apparently, the resulting charts left some shoals unmarked, and one day a lookout announced that the ship was sinking (Lierheimer, 1969). The disaster was said to have resulted from counting courses instead of accounting for competence.

As a matter of fact, the most highly regarded aspect of virtually every teacher preparation program, representing over a third of its professional component, has been something called student teaching, in which competence has been the focal point of both evaluation and training efforts. It may have been highly unrealistic to assume that the student-teaching setting provided adequate opportunity for development of the requisite competencies. Prior training through "microteaching" might well be a highly desirable supplement. Certainly, an implicit understanding has long existed between the institutions that prepare beginning teachers and the schools which employ them so that the teacher-training institutions can assume responsibility only for initial certification-level competence and the schools must assume primary responsibility for the in-service refinement of competence to full professional level. However, it is absurd to assert or imply that student-teaching supervisors and the cooperating teachers with whom they work have not required the demonstration of competence as an essential condition for the earning of credit for successful completion of student teaching.

Nevertheless, it may be objected that while competence may have been given attention in both evaluation and training, several important conditions were lacking: (1) there was no widespread agreement on what the essential competencies are; (2) they were not publicly announced in advance; (3) minimal acceptable performance was not defined; (4) evaluation was subjective because there were no accepted, reliable measures of performance; and (5) evaluators considered overall performance instead of insisting on satisfactory demonstration of each and every competency. Obviously, these objections derive whatever validity they may have from the same arguments as do behaviorally-stated objectives, criterion-referenced evaluation, mastery learning, and outcome accountability.

The critique of these arguments offered earlier revealed that each of these four concepts is attended by a considerable amount of confusion. Consequently, the objections raised to accepted student-teaching practices, while not to be ignored, are far from conclusive. At most, they provide a basis for improving that aspect of teacher education which is most concerned with competence. This aspect constitutes a minor portion of even the professional segment of the total program.

The Interpretive Function

A teacher's "tool kit" comprises not so much a series of skills as a set of concepts, principles, and attitudes. These abstractions derive their meaning from their interrelationships and from the arguments and evidence on which they are based. The various concrete situations in which such cognitions may be applicable are not suitable occasions for their acquisition because specific practical situations do not reveal either the intellectual bases of ideas or their interrelationships.

There seems to be a certain body of opinion that abstract knowledge is useless. On the contrary, it can be viewed as being the most useful form of knowledge, since it is not situation-bound. Knowledge gained in a particular practical context is applicable only in situations that are obviously highly similar; abstract knowledge is applicable in a large variety of situations that may superficially appear to be quite dissimilar. Each situation must be correctly interpreted before any application can occur.

Interpretation requires appropriate concepts, principles, and attitudes that are not derived from the polishing of skills in the "field."

There is, indeed, something puzzling about the line of argument that begins with the untenable premise that the schools are disastrous failures and ends with the unwarranted conclusion that they are precisely the place in which to prepare the teachers of the future. The schools are not disasters, but to the extent that they have shortcomings, even their severest critics maintain that the chief cause is not their doing poorly what they are doing but rather their emphasizing the wrong goals or not knowing how to achieve the right goals. The corrective for these short-comings is greater knowledge, not increased skill, and the source must be largely outside of the schools themselves.

Moreover, the most significant performance capabilities that teachers can possess are, as argued earlier, not those practiced in the classroom itself. One does not need the school setting to develop competence in performing such tasks as:

Deriving specific instructional goals from broad educational purposes.

Recognizing hierarchical structures in a field of knowledge.

Deciding what ought to be learned in an instructional episode or sequence.

Identifying exemplars and other instrumental content appropriate in spe-cific instructional situations.

Selecting and developing materials that display desired content effectively for particular learners.

Designing learning activities suitable for particular learnings.

Distinguishing among statements as being universals, particulars, or singu-lars; definitions, explanations, assumptions, observations, judgments, em-pirical generalizations, or justifications.

Planning reliable evaluation procedures for obtaining valid data for various instructional decisions.

Interpreting evaluative data correctly for a diagnosis of learning progress and difficulties.

Prescribing appropriate activities and materials for various learners and situations.

Performance of planning tasks of this sort requires such judgmental abilities as translation, inference, prediction, analysis, synthesis, and evalua-tion. All of these intellectual abilities rest in turn on the possession and application of relevant, high-order cognitions. The cognitions derive from various modes and traditions of scholarly and pedagogical inquiry, and their meaning depends heavily on their relationships to other cognitions within particular conceptual structures. These meanings cannot be developed piecemeal in the course of attaining a series of competencies in a practical rather than an intellectual context. Neither is the practical setting appropriate for the acquisition of the various judgmental abilities mentioned, because their development requires extensive, carefully sequenced practice of a kind that does not arise in the application situation. Indeed, these intellectual abilities cannot even be acquired within the professional component of teacher education, nor need they be more than refined there if proper attention has been given to them in precollegiate general education and in the liberal and specialization components of higher education.

The devolpment of competence in instructional planning is, however, an appropriate responsibility of the professional component, and it is currently not being done systematically and thoroughly enough. But the correction of this weakness does not necessitate either a "field-centered" approach or the transformation of the entire teacher education program into a "performance-based" format. Prospective teachers will need to practice and learn to coordinate planning tasks in the practical "field" setting, but their initial development of these competencies is probably most effectively achieved in a "laboratory" context closely linked to the acquisition of the cognitions that furnish the interpretive basis for the application of the judgmental abilities inherent in the competencies.

Theory and Training

A far more sensible reform of teacher education than any proposal to be found in the burgeoning promotional literature on PBTE was suggested by B. Othanel Smith in the volume entitled *Teachers for the Real World*, issued by the AACTE. This reform called for a program with three components: a teaching-field component with three main aspects, a two-phase theoretical component comprising systematic courses and situational analysis provided in an academic setting, and a two-phase practical component consisting of systematic practice in a "training complex" followed by a supervised internship in an employment context (see Fig. 1). Perhaps this program qualifies as "performance-based," since the professional portion is grounded in an identification of the "tasks that must be performed" in the teaching job, "the abilities required for the performance of these tasks," and "the skills or techniques through which the abilities are expressed" (Smith, 1969, p. 77). But performance is truly the *base* for the program and not the whole edifice. Nowhere is it suggested that a string of "modules" constitutes a total program or that satisfactory completion of it can be demonstrated solely by checking off a list of merit badge requirements.

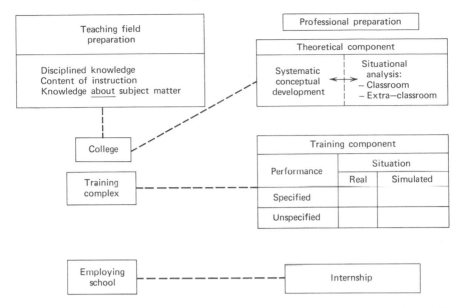

Figure 1. Summary of B. O. Smith's program for "teachers for the real world."

The "real world" proposal was prompted by much the same appraisal of existing teacher education programs that underpins the PBTE movement.

> Almost all teachers are now prepared in programs that provide little or no training in teaching skills. These programs consist of courses in the sociology and philosophy of education, learning theory and human development, and in information about teaching and management of the classroom. These are taught apart from the realities that the teacher will meet and are considered preparatory to student teaching . . . [which] frequently has little relationship to them, and is ordinarily inadequate preparation for the responsibilities given the beginning teacher. The trainee studies theories that lead nowhere, then does his teaching with litle theoretical understanding of the situations he meets (Smith, 1969, pp. 69-70).

In the corrective he advances for this state of affairs, Smith makes a number of very important distinctions that are seldom, if ever, noted in the PBTE literature. He distinguishes between knowledge and competence; between the interpretive use of knowledge in gaining an understanding of a situation and its replicative use in proficiently employing the procedures and devices that are appropriate in that situation; between the situational context in which concepts and principles find their relevance and the theoretical context from which they derive their validity and meaning; and between the replicative task of "applying" available solutions and the applicative task of creating new solutions. Clearly, "performance" is an element in all of these distinctions, but the word is not used as an all-purpose term to denote a variety of referents, as is the case in the writings on PBTE.

Confusion about Performance

Within this genre, an article by Schalock (1970) is noteworthy in that the author explicitly recognizes three distinct meanings of performance, a term that he finds ". . . is not at all clear—either in the literature or in the heads of teacher educators" (p.43). Other writers seem either to be unaware that the meanings vary or unconcerned that they do, so long as one uses the term and believes in the cause. Schalock designates the three meanings as focusing respectively on knowledge, skill (teaching behavior), and competence (products) as criteria for evaluation (and certification). These are, indeed, the primary connotations, but there are second-order uses as well.

Both the distinctions and the relationships among the three types of performance are most readily explicated through the use of symbols. Let Pt represent a performance associated with the teaching profession, something a teacher might be required or expected to do. To do it, for instance to perform, the teacher must have appropriate performance capabilities (skills). This is what is meant by competence, that is, the ability to perform effectively (or proficiently or skillfully). Let Cpt represent this attribute of teachers. The acquisition of this capability usually depends on the possession of some kind of pertinent knowledge (Kt). The only evidence that someone is in possession of such knowledge is, again, some kind of performance that is accepted as indicative of knowing. Let Pkt be the performance that is evidence of knowledge possessed by a teacher. But at least some of the teacher's performances (Pt) are directed at the goal of inducing their students to learn, that is, to acquire knowledge (Ks) and performance capabilities (Cps) of their own. And of course the only evidence of Ks is, once more, some kind of performance (Pks) and the demonstration of Cps is still another performance (Ps).

Therefore, what the term "performance" is being called upon to subsume turns out to be four different performances (Pt, Pkt, Ps, and Pks) and four nonperformances (Cpt, Kt, Cps, and Ks). Now, although all four of the performances stand in an evidential relationship to the four nonperformance attributes of which they are operationalizations, one performance (Pt) also stands in an antecedent relationship to two attributes, Cps and Ks (see Fig. 2). The "accountability" issue revolves around whether Ps

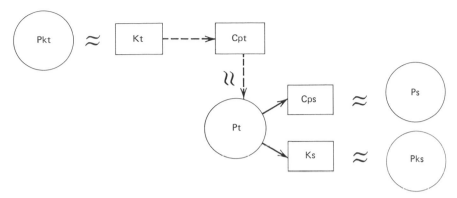

Figure 2. Schematic of various uses of term "performance." The major issue is whether evidence of teacher's competence (Cpt) should be teacher's performance (Pt) or students' performance as evidence of learning (ps and Pks).

Key: Kt — Teacher's knowledge
  Cpt — Teacher's performance capability (competence)
  Ks — Student's knowledge
  Cps — Student's performance capability
  Pkt — Performance evidence of teacher's knowledge
  Pt — Teacher's performance (evidence of competence)
  Pks — Performance evidence of student's knowledge
  Ps — Student's performance (evidence of competence)

and Pks, as indicators of Cps and Ks, shall be required as evidence of Cpt for certification (and later retention) purposes, or whether direct observational evidence of Pt is satisfactory. Current certification policies rely on Pt along with Kt, although neither the former nor the Pkt that is evidence of the latter is explicitly stated and publicly announced, before or after the teacher is prepared and certified.

PBTE proposals usually stress explicitness, but tend to mix Pt and Pkt together. Moreover, unlike Smith's plan, they make no distinction between interpretive and replicative (executive) performances, the one having to do with being able to decide what should be done in a situation and the other with being able to do what has been decided upon. Since Smith derives four different professional preparation settings on the basis of his careful distinctions, any plan would appear to be overly simplistic that entails a single series of instructional modules based on an undifferentiated concept of "performance" and a vague claim to "field-centeredness."

Conclusion

Greater attention to the application of theory to practice is needed in teacher education. To a large extent such application entails the interpretation of specific situations and the exercise of judgment regarding appropriate courses of action. To a much lesser extent does it involve skillful performance in the classroom.

Performance in "teachering" taken broadly (rather than a narrow conception of classroom *teaching*) does provide a basis for designing a teacher education program. But the literature on PBTE gives the impression that the entire program can be directed toward and organized for the development of the acquisition of a series of "competencies." Decisions to base certification on demonstrated competence are premature, but in any event they should not be permitted to dictate the substance and form of teacher preparation programs. Nevertheless, research, development, and conceptual clarification should be encouraged.

On the single peripheral question of whether competence should be judged by observing the behavior of teachers or measuring the achievement of their students, one proponent of PBTE was able to identify 14 unresolved issues (Schalock, 1971, pp. 46-48). A dedicated opponent could raise many more vexing questions and related issues. The possibilities for research and development are almost limitless. After all of it is done, it may turn out that a teacher's professional knowledge is a better basis for continued growth in effectiveness than is initial demonstrated competency on a meager conceptual base. If PBTE is a valid idea, premature adoption can doom it; if the idea is not valid, any adoption is premature, serving only to show those who believe that things could not be worse than they are at present that they can indeed.

References

Bloom, Benjamin S., J. Thomas Hastings, and Gordon F. Madaus, *Handbook on Formative and Summative Evaluation of Student Learning* (McGraw–Hill, 1971).

Burdin, Joel T., and Margaret T. Reagan, eds., *Performance-Based Certification of School Personnel* (ERIC Clearinghouse on Teacher Education and Association of Teacher Educators, 1970).

Burkhart, Robert, ed., *The Assessment Revolution: New Viewpoints for Teacher Evaluation* (New York State Education Department and State University College at Buffalo, n.d.).

Elam, Stanley, *Performance-Based Teacher Education: What is the State of Art?* (American Association of Colleges for Teacher Education, 1971).

Elfenbein, Iris M., *Performance-Based Teacher Education Programs: A Comparative Description* (American Association of Colleges for Teacher Education, 1972).

Giles, Frederic T., and Clifford D. Foster, *Changing Teacher Education in a Large Urban University* (American Association of Colleges for Teacher Education, 1972).

Houston, W. Robert, and Robert B. Howsam, *Competency-Based Teacher Education* (Science Research Associates, 1972).

Lierheimer, Alvin P., "Give up the Ship: A New Basis for State Certification," *The English Record* (October 1969), pp. 64-70.

New York State Education Department, *Unit 2: In the Preparation and Practice of Professionals for Elementary and Secondary Education* (The Department, November 1, 1972). (Also in: *PBTE* 1, November 1972, pp. 1, 5-6.)

Rosner, Benjamin, *The Power of Competency-Based Teacher Education* (Allyn and Bacon, 1972).

Roth, Robert A., *Performance-Based Teacher Certification: A Survey of the States* (New Jersey State Department of Education, 1972, mimeo).

Schalock, H. Del, "The Focus: Knowledge, Teaching Behavior, or the Products?" in Burdin and Reagan, op. cit., pp. 43-49.

Schmeider, Allen A., *Competency-Based Education: The State of the Scene* (American Association of Colleges for Teacher Education and ERIC Clearinghouse on Teacher Education, 1973).

Shanker, Albert, "Teacher Training and Certification: The Search for New Programs," *PBTE* 1 (February 1973), pp. 3-4.

Smith, B. Othanel, *Teachers for the Real World* (American Association of Colleges for Teacher Education, 1969).

6. *Can Education Find Its Lost Objectives Under the Street Lamp of Behaviorism?*

Hugh G. Petrie

There is no need to document the extent to which behavioral objectives (or some variant thereof) have taken over in education. Colleges of education are urged to institute plans for performance-based teacher education. State departments of public instruction demand that school systems institute schemes for writing behavioral or instructional objectives. Private firms have been contracting to increase levels of student "performance," where such performance is usually stated as a certain level of test scores. Legislatures and school boards, faced with constricting financial resources, demand that education be made accountable, from institutions through teachers, for the public funds allotted to them. And underlying all these phenomena is the recurring theme of behavioral objectives as a universal panacea.

Yet the more closely one looks at these varying manifestations of the increased influence of that peculiar social scientific doctrine known as behaviorism, the more one is struck by how out of phase are the ills being attacked with the cures being offered. One cannot help but be reminded of the story of the drunk crawling around on his hands and knees under the street lamp. A passerby notices this odd behavior and asks, "Lose something?" "My watch," replies the drunk. The well-intentioned samaritan proceeds to help the drunk look with no success. Finally, he asks, "Just where did you lose your watch?" "Over in that doorway," replies the drunk, pointing down the street a hundred feet or so. "Well, why in the world are we looking for the watch here, then?" explodes the samaritan. "Oh, the light's better here," comes the reply.

This article was especially prepared for this volume.

It would appear that if one could show that the current emphasis on behavioral objectives is as out of touch with reality as the drunk's behavior, we would not have to await the empirical evidence to know that education will not be able to find its way under the street lamp of behaviorism. It is my contention that there are so many conceptual confusions rampant in applying the doctrines of behavioral objectives to education that no matter how bright the light, it is falling on inappropriate ground. In this paper, I want to isolate some of the more important of these confusions and attempt to show both the justifiable kernel of truth along with the overlay of misunderstanding and error. My hope is that once these confusions are laid bare, the individual institution, principal, teacher, student, or layman can intelligently separate the wheat from the chaff.

I.

One of the central confusions in this general area is the conflation of accountability with measurement—and a peculiar kind of measurement at that, specifically, the measurement of efficiency. One cannot seriously challenge, for example, the request from legislators that schools must be held accountable for their contribution, or lack thereof, to the public good. Indeed, hard though it may be to swallow, there is nothing inherently wrong about a society asking itself whether it values welfare for its poor more than education, or decent housing more than either, or if nuclear deterrence is the highest value of all. Social values do not come automatically ranked and in an economy of scarce resources; it is surely plausible that sometimes hard decisions must be made.

Schooling as a social institution will have to continue to make its case as best it can—sometimes in competition with other social goods. The one change I would urge is that more effort be made to justify the products of schooling, for example, education, as good in itself rather than solely on the basis of schooling's instrumental value to other goods. The opposite kind of justification has been the more prevalent. During the 1960s one could scarcely pick up a Sunday newspaper supplement without reading an article on how much more money college graduates would make than nongraduates, or on how desirable liberal arts graduates were in business, never mind their major. This line of reasoning clearly holds up schooling as an instrumental value; it is a means to other ends. It is small wonder, then, that when the bubble burst in the early seventies and schooling was no longer a means to a better job, support for schooling fell off sharply. Had schols paid even a modicum of attention to justifying the intrinsic value of education, they would not look so stupid now—they would have some kind of intellectual ground to fall back on to justify their ultimate value.

The point, however, is that it is surely acceptable to hold schools accountable for their contribution to the public good. This sense of accountability means nothing more than holding responsible in the typically ethical sense. We hold government responsible in this sense for the rapprochement with China and for Watergate. We hold industry and technology responsible in this sense for increasing our standard of living as well as for polluting our environment. Schools are no different in this respect.

There is another sense of "accountability," however, which is all too easily confused with the above sense. This second sense is the one from which the profession of accounting is derived. In an almost literal way it has come to mean to count up or measure. And it is most important to notice here that for this "counting" sense of accountability to get a handhold, the *units* in terms of which we count must be externally determined. Accountability in the measurement sense cannot tell us *what* to measure. Thus, this kind of accountability can only show us how efficiently we are pursuing already agreed-upon goals. It cannot evaluate between alternative goals. It is when accountability in the "holding responsible" sense is confused with accountability in the "measurement" sense that mischief results.

These two senses of accountable can be illustrated quite nicely by considering the case of industry. As long as there is general agreement on profit as a goal of industry and no serious perceived conflict between that goal and other social goals, there is no difficulty in holding industry accountable by measuring how they generate profit. Accountants perform this measurement task by means of financial statements, and a good measure of the efficiency of the business is given by these statements. But when a question is raised as to the desirability of the profit motive as a single all-inclusive value, for instance, when questions of accountability in the sense of ethical responsibility are raised, as in the case of pollution, it simply makes no sense to look at financial statments to find out if business is accountable. A question of goals themselves is being asked, *not* a question of the efficiency with which already agreed–upon goals are being met. Financial statements, can of course, reflect pollution fines and the cost of antipollution measures. What they cannot do is give any answer to whether or not industry ought to be held accountable for their pollution.

Now, on almost anyone's showing, education's goals include as a major part the development of the skill, sensitivity, and intellectual curiosity to reaxamine traditionally accepted goals. There is no doubt some sense in which progress toward such goals can be determined, but "efficiency" models of measurement are precisely the wrong ways. For efficiency models depend on agreed goals, and the goals of educators are to question these agreed–upon goals. It scarcely makes sense to measure the progress of some activity by means of accounting procedures whose very reliability is derived from what the activity is questioning. The way in which accountability is presently being practiced in education is like allowing the men accused in the Watergate scandal to determine the rules for whether they are guilty. You might accidentally get justice, but it would not be very likely.

Thus, in discussions of accountability, educators must be perfectly willing to morally justify the institution of schooling as an important social good with all the intelligence and fervor at their command. At the same time, however, they must demand that the nature of education renders "efficiency" models of measurement wholly inapplicable as guides to whether schools are doing their jobs.

II.

Even if one is clear that the efficiency model of measurement is inappropriate to accountability in the schools, another confusion is rampant in discussions over how one does find out if schools are doing their jobs. This is found in its most general form in the confusion between the desirability of competence as a measure of learning and the actual state of the art of evaluation. In more specific terms it is urged, for example, that what we want are competent teachers and not necessarily people who have gone through some specialized curriculum. Thus we get the push for performance-based teacher education, the use of instructional objectives in the classroom and what have you with a corresponding increase of attention on assessing these competencies.

Now it is clearly an advance conceptually to recognize the distinction between some desired competency on the one hand, and perhaps any number of ways of attaining that competency on the other hand. And it is a good thing for schools occasionally to be reminded that their cherished courses, lectures, and recitations may not be the only way to achieve the competencies aimed at in education. On the other hand, it must be remembered that a standard school curriculum clearly is *one* way of achieving educational competencies.

Nevertheless, this very valuable conceptual distinction between end product and varying ways of getting to the end product is not automatically translatable into practice. If one is going to aim at and certify for competencies actually possessed rather than curricula undergone, then clearly one must be able to judge in some reliable way when the competency actually is present. Thus, the empirical side to the competency-based coin is an adequate, comprehensive, and reliable method of assessing the presence or absence of the competencies. Yet virtually everyone, even those who are in the testing establishment, know that current testing models are really extremely unreliable. Rough distinctions can be made, but current testing procedures cannot even come close to making the fine-grained distinctions that are required if we are, as a matter of policy, to abandon curriculum satisfaction in favor of competency-based criteria for having achieved educational goals.

Let me take just one example of the inability of current tests to make the fine-grained distinctions needed. Scores on the prestigious College Entrance Examination Board (CEEB) tests determine for many students whether or not they will go to a certain college. Yet by the CEEB's own admission, there is only a 68% chance that a score difference of 31 points on the verbal test (34 points on the quantitative) represents a real difference in ability.[1]

Thus, if that difference occurs around the college's cutoff point, one student will be admitted and another not. Of course, college admissions people will be quick to say that they use other indicators as well. It turns out that gradepoint average, clearly a curriculum-based indication, is *the* most reliable indicator of college success. But this just makes my point for me. Judging competencies without taking into account curricula undergone is very, very difficult.

Harry Broudy makes this point in an instructive way.[2] One occasionally finds someone practicing medicine, aparently very successfully, who has never been to medical school. Does the AMA admit that he has the competency to be a doctor and let it go at that? Not at all! But that is just what schols of education are being urged to do. The point is that it may just be that given the present and foreseeable state of the testing art, the very best, although not infallible, way we have of judging whether someone possesses a specific competency is whether he has undergone a standard school curriculum in that area.

Thus, educators should quickly grant the distinction between possessing a given competency and various means by which the competency might have been attained. But until the testing establishment demonstrates *its* competency to detect competencies a *great* deal better than it can now, the prudent response would be to go very slowly in converting to competency-based programs. A good strategy would be to agree with the principle of such programs and then examine very carefully the detailed testing arrangements to be used.

III.

Examining the details of testing programs almost inevitably leads one into another one of the confusions rampant in the educational use of

---

[1] *College Boards Guide for High Schools and Colleges,* 1972-1973 (College Entrance Examination Board, 1972).

[2] Harry S. Broudy, *The Real World of the Public Schools* (New York: Harcourt Brace Jovanovich, 1972), p. 65.

behavioral objectives. This confusion is between the desirability of having some sort of connection between an ascribed competency and the real world on the one hand, and a particular specified kind of connection on the other hand.

It is a truism that any scientific theory must have some sort of empirical import. And likewise, if a supposed educational goal, whether it be a competency or any other kind of educational result, has no conceivable connection with the world as we can observe and experience it, then clearly such a goal is some kind of chimera. Therefore, some kind of publicly testable result surely is a necessary condition of any supposed educational outcome, and the testing establishment is certainly on unassailable grounds in insisting that there be *something* we could observe—sometime, somewhere.

Nevertheless, this truism from the philosophy of science is confused with the idea that the required observability be of a very peculiar behavioristic sort. Behaviorism in general holds as a methodological principle that the only kinds of things that can be observed in the world of human beings are very gross kinds of "behavior," and that all else must be inferred. It turns out, however, that this principle is honored more in the breach than in the observance. If it were strictly followed, behaviorism would have been seen to be impossible long ago. Only constant equivocation on its own methodology gives it even its remote plausibility.

For, if we are to follow behaviorism, we can observe marks on a piece of paper, but we must infer test results and competence. We cannot observe that a student understands the material. We can see a student standing in front of one painting longer than another, but we cannot see that he appreciates one more than another. We can see a student moving around in his seat with knitted brow, but we cannot see that he is confused.

I have argued in technical detail elsewhere that this view of what is observable and what is not is dogmatic and totally unsupported by any argument or evidence.[3] However, the point I wish to make here is that it is extremely poor policy to confuse the necessity for testability of some form or other with a highly controversial specification of just how that testability is to be understood. Public policy in the schools cannot possibly justify *requiring* everyone to implicitly adopt one side of an obviously controversial issue in the methodology of the social sciences. This is especially true since the acceptance of testability does *not* also require the acceptance of behaviorist language and methodology.

Thus, educators should grant the necessity for their educational goals

---

[3] Hugh G. Petrie, "A Dogma of Operationalism in the Social Sciences," *Philosophy of Social Science I* (1971), pp. 145-160.

to "make a difference"—to be testable somehow, somewhere. They should be clear and precise about these goals and desired outcomes, but they should also insist on the necessity for the tests to be appropriate to *their* goals and not vice versa. And where there is an inconsistency between available testing methods and the professed goals of experienced practitioners in any field, it is at least as likely that testers need to be more imaginative as it is likely that the practitioners have not known what they have been doing all that time. In short, educators must insist on the priority of the goals in determining the appropriateness of the tests.

IV.

A fourth confusion has been recently expounded in great detail by Michael Scriven.[4] However, it is so important as to bear summarizing here. It is desirable to be objective (reliable) in one's judgments about educational as well as all other matters. Contrariwise, one should attempt to avoid insofar as possible being subjective (biased). Unfortunately, the pair of terms "subjective" and "objective" have another set of meanings that are often confused with the "biased—reliable" set. Subjective also means relating to feelings, thoughts, emotions, and judgments of a *single* person. Objective as a contrast to *this* sense of subjective simply means intersubjective, that is, referring to the feelings, thoughts, emotions, and judgments of *more* than one person.

Now clearly one can be subjective in this second sense without at all being biased or unreliable. The most obvious example is that any person is usually the most reliable judge of his own internal states of emotion and, for that matter, of his own thoughts. But there are educational examples as well. Indeed, graduate education is based upon the belief that subjective (personal) judgments of the student's adviser are more reliable than the judgments of lots of other people. Even the fact that there are usually doctoral *committees* does not vitiate this point, since one must pick people for the committees who are *qualified*. And how do we know if they are qualified? Are they qualified if their subjective (personal) judgments are reliable and unbiased?

Another example lies in the area of art appreciation. The subjective (personal) judgment of a sensitive art teacher as to the progress and competence of a student in coming to appreciate art is almost certainly far more reliable than any intersubjectively verified test. As a related example, any sane person would surely prefer Leonard Bernstein's subjective (personal) judgment as to the quality of a student violinist to the satisfaction

---

[4] Michael Scriven, "Objectivity and Subjectivity in Educational Research," *Philosophical Redirections of Educational Research*, Seventy-first Yearbook of the National Society for the Study of Education (Chicago: University of Chicago, 1972).

of so-called "objective" behavioral objectives. Nor did Bernstein attain his eminence by satisfying behavioral objectives.

And yet the confusion is so rampant that not only behavioral objectives buffs, but many others as well would prefer an objective intersubjectively verified test to a subjective judgment every time—even in areas where we *know* that the objective measurement is not as reliable as the subjective judgment. The results of this confusion are to be seen in the dreary sameness of our schools. The intersubjective tends to reduce everything to the lowest common denominator. Even worse are the effects that a denial of the reliability of subjective judgments has upon individual students. We are faced with students being labeled as mentally retarded and largely condemned to a certain kind of education largely independent of subjective judgments of his ability. And yet the push for behavioral objectives can only intensify the denigration of subjective judgment and the tendency to replace reliability with intersubjectivity, whether such replacement can be justified or not.

Thus, the educator should embrace reliability and shun bias. But he should be very careful to understand in each case wherein reliability resides. Quite clearly it is not always in majority opinion. Traditionally the judgment of trained experts has been considered most reliable in source areas. When asked to replace that judgment by something "more objective," the educator should very carefully ask whether reliability is likely to be increased or whether results will simply be homogenized to the benefit of no one except the "objectifiers."

V.

The next confusion is closely related to the last one between subjective and biased and objective and reliable. It also arises in discussions emphasizing student competence as over against teacher performance and so is related to the earlier discussion of competence and curriculum and the difficulties of determining competence independently of curriculum. This present confusion is between an emphasis on student outcomes and competences as desirable educational goals on the one hand and appropriate ways of assessing teacher performance on the other hand.

Surely *what* the student learns should be a major part of any set of educational goals. The goal of education is *not* for a teacher to go through a rigid lesson plan independently of whether or not students learn anything from that lesson plan. The teacher's performance must be relevant to the student's learning in some sense or other. Obviously it would be senseless to suppose that teaching performance has no connection whatever with student learning performance.

On the other hand, it seems equally obvious that teacher performance cannot be wholly, or perhaps even mainly, judged on the basis of student outcomes.[5] There are simply too many factors other than the teacher's performance that go to determine the student's ultimate performance. The student may be lazy and not learn from the brightest teacher. He may be highly motivated and learn from the dullest teacher. The student may not have the competence to learn, or he may be so bright that he learns from *any* teacher. Are teachers in high socioeconomic neighborhoods that good, or is their job so much easier? Are ghetto teachers all bad or are they contending with virtually insuperable environmental problems? In short, there are clearly many occasions on which the best teaching efforts will fail and many other occasions on which very poor teaching may, nevertheless, be associated with good student learning.

Consider an analogy from baseball. One of the goals of the shortstop is to commit as few errors as possible. Indeed, one could not understand someone "playing shortstop" and being totally unconcerned with the number of his errors. However, there can be very bad shortstops who commit very few errors. They never try very hard so they never get close enough to the ball to commit many errors. On the other hand there can be very good shortstops who commit many errors. They are trying for everything. Evaluation of good shortstops cannot be tied too closely to one outcome.

Analogously, one can imagine situations in which the very best teaching would result in *no* student learning of what was taught. Consider the case of the student who in terms of interest or ability simply should not be taking a certain course. The best teaching in such a situation would result in getting the student *out* of the course and hence in his not learning anything about the course at all. Therefore good teaching is and must be kept conceptually distinct from actual student learning.

Thus the educator should grant that one of the goals of teaching may well be student learning. Occasionally teachers forget this and seem to think schools would be great places if only there were not any students. They should not be allowed to forget their responsibilities to students. But, likewise, neither should judgments of their professional competence be judged solely or even mainly on their student's performances. Schemes of teacher evaluation should be developed that rely on student progress to an *appropriate* degree but that also have provision for significant weight to be given to professional, peer, and self-evaluation.

VI.

The last confusion is one that really should not have to be mentioned. Unfortunate as it is, proponents of many of the accountability-type pro-

---

[5] See Israel Scheffler, *The Language of Education* (Springfield, Ill.: Charles C Thomas, 1960), Chap. 2, for a classical statement of the issues surrounding the conceptual connection between teaching and learning.

grams discussed in this paper seem unable to distinguish between criticism of the concepts they use and criticisms of the people who employ these concepts. Time after time, when it is pointed out that behavioristic concepts have this or that kind of implication, the response is that the practitioners do not actually do such nasty things. In logic this response constitutes the fallacy of *ignoratio elenchi*—missing the point.

A person who is committed to any set of principles is also logically committed to the logical implications of those principles. If he at the same time does not wish to be committed to those implications, then he is simply inconsistent and, of course, literally anything and everything logically follows from inconsistent premises. Is it any wonder that accountabilists tend to be so hard to pin down? If one is allowed to take contradictory stands, then one is bound to be right half the time *and* bound to be wrong the other half, and, worse, one cannot tell which is which.

The saddest thing, however, is that the accountabilists seem to feel no necessity to respond to the criticisms offered of their programs other than to say they do not behave in the undesirable ways indicated by the logical consequences of their principles. Now it may well be that by acting inconsistently with their own principles, accountabilists can avoid, for a time, the implications of those principles. But ideas have a way of catching up with inconsistent uses. If the ideas are mistaken or confused, the action taken in the name of those ideas will likewise in the long run be mistaken or confused. History allows no more lenient interpretation.

Thus, the educator should continue to point out the intellectual confusions, where they exist, to the accountabilist. And if the accountabilist responds as if he were being personally attacked, the educator must gently, but firmly, point out to the accountabilist that he has simply missed the point of the criticism. The truth or falsity of ideas is sometimes hard to grasp, but false ideas cannot stand the light of reason forever.

VII.

My initial analogy between the drunk looking for his watch under the streetlight and the use of behaviorism in many areas of education can now be seen to have been quite generous to behaviorism. To fully reflect the confusions I have tried to illustrate in this paper the story would have to run something like this: The drunk would have to be very pleased with himself if he elaborately and *efficiently* covered the ground under the street light even without finding his watch (the confusion between accountability and measurement of efficiency). Furthermore, the drunk should find a child's toy watch, be unable to tell the difference between that one and his own, and still be perfectly satisfied. After all, the end product was achieved, finding a watch (the confusion between concentrating on the end product and the sorry state of our ability to determine whether the end product has actually been achieved). The drunk's original behavior of looking under the street light for the watch because the light was better there, even though he knew the watch was not lost in that area, would be retained (the confusion between needing observability for an empirical theory and thinking it must be behaviorist observability). The drunk ought to be looking for a "time" he had forgotten rather than a watch, but still be visually looking under the street light because others might be able to help him in such a public "objective" search (the confusion of intersubjectivity with reliability and bias with personal feelings or thoughts). The drunk would have to feel that he, the drunk, was a superb searcher if the samaritan found the watch and gave it to the drunk (the confusion between good teaching and student learning as the sole criterion of good teaching). Finally, if the samaritan were to criticize any or all of the drunk's ideas, the drunk would have to get mad and claim that he really does not act absurdly (the confusion between the implications of ideas and behavior inconsistent with those ideas).

If all of these changes were made to the original story, one would get a very confused drunk. One would also have a very good analogy with the curent situation of accountability and its cousins in education. It really is that bad.

7. *Instructional Objectives and Observable Behavior*

Philip G. Smith

In the more than two and one-half centuries since Berkeley published his *New Theory of Vision* and his *Principles of Human Knowledge,* a very substantial body of literature has been developed concerning the relation of what can be known to what can be observed. The overall import of this literature was rather neatly put by Norwood Hanson (1961) in his now famous dictum "There is more to seeing than meets the eyeball." There is also a body of technical literature concerned with the problems of sampling in relation to testing or assessment. And we all know there is more to assessment than giving a test.

For the purpose of this essay, however, we may resist the fascinating perceptual-epistemological problems investigated in the philosophical literature and bypass the technical problems discussed in the literature of measurement. Let us construct instead, a simple analysis based upon the common sense distinction between what can be directly observed and what can reasonably be inferred from what can be observed.

Performance Objectives

From the standpoint of the teacher or curriculum–maker, the question arises as to what, if any, instructional objectives are such that *their attainment* can be directly observed. The answer seems to be that when what is to be learned is, actually, an observable performance exhibiting clearly specified behaviors or resulting in an observable product with specified characteristics, then such an instructional objective may properly be called

This article was prepared especially for this volume.

a *performance objective,* and its attainment or lack of attainment can be directly observed. The logic of the testing or evaluation is certainly straightforward. The objective is attained if and only if the specified behaviors are exhibited (under appropriate conditions).

There appears to be two general types of performance objectives utilized by classroom teachers: replicative performance and applicative performance. This distinction is based upon a difference in the way in which what is learned is lated used—especially in out-of-school situations (Broudy, Smith, Burnett, 1964). When what is learned is later used in substantially the same form in which it was learned, we speak of learning for replicative use. For example, in school a student memorizes and learns to recall the correct spelling of a large number of commonly used words. For the rest of his life he may recall and spell these same words in the same way.

On the other hand, a student learns a number of principles and procedures for solving problems in, say, mathematics. Later he *applies* what he has learned to many problems that were not encountered in the study and practice involved in learning the principles and procedures. The transfer of learning that takes place in the applicative use ranges, of course, across differences from those that are barely distinguishable from replication to those that are so greatly different that application involves a highly imaginative and creative ability.

It follows that in teaching for performance objectives, the instructor should make very clear to the students (usually by demonstration as well as verbally) all of the criterial characteristics of the performance. In the case of replicative performance, the instructor should then *teach for the test.* In teaching spelling, for example, it is obvious that students should be told exactly what words they are to learn to spell and what the correct spellings are. And the same words are used in both instruction and testing.

Or suppose the instructional objective is "to swim two lengths of the school pool using only the back stroke, in not more than three minutes." Certainly students should not be kept in the dark concerning the criterial attributes of the back stroke and the instruction and guided practice should be directed toward bringing the student up to these criteria of performance. Again, the teacher teaches for the test. Even though in later life the student will swim in other pools and under other circumstances, he will substantially *replicate* this performance.

By contrast, suppose the objective is "to use simultaneous equations to solve problems not encountered in the preparatory instruction and practice." Obviously the instructor should not teach for the test in the same way one does for replicative performance. The principles and procedures to be used in the test should be made clear (by instruction and practice), but the test problems are deliberately designed to require something more than a simple, mechanical, or routine replication *of the behavior* involved in the instructional practice. When the objective is application rather than replication, the test performance is at best a demonstration of only a *sample* of the ability or skill the student has acquired through instruction and practice.

It may be useful, at this point, to draw a distinction between a pedagogical purpose and its corresponding instructional objectives. After all, an instructional objective is not an end in itself—it is designed to serve some larger purpose. Even in the case of a basic replicative performance, such as spelling, the purpose for teaching runs far beyond any in-school testing situation. And it is just because it is so easy to justify the inclusion of such elementary skills in any instructional program that there is little objection to teaching for replicative performance in relation to these skills, and for treating this performance as if it were an end in itself. As the student demonstrates his ability to spell the assigned words, the teacher *observes* that the instructional objective has been attained and tacitly *assumes* that the purpose for which spelling has been taught has been properly served.

In the case of an applicative performance, however, the relation between pedagogical purpose and instructional objectives is both more tenuous and more complex. Why should algebra be in the curriculum at all? Why should we teach algebra in such a way as to foster applicative rather than replicative ability? And does applicative performance adequately serve our pedagogical purpose for teaching algebra? At the very least, we see that adequate performance on a test sample of new problems should never be treated as an end in itself, and the tacit assumption that could be treated as *safe* in connection with spelling now becomes more nearly a matter of *faith*.

Or, suppose the instructor adopts the following as a performance objective.

> To write an analysis of a newspaper editorial argument indicating (1) The premises of the argument, (2) The conclusions of the argument, (3) The empirical propositions (if any) offered as evidence, (4) The critically important definitions stipulated or assumed by the editor.

The written analysis certainly constitutes an observable performance product that can be evaluated (by persons with some expertise in these matters) with considerable reliability. And this is true even though a satisfactory performance requires the student to use some degree of judgment and creative skill in the application of the distinctions involved. It follows that the meaning of these distinctions, for example, "critically important definitions," should be taught and learned in a manner different from the memory and recall of a list of correctly spelled words.

As the degree of creativity and skill required for adequate performance is increased, then, the level of expertise required for reliable evaluation or grading rises proportionately. This is true with physical performance, such as diving or gymnastics, artistic performance (musical, dramatic, etc.), and intellectual performance. The notion that performance objectives makes possible "expert-proof" evaluations is even more absurd than the notion that they make possible "teacher-proof" curricula.

If all school learning were intended for replicative or applicative use, then all instructional objectives could be cast in the form of observable performances, or performance products. And to the extent that the behavioral objectives movement has encouraged such a conclusion it has, in spite of its emphasis on clarity, contributed to "fuzzy thinking" in education.

Indeed, the old fashioned distinction between training and education may be helpful at this point. If the schools are interested in doing more than producing trained performers, then something more than performance objectives is needed. And to say this does not in any way denigrate the importance of training which, as we have seen, may include highly creative applications that require very high level intellectual and artistic ability. The development of such abilities is surely an important goal of schooling.

But it is sometimes said, and I think correctly so, that the central purpose of schooling ought to be *education*, that is, fostering the ability and inclination to engage in independent thought and judgment. The critical question then becomes whether all of the thought and judgment the school should foster can (or ought to be) incorporated into specified observable performances or performance products. On the face of it there seems to be some conflict between thought and judgment that is *independent*, and a performance that can be *fully specified in advance of instruction*. Said differently, although one can be *trained* to perform certain functions, from firing a machine gun to performing a surgical operation, it is not clear that one can be trained *to behave as if* he were educated.

In short, not everything that is worth learning is used either replicatively or applicatively. Some important learning is used associatively and some, interpretively (Broudy, Smith, Burnett, 1964). And the *attainment* of learning intended for these uses is not generally directly observable.

Behaviorally Indicated Objectives

Consider, for example, instruction in history, general science, geography, and literature, in short, all of the subject matter of liberal or general education. What is the purpose of instruction in these areas? Is it to teach students to perform?

There is much in such subjects that could be thought of in terms of observable performance and, no doubt, some of it should be. For example, a geography teacher could and probably should teach students certain map-reading procedures. Not only is skill in the use of various kinds of maps something that may turn out to be useful in later life but the learning of such procedures may also be one way to develop interest in geography. But the point is that "learning to perform with maps" hardly scratches the surface of the purpose of including geography as part of liberal or general education.

When the pedagogical purpose is to foster the ability and inclination to engage in independent thought and judgment, then the corresponding instructional objectives are not directly observable performances, but knowledge, insight, grasp of relationships, a sense of the significant, a disposition to investigate, and the like. We may still ask the question: "What (observable behavior) will the student be able to do when the objective is attained?" But the relationship between attainment and observable behavior is now significantly different. And the logic of the evaluation or testing has changed (P. G. Smith, 1972).

Suppose, for example, that a social studies teacher reasons that after instruction (assigned readings, classroom discussion, etc.) designed to develop knowledge and insight concerning the decisions of the U.S. Supreme Court, the students ought to be able *to do* the following:

When presented with three hypothetical descriptions of State Supreme Court decisions, the student will be able to select the one which is least consonant with previous decisions of the U.S. Supreme Court (Popham, 1969, p. 37).

Performing well on such a test is surely *not the objective* of the instruction. Nor is it even a sample of the objective. This kind of *doing* is, rather, a more or less valid indicator of the attainment of the objective. If the objective (i.e. the knowledge and insight) has been attained, then the students will be able to perform correctly on the test. If proper precautions against cheating have been taken and if the test is constructed in such a way that it is very unlikely that one could spot the correct answer without knowledge and insight concerning the decisions of the U.S. Supreme Court, then the teacher may reason that the objective has been attained *if and only if* the behavioral indicators are displayed.

Since in many situations, especially when using so-called "objective tests," it is difficult to establish an *if and only if* relation between the objective and a test behavior, the teacher would be well advised to treat the test results as a hypothesis that *suggests* the attainment of the objective (P. G. Smith, 1972). This approach to evaluation (grading) points to the need for convergence of evidence in a manner not unlike the requirements of a research design.

It should also be obvious that when dealing with *behavioral indicators* (in contrast to performance objectives) the kind of naive operationalism that is frequently urged upon teachers as an antidote for "the fuzzies" (Mager, 1972) is hardly a service to the profession. After all, if we really believe that teachers frequently do not know what they mean by terms such as "knowledge," "insight," and "appreciation" in relation to the content of instruction, how can they possibly select appropriate behavioral indicators for the very objectives they do not understand? If the problem is lack of clarity concerning what the teacher is trying to accomplish by instruction, then this problem had better be worked at before attacking the problem of selecting behavioral indicators (Popp, 1969). It is only in the case of replicative performance—where what is taught *is the test*—that test construction is the same activity as "clarifying the meaning" of the objective.

When instructional objectives are viewed in relation to pedagogical purpose, they typically appear in clusters or networks rather than as isolated, independent items. Various relationships exist among objectives: some are prerequisite to others; some are subsidiary; some are in a part-whole relationship; and some are *merely* instrumental—they would not be in the program at all except as a means for getting to something valuable, a kind of necessary evil. Suppose, for example, that a teacher of American history attains enough clarity about what he is trying to do so that he can decide, in conection with a particular lesson, that what he wants the students to learn is some specified details of the general military situation preceding and following the battle of Gettysburg and the reasons typically given by historians as to why Gettysburg is considered to be a critical battle of the Civil War. If such an objective (as part of a cluster or network) can be defended as serving the pedagogical purpose for teaching American history, *only then* is the teacher ready to consider what behaviors may be accepted as indicators (or suggestors) that the intended learning has taken place. To move directly to test construction before (or as a substitute for) clarification of objectives, is to get the cart before the horse and it results in the tail wagging the dog.

Configurationally Indicated Objectives

Fostering the development of certain *dispositions* frequently occupies a key position in the network of objectives designed to serve the purpose for which many traditional subjects are taught. Since a disposition, by definition, is not a behavior, but a tendency to behave, it follows that no particular behavior at any given time can serve as an adequate indicator that the desired disposition has been formed. What is needed is a series of observations extending over a span of time and a variety of circumstances. A disposition is indicated by what might be called a behavioral configuration.

For example, suppose a social studies teacher has the objective of fostering a disposition toward careful consideration of a range of viewpoints or opinions on controversial issues. (Or, said differently, the objective is to foster a disposition to avoid the fallacy of black or white thinking.) Or suppose the objective is to develop curiosity about the historical antecedents of significant contemporary events. A teacher with such objectives, although well advised to think in behavioral terms, will surely miss the boat if a behavioral configuration is confused with any particular specified test performance.

Clue–Indicated Educational Process Objectives

One type of objective that is frequently alleged to be both fuzzy and grandiose typically starts with the words "To understand. . . ." Now it has been pointed out that arguments about so-called aims of education frequently are really about *the manner* in which something is taught and learned rather than *the matter* (Peters, 1963). For example, "to understand Algebra" probably means "to learn Algebra with understanding" (Waks, 1969).

Actually, of course, neither learning nor the manner of learning can be directly observed. In the case of replicative performance it probably does no harm to think of, say, "watching Johnny learn to swim." But, strictly speaking, since *learning* is a construct used to account for changes in behavior that cannot be attributed to maturation, drugs, fatigue, or the like, a student's learning is not something that can be observed. What is observable are a student's pupiling activities and products. These are the correlative student activities that take place vis-à-vis the teacher's teaching activities. And teaching-pupiling activities can be monitored with respect to manner as well as matter.

Suppose a teacher wants students "to learn with understanding the Bill of Rights," or, "to appreciate the contributions of black culture to the American way of life;" or, "to gain insight into the role and function of the federal income tax in relation to the socioeconomic structures of American society." One can, of course, specify in great detail the subject *matter* that gives meaning to these objectives in a particular context. And one can certainly devise recognition or recall test items appropriate to the subject matter. Furthermore, by asking what the student will be able *to do* (if and only if) he really has gained understanding, appreciation, and insight, in relation to this content, one may even be able to devise additional tests or other behavioral indicators that seem plausible. But at this point, experienced teachers are more likely to depend primarily upon certain *clues* that may be observed within the teaching-pupiling process. For example: How does the student act and react during class discussion? What kind of questions does he ask in connection with home work and reading assignments? Teachers find it plausible to suppose that the manner in which a student goes about pupiling serves as a clue to the manner in which he is learning.

This practice may well be more defensible than any particular formal test that can be devised. For what is at issue, in terms of pedagogical purpose, is not only the particular understanding, appreciation, and insight named by the stated objectives, but the learning of how to pupil in such a manner as to gain understanding, appreciation, and insight.

Incremental Progress Toward Long-Range Educational Goals

Finally, no discussion of instructional objectives would be complete without acknowledgement of certain worthy aspirations held by teachers that, while intimately connected to observable behavior, nevertheless are not appropriate items for grading and certainly not for accountability. Yet are we to say that teachers are in no way responsible for fostering, for example:

(a) A benevolent sensitivity to the needs and wants of others coupled with a feeling of obligation to act on principle rather than entirely on self-interest.

(b) Confidence in human intelligence when it is formed and informed through the processes of free, autonomous inquiry.

(c) An acceptance of imperfection in the self and others as not necessarily indicating malevolence.

These integrative character traits provide the anchor posts around which individual life styles are developed. *Taken as a whole,* a student's behavior sometimes seems to indicate an incremental gain toward such long-range goals. And the fact that teachers sometimes think they can detect such a gain and believe that they have had something to do with it is, no doubt, one of the things that keep them going even while buffeted about by movements such as behavioral objectives, accountability, and the like.

Some Types of Objectives (Summary)

We have briefly identified and differentiated the following types of instructional objectives.

1a. Replicative performance objectives.
1b. Applicative performance objectives.
2.   Behaviorally indicated objectives.

3. Configurationally indicated objectives.

4. Clue-indicated process objectives.

5. Incremental progress toward long-range educational goals.

Frequently, in the literature, all of these types are carelessly mixed together under the label "behavioral objectives." Yet we have seen that it is only in the case of objectives 1a and 1b that the specified behavior *is the objective*. And it is only with type 1a that the test behavior should be modeled as part of the instruction and that the teacher should teach for the test.

No claim is made that an exhaustive list of types of objectives has been presented. What is claimed is that (1) an early mistake of the behavioral objectives movement was a confusion of behavior as an objective with behavior as an indicator of the attainment of an objective, and (2) instructional objectives, whether homemade or mail-ordered, do not classify themselves with respect to their relation to observable behavior.

Each teacher must analyze what he means by the words used to express an objective in a particular context. How will this objective, along with others in the same cluster or network, serve some pedagogical purpose? How will the student use what he has learned—by replication or by application, for interpretation, for association? *After* the meaning of the objective is clarified, *then* it is appropriate to determine what specified performance characteristics, behaviors, configurations, or clues, are plausible indicators that the objective has been attained.

Performance–Based Teacher Education

Even though teaching includes a great deal more than classroom instruction, the various activities of teaching (Green, 1971) may be thought of as a series of performances. The same thing can be said of any professional practice. As with all such practice that is *professional*—that is, that is based upon theoretical knowledge and insight—the *training* must be built upon and intimately connected to a suitable *education*. The key, then, to an adequate performance–based teacher training effort (as part of a program of teacher education) is an analysis of the activities of teaching.

An analysis of intelligent, purposive *action*, however, should not be confused with simple time and motion studies of *observable behavior*. Consequently, an analysis of teaching, or of medical or legal practice, is concerned primarily with (1) the principles and conceptual distinctions that lift the professional practice above just good common sense, and (2) skillfully executed procedures that apply these principles and distinctions in a contextually appropriate manner. In short, a performance–based teacher training program should be conceived in the same general format as the preparation program for any other professional practitioner. The meaning of this format, in relation to teacher education, has been discussed, in broad outline, by Broudy (1965) and this format is fully compatible with the new NCATE Standards for the accreditation of programs of teacher education.

Why, then, is there resistance to the development of performance–based teacher education programs? Perhaps it is because in education there is a considerable history of "commitment without understanding" to various fads and movements. In the light of this history it is no wonder that many are fearful that at least the following two mistakes will be made.

One, when *competence* is thought to be directly observable rather than something that must be judged (by experts) on the basis of systematic observations of behavior, it may be thought that the way to build a performance–based program is to throw out all present courses, textbooks, and the like, and move the students "into the field" where they can learn to imitate what they can *actually see* teachers doing. Under guided practice and a schedule of reinforcement, some students could, no doubt, learn to "perform" rather quickly in ways that, to direct observation, would be hardly distinguishable from the behavior of the teacher. When both the student and the teacher appear to go through the same motions, why should certification be withheld from the student?

Two, when "performance–based" is thought to mean the same thing as "using behavioral objectives," it may be thought that the way to build a performance–based program is simply to rewrite all present course objectives as behavioral objectives. If each step in the program is conceived as a "specified behavior," then surely any student who can waltz through these steps has demonstrated that he can perform.

Probably, neither of these mistakes will be made in the bald form in which they have been described, but, of course, that is precisely what is feared. A program that is obviously absurd will be closed down before it can do much harm; a program whose fundamental mistakes are mitigated by the eclectic "good sense" of dedicated workers can, in the present state of the art, continue indefinitely and thus further delay the badly needed basic reconstruction of teacher education.

Perhaps another source of fear is a presumed connection between PBTE and a nonprofessional version of accountability. Actually, if we were able to develop a sound performance–based program for the preparation of professional practitioners in education, we could then hold our graduates accountable *to the profession* in a manner similar to the professional accountability practiced in the medical or legal profession. The individual practitioner is held accountable for the consequences of departures from standard practice; it is the profession as a whole that is held accountable for the consequences of standard procedures.

At this point, some will say that we are not yet ready to undertake the development of professional standards for competence in teaching performance—we do not yet have adequate empirical evidence linking various pedagogical "treatments" to student learning. Indeed, we do not yet have a set of clearly defined (or standardized) treatments! A review of the research on the effects of behavioral objectives on learning (Duchastel and Merrill, 1973), for example, leaves one in doubt as to what on earth the research was all about.

But there may be a "chicken or the egg" paradox here. We do have a considerable body of principles and conceptual distinctions from education's foundational disciplines (e.g. logic, epistemology, psychology, sociology) to serve, when coupled with pedagogical experience, as the bases for *applicative procedures* for dealing with many of the "critical incidents" or the recurring problems and tasks of teaching. Building a professional practice requires the will and discipline to use what we now *think we know* to develop a professional posture that will enable us to correct and extend, in a systematic manner, our present knowledge base.

If PBTE can be securely linked to the development of a fully professional practice, and if performance evaluation, certification, and accountability can be cast in terms that would be acceptable to any profession, then surely the movement should be supported. To the extent, however, that overly zealous advocates have substituted enthusiasm for insight and political pressure for professional discipline—to that extent—persons with a serious commitment to education and to the public interest will, quite properly, resist the movement.

References

Broudy, Harry S., "Criteria for the Professional Preparation of Teachers," *Journal of Teacher Education,* Vol. XVI, No. 4, December 1965.

Broudy, H. S., B. O. Smith, and J. R. Burnett, *Democracy and Excellence in American Secondary Education* (Chicago: Rand McNally, 1964).

Duchastel, Philippe C., and Paul F. Merrill, "The Effects of Behavioral Objectives on Learning: A Review of Empirical Studies," *Review of Educational Research,* Vol. 43, No. 1, Winter 1973, pp. 53-69.

Green, Thomas, *The Activities of Teaching* (New York: McGraw–Hill, 1971).

Hanson, Norwood, *Patterns of Discovery* (London: Cambridge University Press, 1961).

Mager, Robert F., *Goal Analysis* (Belmont, Calif.: Fearon, 1972).

Peters, Richard S., "Must an Educator have an Aim?" *Authority, Responsibility, and Education,* 2nd edition (London: George Allen and Unwin, Ltd., 1963).

Popham, W. James, "Objectives and Instruction," *Instructional Objectives,* AERA monograph (Chicago: Rand McNally, 1969), pp. 32-52.

Popp, Jerome A., "Operational Definitions in Educational Inquiries," *Philosophy of Education* 1969, Procedings of the Twenty-first Annual Meeting of the Philosophy of Education Society, pp. 200-205.

Smith, Philip G., "On the Logic of Behavioral Objectives," *Phi Delta Kappan,* March 1972, pp. 429-431.

Waks, Leonard Joseph, "Philosophy, Education, and the Doomsday Threat," *Review of Educational Research,* December 1969, pp. 607-621.

8. *Educational Objectives and Existential Heroes*

Leonard J. Waks

The purpose of this paper is to provide substantial reasons for rejecting the still fashionable doctrine of behavioral objectives.[1] To accomplish this I will, in the first part of the paper, divide that doctrine into two sub-doctrines, which will be called the doctrine of technical planning and evaluation (DTPE) and the doctrine of behavioral specification (DBS).

The DTPE formulates the basic pedagogical assumptions underpinning behavioral objectives. These pertain primarily to the role of objectives (aims, goals, ends) in educational planning, in teaching, and in evaluation. The DTPE conceives education as a body of techniques, means to specific ends: hence the term "technical." According to this doctrine, educational episodes are to be initiated solely for the sake of applying these techniques to produce specific outcomes, to achieve specific objectives, which must be formulated in speech or writing prior to these episodes. The DTPE holds that to the extent that these formulations are sketchy, imprecise, ambiguous, or fail to "communicate," that is, fail to have the same meaning to the educator responsible for them and his various audiences, appropriate techniques cannot be determined, so the related episodes will be aimless and incoherent.

According to the notion of educational evaluation implicit in the DTPE, formulations of educational objectives serve to close what I will call the "evaluation space" of educational episodes; that is, these objectives eliminate some among the possible interpretations of what will count as acceptable outcomes for these episodes. A fully adequate set of objectives

Source. This article was first published in *Focus on Learning*, Vol. 3, No. 2 (Fall/Winter 1973), pp. 13–24, and is reprinted here with permission of the author and *Focus on Learning*.

for any episode is one that closes this evaluation space completely; one that determines intersubjectively and with precision the outcome(s) that is (are) to count as acceptable for that episode; and one that permits objective, scientific measurement of the precise degree of pedagogical success and failure. A set of objectives that fails to eliminate the guesswork from evaluation, which leaves it open to subjective interpretation whether given outcomes are or are not acceptable, is to that extent a defective set of objectives. And those educational episodes conducted without any prespecified objectives at all exhibit the limiting case of this defect, since their goal sets (= the empty set) rule out the fewest interpretations of what will count as acceptable—none. Therefore these episodes, according to the DTPE, will be the most aimless and incoherent of all.

The subsidiary doctrine of behavioral specification augments the DTPE by further determining the class of stated objectives that are such that their attainment can be objectively verified, those that do "communicate." The DBS lays down the methodological stipulation that the only objectives in this class are those specified in behavioral terms. What, exactly, does this stipulation mean?

It is not possible, I think, to derive from the literature on behavioral goals a clear and unequivocal set of rules for the application of the expression "behavioral terms."[2] The most common definitions of behavioral terms in the literature define this expression in terms of "behavior," "action," "observable behavior," and "overt doings." These expressions are in turn defined in terms of what may be "seen or heard," of what is "visible."[3] This state of affairs is not altogether satisfactory.

It is a difficult problem of methodology to determine the scope of the observable for specific purposes. Informal definitions in terms of what may be "seen," for example, are inherently unsatisfactory because such terms, in their ordinary, nonspecialized senses were not invented to, and cannot, carry the burden that would be imposed on them. We cannot, for example, appeal with much hope of success to the ordinary and familiar meaning of the verb "to see" to decide who is correct when Alpha claims to see the gracefulness of this dance, while Beta insists that gracefulness cannot be seen and at best must be inferred from such and such movements. Fortunately such problems do not, for ordinary practical purposes, demand a solution. But if what is at stake here is, for instance, the admissibility of "gracefulness" as an educational objective capable of scientific measurement, or (what is the same problem in another guise) as an adequately defined variable in a correlational study (one, perhaps, intended to compare the validity of particular means for achieving important ends of dance education), then of course methodology and not lexicography is the appropriate discipline with which to face the problem. Definitions of the expression "behavioral terms" that fall back on our ordinary perceptual terminology and do not provide a clear and unequivocal set of rules for the ready application of this expression will therefore be unsatisfactory.

Nonetheless, this problem, found in the DBS as formulated in the literature on behavioral goals, is of no importance for the present paper. For it is not my purpose to attack behaviorism *per se.* It is my goal to develop reasons for rejecting the basic assumptions of behavioral goals, not any merely contingent elaborations. The DBS, the stipulation that educational objectives must be formulated in behavioral terms, is an addition to the basic program built on the assumptions about pedagogy embodied in the DTPE. It is this additional stipulation, and not anything basic to the program of educational design and assessment underpinning behavioral goals, which has stamped that program with the misleading label "behavioral goals." There could be, among adherents of that basic program, heated discussion not only about what it would be for an educational objective to be "behavioral," but also about whether or not the objectives used in conjunction with the program ought to be formulated in distinctively behavioral terms (whatever these are) in the first place.

The conjunction of the technical planning and evaluation model with behaviorism is something of an historical accident; whatever the affinity, the DTPE can be isolated logically from its behaviorist elaborations. On the face of it the basic program of technical planning and evaluation that lies at the heart of behaviorial objectives seems to be compatible with the whole gamut of methodologies, behaviorist, and nonbehaviorist. Those who accept the DTPE must in some way contend with the imprecision of the DBS as formulated in the literature. They must decide to reject the DBS, reformulate it, or studiously ignore the problems it raises. However, unlike them, I do not intend to augment the DTPE; rather I intend to develop reasons for rejecting it. As it is independent from the DBS, no argument against it can depend on any features of or problems with the DBS. Thus these problems are irrelevant for my present purpose.

For my purpose it suffices at this juncture merely to disentangle the pedagogical assumptions implicit in behavioral goals, which are embodied in the DTPE, from the behaviorist methodological stipulation that is confusingly peripheral to behavioral goals. Once this distinction is forged, the confusing issues of behaviorism may safely be placed aside while the basic pedagogical questions of behavioral goals are addressed.

At the risk of repetition it may be instructive to look at the relative positions of the DTPE and the DBS in the existing literature on behavioral goals. Of the two subdoctrines, the DBS has tended to occupy a more central place in the literature, both pro and con. Advocates of behavioral goals have tended to make an attempt to support the behaviorist element of their position with arguments; indeed, they have attempted to support the entire behavioral objectives structure with arguments in direct support of only the DBS. They have tended to allow the DTPE, the underlying basis of this structure, to be carried along piggyback fashion, without independent arguments or evidence. That it is open to question and in need of independent justificatory support is rarely noticed.[4]

Robert F. Mager, for example, opens his immensely influential *Preparing Instructional Objectives* with this bald, unsupported proclamation of the DTPE.

> Once an instructor decides he will teach his students something, several kinds of activity are necessary on his part if he is to succeed. He must first decide upon the goals he intends to reach at the end of the course or program. He must then select procedures, content, and methods that are relevant to the objectives; cause the students to interact with appropriate subject matter in accordance with principles of learning; and finally measure or *evaluate* the student's performance *according to the objectives or goals* originally selected.[5] (Mager's emphasis)

Here are all the essential elements of the DTPE. The instructional episode is conceived as nothing but a context for the application of techniques to achieve specific ends, preformulation of which is necessary for instructional success. Notice that it is a logical consequence of the DTPE (it results from the conception of education as nothing but means to an end) that instructional success is defined in terms of the attainment of prespecified objectives and not, as would be at least somewhat more natural, in terms of the value of the results actually obtained! If, contrary to the DTPE, success were to be defined in terms of the achievement of worthwhile results, whether or not these were congruent with such objectives as might have been specified in advance of the episode, then, (a) Mager's confident assertion of the necessity of prespecified objectives for instructional success would cease to be tautologously true, and instead should begin to appear somewhat dubious; and (b) Mager's emphatic restriction of evaluation procedures to measurement of students' attainment of prespecified objectives only, without consideration of other educational values that have possibly been achieved, would clearly be arbitrary and unjustified.

The remainder of *Preparing Instructional Objectives* is devoted to an explanation and defense of the DBS, based of course on the unsupported prior assumption of the DTPE. But nowhere here, or to my knowledge in any other work, does Mager, or for that matter any other prominent advocate of behavioral goals, provide any substantial independent justification for the fundamental DTPE.

Similarly, many criticisms of behavioral objectives have been directed against the DBS. For example, the familiar arguments designed to show that the behavioral approach is overly restrictive because there could not be adequate equivalents in behavioral terms for many important kinds of educational ends (e.g. understanding, creativity)[6] are cogent criticisms of the DBS at most, and leave the more fundamental DTPE unscathed.

Yet despite the more important place of the DBS in the literature, the DTPE may readily be shown to be the more fundamental of the two subdoctrines. The DBS is subsidiary to the DTPE because one may reject it while consistently maintaining the DTPE but not *vice versa*. One may reject the DBS, believing that a less restricted, nonbehaviorist vocabulary is acceptable (or even required) for all relevant theoretical and practical purposes, yet still maintain without inconsistency that educational episodes require appropriately defined objectives and that without them these episodes will be aimless and incoherent. Here "appropriately defined" would be spelled out in terms of the less restricted, nonbehaviorist vocabulary. However, one may not reject the DTPE and still maintain the DBS, because the DBS is an answer to a question that arises only upon prior acceptance of the DTPE. If the DTPE is rejected, that is, if it is denied that educational episodes require exhaustive prespecified objectives to be coherent and successful, then the question addressed by the DBS, "in what terms ought the exhaustive prespecified objectives required for coherent, successful education be formulated?" simply fails to arise. Because in that case there simply would be no such objectives.

So far, I have distinguished the pedagogical component of the doctrine of behavioral objectives from the methodological stipulation of behaviorism that augments it, and have established the relative positions of these within the composite doctrine. If I have been correct so far, the DTPE and not behaviorism ought to be the target of any fundamental criticism of the doctrine of behavioral objectives. This should serve as an adequate preliminary defense for the approach developed below, where I consider the DTPE in isolation from behaviorism and attempt to adduce compelling reasons for rejecting it.

The Case Against the Technical Model

Aims, purposes, ends. To challenge the DTPE, which pertains primarily to the role of objectives in educational design and evaluation, I must ask the reader to consider along with me the following questions.

When, if ever, are prespecified objectives genuinely necessary for coherent, effective teaching? Just what sorts of objectives are needed in those circumstances? Why, precisely, are these objectives needed?

When these questions are raised in the penumbra of the shadow cast by the doctrine of behavioral objectives, they admittedly have an awkward ring. In the first two sections of this second part we will enter into a conversation with a hypothetical advocate of the technical model, the model of pedagogy prescribed by the DTPE, in an attempt to eliminate this ring of awkwardness and imbue these questions with serious import.

We may imagine our hypothetical interlocutor to respond initially to these questions by asking "How can one seriously question the necessity of having clear objectives? Is it not the case that action without an objective (aim, purpose, end) is random, unintelligent and, in short, aimless? And is it not also true that if a person's aims for some action are unclear, vague, or incapable of explicit formulation to any degree, then that action will be aimless to just that degree? How could this be otherwise?"

We may meet this *conceptual* line of defense of the DTPE by asking our interlocutor to notice that he falls back on the tautology that action without an aim is aimless action in defending the DTPE but fails to indicate the precise relationship between the DTPE and the tautology. Tautologies require no support, but the price they pay for this privilege is emptiness. Being empty of content, tautologies cannot figure essentially in the defense of substantive doctrines and policies. The DTPE is a substantive doctrine and the main support for substantive policies of curriculum reform. Although in moments of carelessness it may be confused with the tautology that action without an aim is aimless action, it is obviously stronger than that tautology, and hence more vulnerable to attack.

There are, of course, some conceptual relationships between (i) taking means to an end and (i') taking means to ends of the specificity and extent required by the technical model, (ii) such broader concepts as pursuing aims and acting with purpose, and (iii) acting in an intelligent, nonrandom, nonaimless fashion. But some of these relationships are obscure, and this conceptual defense of the DTPE trades on this obscurity.

The defense presupposes, correctly enough, that aimless random teaching is unacceptable. But it fails to make the relevant distinctions between (i), (i'), and (ii). Instead, it runs these together, creating a spurious relationship between failing to conform to the technical model and acting (as would be unacceptable) in an unintelligent, aimless fashion. The category (ii), which is clearly related closely to (iii), mediates, as it were, between (i) and (i') on the one hand and (iii) on the other. The defender of the technical model reminds us of the importance of acting with purpose, or having aims, when teaching. But few would dispute the importance of that (other than those who are taken in by the assimilation of (i), (i'), and (ii) and believe (falsely) that to admit that would commit them to the technical model). When the notions of category (ii) are run together first with (i) and then (i'), the appearance that a strong conceptual relationship exists between (i') and (iii) is created.

But this conceptual defense of the DTPE must not be made to depend merely on the general relation between pursuing an aim (purpose) and acting intelligently and purposefully. Rather, it must provide reasons for believing that formulating objectives in advance of educational endeavor that are sufficiently exhaustive and precise to permit objective measurement of the extent of success and failure is a necessary condition for teaching in an intelligent, purposeful fashion. So far we have not been given any reason for believing this. Might such reasons be forthcoming?

If so, these reasons will not be of conceptual nature. A decade of intense investigation of the logic of pedagogical concepts and concepts related to purpose has generated substantial reasons for thinking that, however tempting the prospect may have appeared to some, the concepts of pursuing aims and acting with purpose cannot, in the manner required for the defense under consideration, be analyzed in terms of or identified with the more lucid (and hence more appealing) notion of taking means to well–defined ends.[7]

To summarize this phase of our conversation: when the means are at hand for distinguishing the DTPE from the tautology that action without an aim is aimless action, it may readily be seen just how little support for the DTPE may be gleaned from the appeal to that tautology. If our interlocutor is to provide reasons for accepting the DTPE, these will not depend upon the relations between concepts. Rather, our interlocutor must find grounds of a different sort.

The magical mystery tour.   Perhaps these grounds may be found in available empirical knowledge. The DTPE is not empty of empirical content, so we must consider the fit between that doctrine and the facts.

At a glance, this fit seems rather poor. The DTPE posits that pedagogical coherence and effectiveness bear a direct relationship to the degree of exhaustiveness and precision of prespecified goals. Yet it is a plain and obvious fact admitted even by proponents of the technical model (in weaker moments, of course) that at least some teachers, in at least some pedagogical intervals, are at least somewhat coherent and effective (whatever nonquestion-begging analyses are reasonably attached to these notions) without positing any objectives of any sort at all, much less a set satisfying the stringent conditions of adequacy laid down by the technical model.

For example, Mr. Alpha enters (e.g. social studies, language arts) class with no idea what to do, only to find student Beta asking for the definition of some term that he, Alpha, habitually uses (e.g. "deployment") and Alpha explains the meaning and connotations of the term, provoking subsequent discussion in which other matters, (e.g. jargon, motives for using jargon) willy–nilly come up and are brought into focus—with Alpha driving home important points at appropriate times.

How, we ask our interlocutor, can you contend with cases of this familiar sort?

We may expect him to reply (as others have before him) that this phenomenon, the creation of educational value without prespecified objectives of the requisite sort, is due to "magic," to the "mysterious gifts" of rare teacher–artists. It is initially perplexing to find the self-proclaimed "tough-minded" advocate of scientific measurement falling back on "soft" notions such as magic and mystery, but there is a method to this madness. These terms are embedded in communications to audiences that generally share with advocates of behavioral goals certain views about the necessity of applying science to educational practice. Among such audiences there is no awe of magic or mystery, excepting the magic and mystery of science itself. Given this leaning in their intended audiences, when proponents of the technical model call this phenomenon magic and a mystery, they emphasize, in a superior tone of voice, that the phenomenon is infrequent and unworthy of the serious attention of serious "scientists."

In other words, these attributions are not serious; they are merely part of the apparatus of self-reinforcing dogmatism which advocates of the technical model utilize to reduce cognitive dissonance. Although these attributions may be successful in this capacity, they naturally beg the question at issue. This question is: Is the DTPE congruent with facts at our disposal? To call the phenomenon of "goal-free" production of educational value magic and a mystery, and in so doing imply that the phenomenon is rare and unworthy of serious consideration, is to reiterate the official position on this question instead of providing any reasons for accepting that position.

The frequency of this phenomenon, and the implications of this for the theory of pedagogy, are at issue. We may allow proponents of the technical model to dub this phenomenon "magic" or anything else they wish, but we must *not* allow them in the next breath to deny that any such magic exists or has any importance. It is, after all, very interesting magic, and we ought to consider how widespread the practice of this magic is within education. How often is teaching a "magical mystery tour?"

Eisner's review of the scanty empirical literature pertaining to the technical model revealed that there has been almost no attempt made to determine with any precision the extent to which educators in their natural settings make their purposes explicit or the form in which any such explicit purposes are cast. Hence very little is adequately understood about these matters. Tied to this, little is known about the empirical connections between either the form or the extent of prespecified aims and the production of educational value.[8] This certainly should be a sobering note for adherents of the DTPE, since it means that they have no solid basis in evidence to support their doctrine concerning the relationship between explications of aims of certain sorts and the coherence and effectiveness of educational undertakings.

Where does this leave us? In the absence of empirical evidence to support the DTPE, we must suppose that the widespread willingness to accept at face value the necessity of having prestated objectives that it posits has rested rather heavily on the apparent conceptual tie between the technical model and acting with purpose, pursuing aims, and the like. But this conceptual foundation for the technical model was discredited in the last section. With the DTPE under attack and certain natural means of defending it repudiated, the following questions, with which I opened part two of this paper,

> When, if ever, are prespecified objectives necessary for coherent, effective teaching? Just what sorts of objectives are needed in these circumstances? Why precisely, are these objectives needed?

should no longer have any awkward ring. Instead they should be seen as the immediately relevant questions to raise in criticism of the technical model and, hence, in criticism of the doctrine of behavioral objectives. Now that these questions have been taken out of the shadow and brought into the light, they may be addressed more effectively.

Existential heroes. There really *is* some "magic" at the heart of the behavioral objectives controversy. But it is the proponents of the technical model themselves, and not any "mysteriously gifted" and "magical" teacher–artists, who are responsible for it. The proponents of the technical model perform a "disappearing act" in the course of their exposition of their doctrine. They eliminate, one by one, all of the essential *sources* of coherent and effective teaching, for instance, the cultural traditions, with their patterns of initiation and orientation, and the individual psychological capacities that in turn depend on these. As in other disappearing acts, that which is made to "disappear" remains in existence, but is lost from view.

At a certain point in this disappearing act, nothing is left (in view) that could provide any explanation of how it is possible for teachers to act coherently and effectively. Because apart from those background forms of tradition, initiation, and orientation, and the in-formed capacities for sensitive and adaptive behavior that depend on these, what is to account for the possibility of coherent, effective teaching? Obviously, nothing! We now find the teacher on the brink of the "despair" of "total emptiness," loaded down with "dread," because there is nothing to fall back on and everything is "up to him." The language by now should be sufficiently "existential."

The image created by the "disappearing act," which eliminates from view the background forms of tradition and initiation, for example, is that of the teacher as an "existential hero," an abject figure in a "meaningless" world, a "naked" individual stripped of the constituents of real individuality, burdened by a "dreadful freedom," with no sense of what he is about or what he is called on to do. The aims that he meaninglessly projects onto an equally meaningless world, his "existential projects," are the only points of reference for such an existential hero.

Recall that familiar scenario of the silent movies—the tramp at the formal dinner party. The tramp has no orientation to the activity of formal dining. He brings nothing with him which fills that world with meaning and purpose. Nothing within the physical surroundings structures his behavior; he has no familiarity with the various artifacts, the silverware and the china, or the purposes they embody. He does not share with other participants a common understanding of the point of the activity, except in terms too gross to be helpful. He has no knowledge of the subtle norms underpinning formal dining.

The tramp looks about abjectly, attempting to form a few simple ideas about what he might do to get him through the evening and out of harm's way. He notices that the guests converse laughingly with one another, so he forms the project of making the surrounding guests laugh. He attracts some attention to himself, sticks his napkin in his ear, and smiles coyly. It may just work! But then again, it may not. Nonetheless, it is all he has to go on. For the tramp, his project, his objective as it were, is a single point of reference in an otherwise booming buzzing confusion. Although dressed in formal attire, the tramp at the formal dinner party is a "naked" individual, an "existential hero."

Existential Heroes and Educational Aims.   The reader will agree, whatever his pessimism about contemporary educational institutions, that the existential hero, the abject, solitary figure whose activities have meaning and direction *solely* by reference to some terminal point or points fixed by or for him, is an unusual figure around educational circles. We must reject any doctrines about educational objectives that can make no better sense than this of the familar figures we find there. These individuals sometimes state aims too, but their stated aims must be understood against the background of their prior experiences and within the framework of the practical social life into which they are initiated and which they are concerned and competent to lead. The familar figures who occupy our educational world, whatever their various shortcomings, are not naked and solitary figures in meaningless worlds. They are "clothed," as it were, by their initiation and training; by their occupancy of roles; and by the manner in which their endeavors are standardized, regularized, influenced, and constrained by morals and custom, made into habit and ready second nature. To put this another way, the teacher is not, regardless of any "disappearing act," an existential hero; rather he is an initiate of a social tradition, a form of life, a whole manner of thinking and acting and feeling.[9]

When we have seen through this disappearing act, and the social and social-psychological background for coherent, effective teaching has been retrieved from the bottom of the magician's storage bin, the teacher may again be seen and understood against that background. This has two implications for the theory of educational objectives.

(i) When the teacher is seen against the appropriate ground (the framework of orientation, initiation, commitment, and shared expectation), then the world he occupies is no longer meaningless. It is no longer the sort of world that requires a constant influx of goals or objectives to provide meaning and structure for behavior. As an initiate of a public form of life, the individual occupies a world with purposes built right into it. That individual has direction provided for his behavior by long familiarity with that form of life; by some sense of its myths, its history, and its traditions; and also by the concrete tools of the trade—the chalk boards, books, and blocks that embody the purposes of the educational world. These purposes are built into the bodies of appropriately oriented individuals, coded into their nervous systems, and reflected in their unconscious habits and inclinations.

This orientation of the teacher to the public form of life does not, by itself, guarantee worthwhile, coherent, and effective education. *Far from it!* But it does give the teacher a lot to go on other than goals or objectives posited in any terms whatsoever for a large range of educational endeavors. Teachers do not generally require explicit prespecified goals merely to give some direction and structure to their teaching activities, since there are purposes implicit in every nonconscious tendency they have and in every artifact that they find around them. The skeptical reader may remind himself that any eight–year–old child who has put in his time at school can give a plausible imitation of a teacher engaged in the activities of teaching, without any reliance on any specified objectives.

(ii) When objectives, aims, purposes are explicitly stated in the familiar educational world, they are stated against this background of orientation and commitment. They are not meant to provide a modicum of direction in an otherwise totally meaningless world, but rather to supplement, to modify, or to reinforce those tendencies and habits that are second nature to the teachers for whom they are stated. These goal statements, when successful, will take forms appropriate to these tasks of supplementation, modification, and reinforcement. As the concrete situations calling out for explicit objectives vary, so too will the forms of objectives appropriate for those situations. There could no more be a goal form that is appropriate for every situation in general than there could be a height for every man in general. Men vary in height, and situations vary in their requirements for explicit objectives.

The one general point worth emphasizing is this: the goal statements appropriate for the concrete educational situations that call out for them will generally be inappropriate for existential heroes and will not provide these lost souls with adequate direction to get around their otherwise meaningless worlds. The teacher's mind may be imagined as saturated with ideas, and stated objectives need only crystallize what is already there. By way of contrast, for the existential hero, each educational objective is merely a drop in an empty bucket. Therefore, when explicit educational objectives are assessed, we must be careful not to allow them to be judged by standards that, while relevant to the existential projects of existential heroes, are thoroughly irrelevant to objectives addressed to those practical social individuals who know where they stand and have in mind and body, and find in the world around them, the means for coherent, effective teaching.

The analysis of directive language. As we have seen, goal statements addressed to the familiar teachers we all know, and not to existential heroes, are not intended to and cannot provide a single sufficient point of reference in an otherwise meaningless world. Instead, goal statements are generally intended to be a small contribution to that already extensive set of factors that together determine the behavior of teachers. Because of this, these goal statements do not *have* to carry solely within the lexical meanings of their constituent terms the message that they convey to those to whom they are appropriately addressed.

At this point we may imagine our imaginary interlocutor breaking in to ask, "Isn't *this* a mystery? How can goal statements provide direction if that direction is not somehow a function of the meanings of the constituent terms?"

Consider an example: two workmen, Alpha and Beta, are working together on a project (e.g., an engine job). Each is in a position to see that XYZ are the relevant facts of the situation and each has tacit knowledge[10] of the norm that, when facts XYZ obtain and a circumstance C arises, a certain act A must be done. This norm is unspoken, indeed, it is unrehearsed in consciousness, although it may be that at some time in the past this norm, or some other norm relating to it in one of a number of possible ways, was explicitly formulated in a training manual or demonstration, or was acquired through and formulated in previous experience. As competent workmen, Alpha and Beta can each trust the other to have perceived and understood this much.

As they are situated, Alpha perceives that Beta is in a better position to observe for circumstance C, while he, Alpha, is in a better position to do act A should C arise. So Alpha, at the crucial time, watches Beta intently. Here, Beta may indicate by any of an enormous range of signs (e.g. a grunt of an appropriate sort, a shout, an utterance of "do it," etc.), signs that have not necessarily been previously assigned the value of symbols, that Alpha is to do act A.

Seen from the external point of view, in isolation from the background of practical competence and shared understanding against which this sign is indicated, the fact that Alpha could get any direction from a sign devoid of meaning, such as a grunt, would certainly seem to be "magical" and "mysterious" indeed. Beta's communication would, from this point of view (the view created by the now infamous "disappearing act" of several sections back), have to remain unexplainable, except perhaps through reference to the magical, mysterious, and "artistic" gifts of Alpha and Beta.

However, seen from the inside, against the appropriate ground, there is nothing the least magical or mysterious about this communication.

Policy implications of this analysis of directive language. Those theorists insisting on retaining the external point of view, and doing a "disappearing act" to get rid of the background of initiation and training that make competent mechanics out of Alpha and Beta, can look only at the grunt to find the direction Beta conveys to Alpha. This grunt, first bracketed and then isolated from the context where it was made with assignable sense, would certainly appear to be defective on semantic grounds. How *could* anything as vague, indefinite, and meaningless as a grunt provide anyone with adequate direction?

Thus, when the external, disappearing act point of view is taken of the transaction between Alpha and Beta, they are stripped in perception of that which makes competent workmen out of them. Policy that is based on this deficient perception of Alpha and Beta may be expected to finish up the job and rob them *in reality* of the competences that at first were lost only *in appearance* to those unprepared to accept (and those rendered by a disappearing act incapable of understanding) Alpha and Beta on their own turf. After all, "realistic," "tough-minded" policy-makers cannot be expected to put much stock in any "magic."

And this is an exact parallel to the approach of the advocates of policies of technical design and evaluation (e.g., accountability schemes based on objectives) as that approach relates to familiar forms of goal statements in education. That variety of forms of goal statements found in advising, supervision, and informal discussion among teaching colleagues is attacked; the forms are criticized on semantic grounds as vague, indefinite, and meaningless. Removed by a disappearing act from their social and social-psychological backgrounds, these objectives indeed do appear to be semantically defective and incapable of providing direction.

Finally, on the basis of this misperception created by the "disappearing act," it is persuasively argued that a new set of educational policies requiring fully explicit, precise, and exhaustive objectives be substituted for those serviceable forms of directive speech found around educational circles and the competences required for using and understanding objectives of those forms.

Advocates of behavioral objectives like to speak of "reducing"the more familiar sorts of educational objectives found around schools to behavioral terms. But to the extent that these new policies involving the use of behavioral objectives in planning and evaluation interfere with the exercise of those practical competences of educators, it will be those educators and not their objectives that are reduced . . . reduced to existential heroes, solitary and naked individuals in meaningless worlds.

Reform or reaction?   It may be anticipated that adherents of technical planning and evaluation in education, who tend to see themselves as liberal reformers using the best available scientific knowledge to find the best replacements for what they see as hidebound traditional approaches to education, will object to what they will perceive as the conservative assumptions that lie behind the argument of this paper. Just what do these assumptions amount to?

I assume only that the second nature that teachers acquire during their days as students and later as teacher trainees counts for something, that it provides something of a frame of reference and point of departure for school practice. This point seems to me to be independent of the pessimistic attitudes some readers will have about ordinary teachers and schools. If the teacher has *something* to go on because of his prior experiences (and he certainly does, because he is called upon to act in similar circumstances, and not, e.g., on Mars), then goal statements issued in contexts of preplanning do not have to carry the burden of providing *everything* necessary either for direction or assessment.

For this reason the claim that there is a general need for precise and exhaustive objectives and, without these educational episodes, cannot be conducted coherently or effectively, must be rejected. The advocate of the DTPE, on the other hand, by his "disappearing act" logic is committed to the absurd proposition that what the teacher brings with him to the educational encounter counts for nothing, that all teachers everywhere are either occult "magicians" or else empty headed idiots.

The second natures that we acquire through participation in our public forms of life are the living residues of what is good and bad in our cultural history. We can, and certainly we should, examine this heritage of ours and struggle to free ourselves from the grip of those activities and attitudes that no longer have any value for us. But what are we to do when new policies negate our second natures altogether, eliminating the good with the bad, conferring upon us that "dreadful freedom" that results when everything is "up to us," reducing us to abject existential heroes in meaningless worlds?

Part of the answer lies in the admission that the image of the brave new educator as existential hero in a meaningless world is overdrawn. There is more to our world than our institutions of education; and the powerful forces that remain when our humanistic educational heritage is negated may be expected to rush in, fill the vacuum, and turn the ghost of education to account. Will it be education? Humpty Dumpty reminds us that we may use words any way we wish, and that the real questions is:

WHO IS TO BE MASTER?

It should hardly be surprising, then, that adherents of the technical planning and evaluation model in education have borrowed not merely their support funds from increasingly authoritarian government, the military establishment, and oligarchic capitalist enterprise, but their very self-image as well.[11]

Notes

[1] Although heralded as a new development, the doctrine of behavioral objectives is merely the current projection of one of the dominant images of education in the twentieth century. The story of the early precursors is told admirably by Raymond E. Callahan, *Education and the Cult of Efficiency* (Chicago: University of Chicago Press, 1962). A more recent precursor is Ralph Tyler, whose "rationale" is developed in *Basic Principles of Curriculum and Instruction* (Chicago: University of Chicago Press, 1950).

The term "behavioral objective" was used prior to the sixties, in, for example, Will French et al., *Behavioral Goals of General Education in the High School* (New York. Russell Sage Foundation, 1957); but it gained wider currency after the publication of Robert F. Mager's manual, *Preparing Instructional Objectives* (Palo Alto, Calif.: Fearon, 1962). This manual stimulated a spate of critical articles, among the most important of which are: J. Myron Atkin, "Some Evaluation Problems in a Course Content Improvement Project," *Journal of Research on Science Teaching*, Vol. 1, No. 2 (June 1963), pp. 129-132, and reprinted in Peter A. Taylor and Doris M. Cowley, eds., *Readings in Curriculum Evaluation* (Dubuque: Wm. C. Brown, 1972), pp. 20-22; J. Myron Atkin, "Behavioral Objectives in Curriculum Design: A Cautionary Note," *The Science Teacher*, Vol. 35, No. 5 (May 1968), and reprinted in Miriam B. Kapfer, ed., *Behavioral Objectives in Curriculum Development* (Englewood Cliffs, N.J.: Educational Technology Press, 1971), pp. 368-374; Philip W. Jackson and Elizabeth Belford, "Educational Objectives and the Joys of Teaching," *School Review*, Vol. 73, No. 3 (Autumn 1965), pp. 267-291; Elliot Eisner, "Educational Objectives: Help or Hindrance?," *School Review*, Vol. 75, No. 3 (Autumn 1967) and reprinted in Kapfer, ed., pp. 358-366 and in Taylor and Cowley, eds., pp. 23-27; and Elliot Eisner, "Instructional and Expressive Educational Objectives: Their Formulation and Use in the Curriculum," *Instructional Objectives,* AERA Monograph Series on Curriculum Evaluation (Chicago: Rand McNally, 1969), pp. 1-18.

Despite these criticisms, more and more manuals on how to write behavioral objectives have continued to appear. Among recent publications of this sort are included: Robert J. Armstrong et al., *The Development and Evaluation of Behavioral Objectives* (Belmont, Calif.: Wadsworth, 1970); N. E. Garland, *Stating Behavioral Objectives for Classroom Instruction* (New York: Macmillan, 1970); H. H. McAshan, *Writing Behavioral Objectives: A New Approach* (New York: Harper & Row, 1970); W. James Popham and E. L. Baker, *Establishing Educational Goals* (Englewood Cliffs, N.J.: Prentice Hall, 1970); David E. Hernandez, *Writing Behavioral Objectives: A Programmed Exercise for Beginners* (New York: Barnes and Noble, 1971); Richard W. Burns, *New Approaches to Behavioral Objectives* (Dubuque: Wm. C. Brown, 1972); and Julie S. Vargas, *Writing Worthwhile Behavioral Objectives* (New York: Harper & Row, 1972). Despite minor differences, these manuals all presuppose the doctrines under examination in the present paper.

One significant attempt to deal systematically with the range of criticisms which have been developed to date against the doctrine of behavioral objectives is W. James Popham, "Objectives and Instruction," in *Instructional Objectives,* pp. 32-52. This is reprinted with some additional material in Kapfer, ed., pp. 391-397 under the title "Probing the Validity of Arguments Against Behavioral Goals." A detailed response to this is Leonard J. Waks, "Re-examining the Validity of Arguments against Behavioral Goals," *Educational Theory,* Vol. 23, No 2 (Spring 1973), pp. 133–43.

[2] This is reflected in extremely variable usage; "behavioral" goals range from those stated in terms of colorless movements to these from French, et al. op. cit.: 1.114a sees learning as a continuous process throughout life, and 2.133c endeavors to be prompt in his responsibilities to the group. The problem is this: the more closely a behavioral goal adheres to the restrictions of a behavioristic methodology, the less plausible it will appear as a genuine goal of education, and the more plausible, the greater the reliance on the full-blooded language of human action and attitude.   .

[3] See, for example, Mager op. cit., pp. 2; Hernandez, op. cit., pp. 1, 3, 45; McAshan, op. cit., pp. 16-17; and Vargas, op. cit., pp. 32.

[4] See Eisner, "Instructional and Expressive Educational Objectives . . .," pp. 10-13.

[5] Mager, op cit.

[6] See, for example, Eisner, "Educational Objectives: Help or Hindrance," in Kapfer, ed., p. 362; also Leonard J. Waks, "Philosophy, Education, and the Doomsday Threat," *Review of Educational Research,* Vol. 39, No. 5 (December 1969), pp. 615-618. Not all prior criticisms of behavioral goals have been directed against the DBS; once the two subdoctrines are clearly distinguished, the criticism of Jackson and Belford, those of Atkin, and some of those of Eisner, may be categorized as arguments against the DTPE.

[7] See especially Richard S. Peters, "Must an Educator Have an Aim?," Chap. seven of *Authority, Responsibility, and Education,* Revised edition (London: George Allen and Unwin, 1963) and reprinted in C. J. B. MacMillan and Thomas W. Nelson, eds., *Concepts of Teaching: Philosophical Essays* (Chicago: Rand McNally, 1968), pp. 89-98; and C. J. B. MacMillan and James E. McClellan, "Can and Should Means–Ends Reasoning be used in Teaching," in MacMillan and Nelson, eds., pp. 119-150. MacMillan and McClellan opt for a model of teaching closely related to the technical model, however.

[8] Eisner, "Instructional and Expressive Educational Objectives . . .," pp. 10-13.

[9] The notion of a form of life was developed by Ludwig Wittgenstein; see especially

his *Philosophical Investigations* (New York: MacMillan, 1953). The notion is utilized effectively in Arthur E. Murphy, *The Theory of Practical Reason* (LaSalle, Ill.: Open Court, 1965). See also A. I. Melden, "Utility in Moral Reasoning," in Richard deGeorge, ed., *Ethics and Society* (Garden City: Anchor Books, 1966), pp. 173-196.

[10] The concept of tacit knowledge (also called personal knowledge) has been explicated by Michael Polanyi, *Personal Knowledge* (Chicago: Chicago University Press, 1958), and *The Tacit Dimension* (Garden City: Anchor Books, 1966). Knowledge is tacit (personal) if acquired through practice rather than by reference to explicit formulations, and cannot be articulated.

[11] In writing this paper I could not have gotten by without a *lot* of help from my friends. The paper got its start in a series of intense conversations with Decker Walker in April–June 1970 at Stanford. He later suggested (August 1971) ways of clarifying several points, and contributed the crucial Chaplinesque example to explicate the notion of an existential hero. Subsequently, my colleagues in the department of Foundations of Education at Temple University gave the paper a going over; William Cutler was particularly helpful. Donald Arnstine wrote a very strong critical letter, in response to which the paper became much improved. A letter from William Hay was also helpful. The paper was read at the Spring 1972 meeting of the Middle Atlantic States Philosophy of Education Society at Rutgers University, April 29, 1972. It has subsequently been expanded and revised.

As I was writing this final footnote, in January 1973, I received the Fall 1972 *Review of Educational Research*, and there I found James G. March, "Model Bias in Social Action," pp. 413-429. That paper, which was read at the 1972 AERA meeting in Chicago, makes a case against the technical planning model similar to the one found in this paper.

9. The Adequacy of Systems Management Procedures in Education

Michael W. Apple

A few years ago, a well-known curriculum worker began his arguments for behavioral objectives—one of the precursors and usually a basic tenet of "sytems management procedures" in education—with some rather interesting comments. Even though pointing to the necessity of dialogue for examining the respective worths of different positions on the controversial subject of designing educational activities in terms of "measurable learner behaviors," he had a few remarks to say that are quite pertinent to this paper. He writes:

> Within the last few years a rather intense debate has developed in the field of curriculum and instruction regarding the merits of stating instructional objectives in terms of measurable learner behaviors. Because I am thoroughly committed, both rationally and viscerally, to the proposition that instructional goals should be stated behaviorally, I view this debate with some ambivalence. On the one hand, it is probably desirable to have a dialogue of this sort among specialists in our field. We get to know each other better—between attacks. We test the respective worths of opposing positions. We can have hopefully stimulating symposia such as this one. Yet as a partisan in the controversy, I would prefer unanimous support of the position to which I subscribe. You see, the other people are wrong. Adhering to a philo-

Source. This article was first published in the *Journal of Educational Research*, Vol. 66, No. 1 (September 1972), and it is reprinted here with the permission of the author and the *Journal of Educational Research*.

sophic tenet that error is evil, I hate to see my friends wallowing in sin.

He then goes on to say

Moreover, their particular form of sin is more dangerous than some of the time—honored perversions of civilized societies. For example, it will probably harm more people than the most exotic forms of pornography. I believe that those who discourage educators from precisely explicating their instructional objectives are often permitting, if not promoting, the same kind of unclear thinking that has led in part to the generally abysmal quality of instruction in this country.[1]

This quote is rather interesting. First, it documents the intellectual state of the curriculum field. Although many of Schwab's specific criticisms of the curriculum field are tautologous, I tend to agree with his suggestion that the imminent death of a discipline is seen in its increasing use of *ad hominum* arguments[2] such as the one just quoted. Secondly, and of more important concern, is the set of assumptions mirrored in the statement just quoted, assumptions that provide the ideological foundation for systems management in education. These assumptions are concerned with the tacit advocacy of a view negating the importance of intellectual conflict, a rather limited perspective on scientific endeavor, an inability to deal with ambiguity and, finally, an outmoded separation of moral and technical questions. The increasing use of systems terminology in education rests on this set of beliefs that, when examined, is often unrealistic and socially and politically conservative.

At the outset, let me make certain of my perspectives clear. In my mind, schooling cannot be considered apart from the other economic and social institutions of a collectivity. It is intimately involved with and mirrors the dominant institutions of a society. Our thought about schooling and curriculum design is also fundamentally linked to the structure of the social order in which we exist.[3] While I would like to avoid a vulgar Marxist interpretation of consciousness, I would take the position that the basic framework of most curriculum rationality is generally supportive and ac-

---

[1] W. James Popham, "Probing the Validity of Arguments Against Behavioral Goals," reprinted in Robert J. Kibler, et al., *Behavioral Objectives and Instruction* (Boston: Allyn and Bacon, 1970), pp. 115-116.

[2] Joseph J. Schwab, *The Practical: A Language for Curriculum* (Washington, D.C.: National Education Association, 1970), p. 18.

[3] Cf., the excellent analysis of the relationship between knowledge and institutions in Peter L. Berger and Thomas Luckmann, *The Social Construction of Reality* (New York: Doubleday Anchor Books, 1966).

cepting of the *existing* economic, political, and intellectual framework that apportions opportunity in American society. I do not ask persons to share my perceptions that this framework tends toward the sublimation of basic human sentiment and the repression of a large portion of people within it. What I do ask is that the perceptions not be dismissed offhandedly and that curriculists cease to act on tacit assumptions that prevent them from focusing upon the definite ideological and epistemological commitments they possess. Part of the task of curriculum scholarship is to bring to a level of awareness the latent dysfunctions of our work, since values continually work through us and are sedimented within the very mind set we apply to our problems. It may very well be the case that the often inhuman and problematic activities and consequences of schooling will not be fundamentally altered until we cease searching for simple solutions to our problems. Part of the answer, but only part, is to illuminate our political and conceptual orientations. It is possible that the two are considerably interwoven.

I would like to point to tendencies in systems management procedures that often have some interesting things to say about the curriculum field's social commitments. For example, I shall consider systems language as conservative social rhetoric and shall look behind it to portray its incorrect view of science. First, let us look at systems thought as a general intellectual framework in education. The points to be made, however, apply to the educational uses of systems logic and not necessarily to systems thought, *per se* (though this latter point does remain moot).

Systems and Technical Control

Usually, one engages in systems approaches to obtain a more exact and "scientific" analysis. However, the view of scientific activity underpinning the use of systems strategies in education and curriculum design is based less upon an accurate view of scientific processes than it is upon an after-the-fact examination of scientific products. A distinction that is helpful here is one between the *logic-in-use* of a science and its *reconstructed* logic.[4] The former connotes what scientists actually do; and that is *not* necessarily the linear progression of stating goals absolutely clearly, of hypothesis testing and verification or falsification through statistical or other analyses, and so forth. The latter connotes what observers, philosophers of science, and others say that the *logic* of scientific inquiry looks like. There has been an exceptionally long history in educational thought, from Snedden up to the present, of borrowing a reconstructed logic of

---

[4] Abraham Kaplan, *The Conduct of Inquiry* (San Francisco, Calif.: Chandler, 1964), pp. 3-11.

scientific activity and expecting it to be sufficient for treating the complex problem of curriculum design, to say nothing of curriculum "research."

This has usually taken the form of the development of procedures to guarantee certainty and to rationalize and make explicit as many aspects of people's activity as possible—be it the researcher, the educational decision-maker, or the student. Huebner has described this approach as "technological" in that it seeks to use strict forms of means-ends or process-product reasoning and is primarily interested in efficiency, thus, tending to exclude other modes of valuing.[5] Examples include the early work of Bobbitt on activity analysis, which seemed to crystallize the basic paradigm of the field of curriculum, and the later emphasis on behavioral objectives. Each of these has sought to specify the operational boundaries of institutional interaction and has been motivated by a need for closure and, especially, surety. The behavioral objectives movement, for instance, in both its weak and strong senses, has sought to reduce student action to specifiable forms of overt behavior so that the educator can have certitude of outcome. Although the need for certainty is understandable given the large sums of money spent on education, its superficiality is disturbing. The behavioral orientation itself (as well as many constitutive aspects of systems management approaches) has been effectively dealt with by such early treatments as Ryle's analysis of knowing in its dispositional versus achievement senses, by Polanyi's exploration of forms of tacit knowing, and in Hannah Arendt's masterful examination of how the need for certainty often precludes the creation of personal meaning and effectively weakens the base of political action.[6] These analytic concerns aside, however, the perspective on systems as enabling a more "scientific" approach to educational problems requires further investigation.

Unlike the unceasing quest for surety among educators, scientific activity has been characterized less by a preference for certainty, for the slow and steady accumulation of technical data, than we have supposed. What most members of the scientific community would label good science is a process that is constituted upon the leap of faith, an aesthetic sensitivity, a personal commitment, and of great importance, an ability to accept ambiguity and uncertainty.[7] Without such qualities, ones that maintain

[5] Dwayne Huebner, "Curricular Language and Classroom Meanings," *Language and Meaning,* James B. Macdonald and Robert R. Leepter, eds. (Washington, D.C.: Association for Supervision and Curriculum Development, 1966), pp. 8-26.

[6] Cf. Gilbert Ryle, *The Concept of Mind* (New York: Barnes and Noble, 1949), Michael Polanyi, *The Tacit Dimension* (New York: Doubleday Anchor Books, 1966), and Hannah Arendt, *The Human Condition* (New York: Doubleday Anchor Books, 1958).

[7] See, for example, the discussion of wave versus particle theories of light in Thomas S. Kuhn, *The Structure of Scientific Revolutions* (Chicago: University of Chicago Press,

the scientific enterprise as an essentially human and changing artifact, science becomes mere technology. The view of science that is used to give legitimacy to a good deal of curriculum thought, especially that of systems approaches, is more reminiscent of a nineteenth–century brand of positivism than it is of current scientific and philosophical discourse. While the trend toward naive reductionism, for example, in approaching human action was stemmed in philosophy by 1930 or so,[8] as we shall see much of curriculum rationality today has progressed no further.

The problem of drawing upon a reconstructed logic is further compounded by our belief in the inherent neutrality of systems management. There seems to be a tacit assumption that systems management procedures are merely "scientific" techniques; they are interest-free and can be applied to "engineer" nearly any problem one faces. A searching analysis discloses some provocative questions about this assumption, however.

To be accurate, systems management procedures are not interest-free. Their own constitutive interest lies primarily in, and has the social consequence of, effecting and maintaining *technical control* and *certainty*.[9] Like the reconstructed logic of the strict sciences, it is aimed, fundamentally and unalterably, at the regularities of human behavior, the language of "individual differences" to the contrary. It is, hence, essentially manipulative. The manipulative perspective is inherent in the quest for certainty. In fact it is difficult to envision how an unflinching requirement for exactitude in goals and behavioral specifications can be less than manipulative given the propensities of man to exist in a dialectical relationship with his social reality—that is to make meaning his own and go beyond the framework and texture of social meanings and institutions.[10] It is here that we find a primary example of the conservative orientation so deeply embedded in "technological" models of educational thought.

A similar point is made by Sennett in his discussion of the tendency of city planners to create systems whose ideal is that nothing "be out of control," for institutional life "to be manipulated on so tight a reign [that] all manner of diverse activities must be ruled by the lowest common de-

---

1970). See also Imre Lakatos and Alan Musgrave, eds., *Criticism and the Growth of Knowledge* (Cambridge: Cambridge University Press, 1970) and Michael Polanyi, *Personal Knowledge* (New York: Harper Torchbooks, 1964).

[8] J. O. Urmson, *Philosophical Analysis* (London: Oxford University Press, 1956), p. 146.

[9] Trent Schroyer, "Toward a Critical Theory for Advanced Industrial Society," *Recent Sociology* 2, Hans Peter Dreitzel, ed. (New York: Macmillan, 1970), p. 215; and Jurgen Habermas, "Knowledge and Interest," *Sociological Theory and Philosophical Analysis*, Dorothy Emmet and Alasdair Macintyre, eds. (New York: Macmillan 1970), pp. 36-54.

[10] Peter L. Berger and Thomas Luckmann, op. cit., p. 129.

nominator."[11] Here, he summarizes his analysis of the propensity for systems planners to use technological and production models.

> Their impulse has been to give way to that tendency . . . of men to control unknown threats by eliminating the possibility of experiencing surprise. By controlling the frame of what is available for social interaction, the subsequent path of social action is tamed. Social history is replaced by the passive "product" of social planning. Buried in this hunger for preplanning along machine—like lines is the desire to avoid pain, to create a transcendent order of living that is immune to the variety, and so the inevitable conflict, between men.[12]

The philosophical naiveté and the strikingly deterministic aspect of systems management as it is applied in education is perhaps most evident in the dictum that requires of those building instructional systems, for instance, to "formulate specific learning objectives, clearly stating whatever the learner is expected to be able to do, *know,* and *feel* as an outcome of his learning experiences."[13] Even a surface examination of the psychological and especially the philosophical analyses of the nature of dispositions, attainments, and propensities, and how these are "taught" and linked with other types of "knowledge," shows the lack of any significant amount of thought being given to how human beings do, in fact, operate in real life.[14] Furthermore, the reductive mentality, one in which the components of cognition are divorced from "feeling" and can be behaviorally specified, fundamentally misconstrues the nature of human action.[15] The very idea that educators should specify *all* or even the primary aspects of a person's action substitutes the slogan of manipulation for the arduous task of making moral choices.

It should be made clear that curriculum design, the creating of educative environments in which students are to dwell, is inherently a political and moral process. It involves competing ideological, political, and intensely personal conceptions of valuable educational activity. Furthermore,

---

[11] Richard Sennett, *The Uses of Disorders* (New York: Vintage Books, 1970), p. 94.

[12] Ibid., p. 96.

[13] Bela H. Banathy, *Instructional Systems* (Palo Alto, Calif.: Fearon, 1968), p. 22. My stress.

[14] Cf., Donald Arnstine, *Philosophy of Education: Learning and Schooling* (New York: Harper & Row, 1967) and Stuart Hampshire, *Thought and Action* (New York: The Viking Press, 1959).

[15] This naive separation and the destructive aspects of behavioral specification can often best be seen in discussions of scientific thought, especially that of Michael Polanyi, op. cit. Susanne Langer's analysis of "mind" in *Philosophy in a New Key* (New York: Mentor, 1951) is also quite helpful here.

one of its primary components is the fact of influencing other people—specifically, students. Our common sense thought in education, however, tends to move in a direction quite the opposite from moral and political considerations. Instead, spheres of decision-making are perceived as *technical problems* that only necessitate instrumental strategies and information produced by technical experts,[16] thereby effectively removing the decisions from the realm of political and ethical debate. In other words, even though rationales such as systems procedures cloak themselves in the language of "being realistic," there is a strong tendency in their use to flatten reality, to define the complex valuative issues out of existence by using a form of thought that is amenable only to technical competence. In essence, the employment of systems procedures qua formula tends to obscure for the educator the fact that he is making profound ethical decisions about a group of other human beings.

Now the real issue is not that systems techniques yield information and feedback that may be used *by* systems of social control. They themselves *are* systems of control.[17] What is of equal importance is the fact that the belief system underlying them and a major portion of the curriculum field stems from and functions as a technocratic ideology which often can serve to legitimate the existing distribution of power and privilege in our society.[18] The very language used by a number of proponents of systems management in education conveys their assumptions. While change is viewed as important, it is usually dealt with by such notions as system *adjustment*.[19] The basis of the system itself remains unquestioned. The use of systems procedures assumes as its taken-for-granted foundation that the institutions of schooling are fundamentally sound. That is, while the "quality of instruction" is often poor, the same general pattern of human interaction is sufficient for education, if the institution can be tuned up, so to speak. The problems of schooling are to be solved by "modest inputs of centralized administration, along with expert services, research and advice." The lack of quality in education is viewed in terms of only a lack of technical sophistication and can be effectively solved through engineering.[20] The increasing disaffection with much of the obligatory meaning structure of schooling by students belies this perception.

Like the Tyler Rationale before it, systems management assumes that the effectiveness of a system can be evaluated by "how closely the output

---

[16] Schroyer, op. cit., p. 212.

[17] Alvin W. Gouldner, *The Coming Crisis of Western Sociology* (New York: Basic Books, 1970), p. 50.

[18] Schroyer, op. cit., p. 210.

[19] Banathy, op. cit., p. 10.

[20] Gouldner, op. cit., p. 161.

of the system satisfies the purpose for which it exists." [21] However, in the quest for orderliness, the political process, in which competing visions of purposes often deal with each other and come to some sort of understanding, is virtually ignored. Again, like Tyler, one—the manager of an institution perhaps—"engineers" in an unreal world. An understanding of the difficult ethical, ideological, and even aesthetic problems of who decides what, and exactly what these purposes should be that exist in the real world of education, are advanced no further.

Now, systems design itself is an analytic procedure in its own right with its own history and, usually, its own modes of self-correction when kept *within* its tradition. However, the educational-orientation labeled systems design does not approach this sophistication; nor does it borrow more than a veneer of terminology that is used to cover the dominant metaphor that curriculists have used to look at schooling for over 50 years. This metaphor or model pictures the school as a factory, and traces its roots back to the beginnings of curriculum as a field of study, especially to the work of Bobbitt and Charters.[22] In systems analysis in the field of computer design, inputs and outputs are *information;* in systems procedures in education, they are often children. The school is the processing plant and the "educated man" is the "product." [23] Given the fact that a field's language and metaphoric constructs often determine its modes of operation, the use of the language of child-qua-product is apt to preserve and enhance the already strikingly manipulative ethos of schooling. The ethos is also fostered by the relative lack of insight educators have into the domain of systems thought itself.

One is hard pressed to find more than occasional references in the literature on systems management procedures in the curriculum field, for example, to the most creative systems theorists. The structuralism of a Von Bertalanffy is nearly absent as is the subtlety of the way he attempts to grapple with problems. Although one does find a few references to him, it is quite obvious that the fundamental notions about systems procedures are not drawn from this school of thought. Rather, one sees a model that is actually taken from such fields as weapons technology and industry.[24] What is not found is of considerable moment given our attempt to be

---

[21] Banathy, op. cit., p. 13.

[22] Herbert M. Kliebard, "Bureaucracy and Curriculum Theory," *Freedom, Bureaucracy, and Schooling,* Vernon Haubrich, ed. (Washington, D.C.: Association for Supervision and Curriculum Development, 1971), pp. 74-93. This is not an unconscious linkage to the work of early theorists such as the sometimes quite problematic work of Bobbitt. See, for example, Robert Kibler, et al., *Behavioral Objectives and Instruction* (Boston: Allyn & Bacon, 1970), p. 105.

[23] Banathy, op. cit., p. 17.

[24] Ibid., p. 2.

"scientific." What is found, though, is the encasing of the school-as-factory model in a layer of slogans to give a field intellectual and economic legitimacy and a sense of neutrality. Systems design as a field of scientific study has within itself self-correcting mechanisms. The continual criticism of research and thought, and the intellectual conflict within the systems field among members of varying persuasions, provide a context for keeping it vital. Educators have borrowed only the language, often only the surface language (what I have called the reconstructed logic) and have, hence, pulled the terminology out of its self-correcting context. Thus, they have little insight into the continuing critical dialogue in the field of systems design that enables it to remain potent. We have yet to learn the dangers of appropriating models from disparate fields and applying them to education. All too frequently, the models are quickly outmoded, are intellectually inaccurate representations of those developed in the lending field,[25] and provide little in the way of the conceptual resources needed to grapple with the complex problem of designing environments that mediate between a student's search for personal meaning and a society's need to preserve its social fabric of institutions and knowledge.

Systems analysis began *not* as a management technique but as a mode by which the complex nature of problems could be illuminated. It sought to show how components of a field were interrelated and acted upon one another. Systems analysis was a mode of thought that sought to enhance our comprehension of change and stability—subsystem A is related in X fashion to subsystem B, which in turn is related in Y fashion to subsystem C. The combination created a different relationship, Z. Any alteration of C, therefore, would have profound repercussions in A and B, and in all the linkages among them. Systems thought, then, was a model for understanding, not necessarily for control. However, many curriculists seem to be employing it to manage their problems without first understanding the complexity of the relationships themselves. This is one of the points in which Schwab is correct. Only when we begin to see the intricate nature of the relationships among the aspects of the educational environment[26]

---

[25] Perhaps one of the more interesting examples of this is reflected in the work of Snedden. His appropriation of the worst of sociology served conservative ideological concerns. See Walter Drost, *David Snedden and Education for Social Efficiency* (Madison: The University of Wisconsin Press, 1967). Yet another instance is our increasing use of learning theory. Not only has it told us little that is applicable to the complex day-to-day reality of educational life but we have been persistently unaware of the problems learning theory itself has within its own scholarly community. The most complete analysis of the conceptual difficulties can be found in Charles Taylor, *The Explanation of Behavior* (New York: The Humanities Press, 1964); and Maurice Merleau-Ponty, *The Structure of Behavior* (Boston: Beacon Press, 1963).

[26] Schwab, op. cit., pp. 33-35.

can we begin to act as more than technicians. As a model for disclosing possibilities, not as a picture of what should be, systems analysis has its place. As a management structure for making institutional meanings obligatory, it is less than neutral to say the least.

While the advocates of systems procedures seek to enhance the scientific status of their work, as I have pointed out, the systems thought that they have borrowed is not from the scientific branch of systems logic. Rather, they have chosen to appropriate the models of operation of the business community.[27] However, this is not new by any means.[28] Although it would be unfair to point out that such "successful" concerns as Lockheed are the major proponents of systems procedures for large scale endeavors, the business and economic substructure of the United States continues to generate avenues that provide extremely limited opportunities for nearly *one-sixth* of the total population. One has to wonder if their models are indeed appropriate for dealing with students.

There are other issues that could be raised about the idea that systems procedures are "scientific" and are neutral techniques for establishing better educational practices. As I have noted, it is one of the basic assumptions that must be examined rather closely. I would like to delve a bit further and raise a few questions about its possible latent conservatism. One question concerns itself with systems language as a social rhetoric; the other concerns a constitutive aspect of systems procedures as they are applied today in education—namely the specification of precise instructional and usually behavioral objectives as tacitly preserving in an unquestioning manner, the dominant modes of institutional interaction in an industrial economy. I will then examine how the penchant for order in curriculum today serves a similar function. Let us examine the issue of systems as a language first.

Systems Procedures as Rhetoric

The Wittgensteinian principle that the meaning of language depends on its use is quite appropriate for analyzing systems language as it is applied in curriculum discourse. Systems language performs a rhetorical and political function. Without an understanding of this, we miss a major point. One of its primary, if latent, uses is to convince others of the sophisticated state of education. If a field can convince funding agencies, government, or the populace in general, that scientific procedures are being employed, whether or not they are in fact helpful, then the probability of increased

---

[27] Bruce R. Joyce, et al., *Implementing Systems Models for Teacher Education* (Washington, D.C.: U.S. Department of Health, Education and Welfare, 1971).

[28] See Raymond Callahan, *Education and the Cult of Efficiency* (Chicago: University of Chicago Press, 1962).

monetary and political support is heightened. Given the high esteem in which science is held in industrial nations, this is important. (Unfortunately, it is not science, *per se*, that is seen positively; rather it is technology and its concrete applicability.) Couching a field's problems in systems terminology evokes tacit meanings from a general audience, meanings that are supportive of a quasi-scientific belief system. But more important, since funding is becoming increasingly centralized in governmental control and since educational experimentation almost always follows funding, systems language has a primary function: the political task of generating money from the federal government. Hence we can expect the "little science, big science" controversy that still rages in the physical sciences to rear its head in education as well.[29] Given the alternative pressure for decentralization, the question of funding and control *cannot* be ignored. Systems management procedures have a tendency toward centralization even without the issue of funding and rhetoric. In order to be most effective, as many variables as possible—interpersonal and economic, for instance—must be brought under and controlled by the system itself. Order and consensus become strikingly important; conflict and disorder are perceived as antithetical to the smooth functioning of the system. The fact that conflict and disorder are extraordinarily important to prevent the reification of institutional patterns of interaction is, thus, ignored.[30]

Now the *content* of systems procedures is empty. Systems thought is a formal set or methodology, if you will, that can be applied to educational problems. That is, its conceptual emptiness enables its application in a supposedly "neutral" manner to a range of problems requiring the precise formulation of goals, procedures, and feedback devices. Since systems methodology communicates this sense of neutrality, it is ideally suited to foster consensus around it.[31] This process of consensus formation, and the avoidance of conflict, enables the interests of the administrative managers of institutions to direct the questions that one asks about schooling.

This evocation of tacit meanings is crucial in examining systems management thought. Not only are supportive feelings generated, but political quiescence is also enhanced. For example, it may be the case that the common school and the ideological underpinnings that support it have *never* served to educate, say, racial minorities in the United States.[32] It

[29] Cf., Derek J. de Solla Price, *Little Science, Big Science* (New York: Columbia University Press, 1963) and Warren O. Hagstrom, *The Scientific Community* (New York: Basic Books, 1965).

[30] Michael W. Apple, "The Hidden Curriculum and the Nature of Conflict," *Interchange*, 1971, 2, 4, pp. 27-40.

[31] Gouldner, op. cit., p. 445.

[32] Colin Greer, "Immigrants, Negroes, and the Public Schools," *The Urban Review*, III (January 1969), pp. 9-12.

may also be the case that schools have served basically to apportion and distribute opportunities that are consistently unequal in terms of economic class. What the employment of sophisticated "scientific" rationales can do by evoking supportive sentiment, then, is to prevent a portion of the population from seeing that schools as they exist by and large simply cannot meet the needs of minority and other populations. The very institutional status of schools is caught up in a variety of other institutional forms—economic, for instance—that enhance the existing political and economic structures.

This quiescence is brought about in a two-pronged fashion and is aimed at two publics. First, systems management language is pronounced to critics of ongoing educational activity—again, let us use the example of minority groups—and is often coupled with the notion of "accountability," thereby giving them the feeling that something is in fact being done.[33] After all, it does sound concise and straightforward. But this is not the essential prong. After all, ghetto dwellers, for example, may not be as enamored with technical terminology and have little political power, nor do they influence economic resources and funding as much as the second set of groups to which this language is aimed. The primary audience includes the members of the general population and industry[34] whose sentiments often resonate strongly to technical expertise and industrial logic. Even when the members of minority groups may have determined over a period of time that school life has been made no less overtly repressive, as has been the case so often, the other more powerful public, due to the depth of the taken-for-granted acceptance of the benefits of technical rationality and technical expertise in solving human problems, will probably remain generally supportive.

To be accurate, one other public should be mentioned. These are the users of systems language themselves. Much of the history of curriculum discourse over the last 50 years has been indicative of a need on the part of curriculum workers to have their field become more like a science. I will not dwell upon the possibility of psychoanalyzing this need for prestige. However, a latent function of systems approaches is, no doubt, that it psychologically confirms curriculum workers' ties to a sought–after reference group—here the scientific community and, as we have and shall note, a misperceived scientific community at that.

---

[33] The use of the language of relevance by schoolmen to feed back to educational critics in the ghetto to bring about quiescence is extremely similar in this respect. Michael W. Apple, "Relevance—Slogans and Meanings," *The Educational Forum,* XXXV (May 1971), pp. 503-507.

[34] Murray Edelman, *Politics as Symbolic Action* (Chicago: Markham, 1971).

It should be made clear, then, that systems approaches are not essentially neutral, nor are they only performing a "scientific" function. By tending to cause its users and the other publics involved to ignore certain possible fundamental problems with schools as institutions, systems management also acts to generate and channel political sentiments supportive of the existing modes of access to knowledge and power.[35]

Besides performing these political functions associated with funding and "affective" support, the rhetorical function of systems terminology and of technical methodologies tends to uphold the dominance of existing institutions in another way. Dealing with a type of systems thought in sociology, Gouldner makes the provocative statement that aside from serving "to defocalize the ideological dimensions of decision making, diverting attention from differences in ultimate values and from the more remote consequences of the social policies to which its research is harnessed," supposedly value-free technical perspectives provide the solution to an elite group of manager's problems,[36] not the complex and fundamental valuative issues that we face in, for instance, education concerning the proper ways to educate children, or the issues of education versus training and freedom versus authority. Gouldner summarizes this quite well by saying:

> As . . . funding becomes increasingly available, the emphasis on rigorous methodologies assumes a special rhetorical function. It serves to provide a framework for resolving limited differences among the managers of organizations and institutions, who have little conflict over basic values or social mappings, by lending the sanction of science to limited policy choices concerning ways and means. At the same time, its cognitive emphasis serves to defocalize the conflict of values that remain involved in political differences, and to focus contention on questions of fact, implying that the value conflict may be resolved apart from politics and without political conflict. Positivism [and perspectives such as systems management stemming partly from it, I would add] thus continue to serve as ways of avoiding conflicts about mapping. Yet despite this seemingly neutral, nonpartisan character, [these perspectives'] social impact is not random or neutral in regard to competing social mappings; because of [their] emphasis on the problem of social order, because of the social origins, education and character of [their] own personnel, and because of the dependencies generated by [their] funding requirements, [they] persistently tend to support the status quo.[37]

---

[35] Compare here to the discussion of systems theory in sociology as being a tacit theory of conservative politics as well in Gouldner, op. cit.

[36] Ibid., p. 105.

[37] Ibid.

Gouldner's argument is rather interesting and is one we all should reflect upon. Is systems management "merely" a mode by which an institutional and managerial elite avoids conflict over *basic* values and educational visions? By making choices about limited options within the framework of existing modes of interaction, are questions about the basis of the structure itself precluded? How, for instance, would systems management procedures deal with the clash of two competing ideologies about schooling where goals cannot be easily defined? These questions require much closer scrutiny if educational institutions are to be responsive to their varied publics.

I have made the point throughout this paper that the consciousness of curriculum workers themselves as well as other educators can be seen as latently political and often somewhat conservative. That is, they use forms of thought that at least partially stem from and can tacitly act to maintain the existing social and economic substructure and distribution of power in an industrial society such as our own. Systems management procedures offer an intriguing example of this problem. I shall give one more example.

A significant part of the framework of systems management is concerned with and is based upon the precise formulation of goals, on a microsystem level usually with the specification of behavioral goals. For example, a student's behavior is preselected *before* he engages in educational activity and this behavior is used as the end-product of the system so that feedback can be gained. Ultimately this will feed upwards on a macrosystem level for the management of large systems. Let us examine this. The process/product style of reasoning employed here, one that is most evident in the call for behavioral objectives, is quite functional to a society that requires a large proportion of its workers to engage in often boring assembly-line labor or in personally unimportant white-collar work. By learning how to work for others' preordained goals using others' preselected behaviors, students also learn to function in an increasingly bureaucratized society in which the adult roles one is to play are already embedded in the social fabric. Each role has its own brand of thinking *already* built into it,[38] and students will feel comfortable playing these often relatively alienating roles only insofar as they have been taught that this is the proper mode of existing. Curriculists, by internalizing and using an orientation that lends itself to such preordination, cannot help but contribute to the maintenance of a political and economic order that creates and maintains these roles and the meaning already distributed within them.[39] This problem is intricately involved with the perspective on disorder that most educators share.

---

[38] Erving Goffman, *The Presentation of Self in Everyday Life* (New York: Doubleday Anchor, 1959).

[39] Berger and Luckmann, op. cit.

Systems, Science, and Consensus

The view on order and conflict mirrored in a good deal of the way systems approaches are employed in education is striking. It is indicative of a constitutive rule of activity that causes most of us to see order as positive and conflict as negative.[40] Order becomes a psychological necessity. This is rather important. As I mentioned before, systems approaches attempt to bring about a technical solution to political and value problems. There is nothing odd about this occurrence. Most advanced industrial societies seem to transform their ethical, political, and aesthetic questions, for instance, into engineering problems.[41] Profound conflicts between opposing ideological and moral positions are translated into puzzles to be solved by technical expertise. Now, when questioned about the tendency to eliminate conflict, or to redefine it, and search for consensus, proponents of systems management procedures in education could and do take the position that they are merely trying to be scientific about their problems. This is where a basic difficulty lies. The perspective they have of science is notably inaccurate in ways other than those to which we referred earlier in our discussion.

In the quote on precise instructional objectives at the beginning of this paper, we saw a perspective that legitimated intellectual consensus, one that asked for total agreement on the "paradigm" to be used in curriculum thought so that we could be more scientific. In fact, those who looked askance at the accepted paradigm were, in effect, labeled as deviants. Such universe maintaining verbal activity is not wrong in itself nor is it unusual.[42] To link scientific rationality with consensus, however, is to do a disservice to science and shows a profound misunderstanding of the history of the scientific disciplines.

The history of science and the growth of individual disciplines have *not* proceeded by consensus. In fact, most important progress in these fields has been occasioned by intense conflict, both intellectual and interpersonal, and by conceptual revolution.[43] It is primarily by such conflict that significant advancement is made, not primarily by the accumulation of factual data based on the solving of puzzles generated by a paradigm all must share. The very normative structure of scientific communities tends

---

[40] Apple, "The Hidden Curriculum and the Nature of Conflict," op. cit.

[41] See, for instance, the provocative but often overdrawn and analytically troublesome examination in Jacques Ellul, *The Technological Society* (New York: Vintage, 1964).

[42] Berger and Luckmann, op. cit., p. 105.

[43] Kuhn, op. cit. For a more in–depth discussion of the place of conflict in science, see Apple, "The Hidden Curriculum and the Nature of Conflict," op. cit.

toward skepticism and not necessarily toward intellectual consensus.[44] The call for consensus, thus, is not a call for science.

One thing that the quote does make clear, however, is the intense personal commitment that accepted modes of thought generate. This is probably true in any field. It does put somewhat of a damper on our traditional concept of neutrality, though. Accepted thought becomes a psychological and valuative commitment, a norm of behavior. Scientists are intensely and personally committed[45] and this is one of the primary sources of conflict within disciplines. Hence, to call for consensus is to call for a *lack* of commitment and is to ignore the crucial value of the uncertain and of conceptual conflict in a field's progress. The covert request for a lack of commitment is of considerable moment. Systems management terminology, as was mentioned, tends to impose technical solutions on moral dilemmas—what is the proper way to influence another human being, for instance. If moral commitments are less firm, the task of flattening reality is made that much easier.

The Search for Alternatives

There are ways of dealing with some of the possible difficulties associated with the use of systems management procedures in education. First, educators must engage in continuous and in-depth analysis of other forms of systems thought. The lenses of open systems and biological systems could provide excellent disclosure models for further examination. Second, they can immerse themselves in the issues and controversies *within* the systems field so that they are aware of the concrete theoretic and practical difficulties facing systems analysis as a field. In this way, educators may prevent a further recapitulation of their history of borrowing knowledge that is taken out of its self correcting context and, hence, is often surface or one-sided. While the use of systems approaches has an obvious immediate plausibility, we do not do justice to the intellectual complexity associated with systems thought itself or to the intricate nature of institutional relationships in education (which systems approaches can at least partially illuminate) if we base our analyses upon conceptions of systems that may be given only a weak warrant within the larger systems community. There are alternatives within systems discourse that educators have yet to explore in a rigorous fashion.

This rigorous exploration will not eliminate all of the difficulties, however, for there are a number of other questions one could raise concerning

---

[44] Norman W. Storer, *The Social System of Science* (New York: Holt, Rinehart and Winston, 1966), pp. 78-79.

[45] Polanyi, op. cit.

systems management procedures. Perhaps one of the more crucial ones centers on the very real possibility of increasing bureaucratization through the total rationalization of education. This is not to raise the spectre of a bureaucratic machine overrunning human concerns. Rather it asks us to be realistic, if not tragic. Anyone familiar with the growth of urban schools knows that the history of rationalizing and centralizing decision—making, no matter what the humane sentiments behind it, has nearly invariably led to institutional crystallization and reification.[46] The fact that we are not familiar with our own history concerning "reforms" of this nature merely documents the simplicity with which we approach our problems.

There are no easy alternatives to a management and control ideology. One could easily show the epistemological and psychological problems associated with behavioral objectives,[47] for instance; or one could document the fact that the Tyler Rationale in curriculum is little more than an administrative document that does not adequately deal with the concrete reality of schools. Yet this type of activity treats such behavioristic rationales as if they were logically founded and scientifically arguable. It may very well be that they are not. As I have tried to show, what they do seem to be are expressions of a dominant industrialized consciousness that seeks certainty above all else. That is, they are social and ideological configurations stemming from and mirroring a set of basic rules of thought that are part of the taken-for-granted reality of curriculum workers and other educators. The reality inclines us to search for relatively easy ways to eliminate the human dilemmas (even mysteries) of dealing with diversity and alternative conceptions of valued activity.

To ask, then, for *a* substitute or *one* alternative to systems management procedures is to confirm the assumption that utterly complex problems can be resolved easily within the accepted framework, and without the ambiguous and awe-ful necessity of engaging in the crucial task of challenging or at least illuminating the framework itself. The task is not to find the *one* acceptable alternative that will enable us "merely" to control our schools better. Rather, it is to begin to disclose the problems associated with our common sense views of schooling and to begin to open up and explore avenues that seem fruitful and may enable us to see the complexity rather than define it out of existence.

Systems metaphors as *models of understanding* may prove helpful here. But there are prior questions with which we need to grapple. We must

---

[46] Carl Kaestle, personal communication.

[47] Michael W. Apple, "Behaviorism and Conservatism," *Perspectives for Reform in Teacher Education*, Bruce R. Joyce and Marsha Weil, eds. (Englewood Cliffs, N.J.: Prentice Hall, 1972).

learn (perhaps relearn is more accurate[48]) how to engage in serious ethical and political debate. In this educators can be guided by the work in philosophical analysis dealing with modes of moral reasoning and valuative argumentation. Such investigations as Rawls' recent attempt at explicating warranted moral stands[49] takes on an increasing importance given the intense controversy surrounding schools today.

Alternative visions of institutional alignments are also critical to prevent the reification of the present into the future. The field lacks the disciplined aesthetic sense and imagination to envision possibilities of disparate educative environments. It is quite possible that the perceived need for operationally prespecified outcomes mitigates against the development of such imagination.[50]

Finally, a significant part of curriculum as a field must be devoted to the responsibility of becoming a critical science. Its primary function is to be emancipatory in that it critically reflects upon the field's dominant interest in keeping most if not all aspects of human behavior in educational institutions under technical control.[51] Such a responsibility is rooted in seeking out and illuminating the ideological and epistemological presuppositions of curriculum thought. It seeks to make curriculum workers more self-aware. Only when this dialectic of critical awareness is begun can curriculists truthfully state that they are concerned with education and not training. It is then that we may begin to explore in a rigorous fashion the complex problems of designing and valuing educational environments[52] in a variety of ways.

---

[48] Arendt's, op. cit., treatment of the forms of argumentation and political and personal action of the polis is helpful here.

[49] John Rawls, *A Theory of Justice* (Cambridge: Harvard University Press, 1971).

[50] See the interesting debate in *Interchange*, 1971, 2, no. 1, on alternatives to existing modes of schooling. Nearly the entire issue is devoted to the topic. On the necessity of imaginative vision in education, see William Walsh, *The Use of Imagination* (New York: Barnes and Noble, 1959).

[51] Habermas, op. cit., p. 45.

[52] Two papers by Huebner are quite important in this regard. See Dwayne Huebner, "Curriculum as the Accessibility of Knowledge," a paper presented at the Curriculum Theory Study Group, Minneapolis, March 2, 1970 and "The Tasks of the Curricular Theorist," a paper presented at the meeting of the Association for Supervision and Curriculum Development, Atlantic City, March, 1968.

10. The Ideology of Accountability in Schooling

Martin Levit

It is futile to seek significant conclusions about what is and what should be happening in education merely by looking, however closely, at what goes on in schools. That would be like trying to understand and control our many floods—let alone trying to rate the priority of that task relative to other pressing tasks—by looking only at swirling, overflowing water. We understand floods and other events by following out threads leading to causes, correlates, and consequences that are umbilical to, yet outside of, the events. We might try to consider in the same way the now loud calls for accountability in education—and we here consider this movement as a social, mainly an ideological, event. Since a conclusion here is that the generally defining characteristics of the present accountability movement should be rejected as unfit for human beings, we will not get into the details of issues that would arise had we decided to build on accountability foundations. Instead, we will sketch an alternative ideology.

The Argument for Accountability: A Summary View

A brief report of some common features of arguments for accountability in education today might go something like this:[1] Despite worrisome and

Source. This article was first published in abridged form in *Educational Studies*, Vol. 3, No. 3 (Fall 1972), pp. 133-40, and later in Robert L. Leight, ed., *Philosophers Speak on Accountability in Education* (Danville, Ill.: Interstate Printers and Publisher, Inc. 1973), pp. 37-50. It is reprinted here with permission of the author and the Interstate Printers and Publishers, Inc.

[1] Since 1969 the literature on accountability and related topics has grown considerably. A few convenient references are these: Leon Lessinger, *Every Kid a Winner: Account-*

rising educational expenditures, too many schools are failing to educate too many of our youth. School personnel must be held accountable for the fulfillment of educational tasks. This can be done, it is often said, partly by the introduction of a battery of intellectual technologies in management science that were developed in industrial and military organizations. These procedures include management-by-objectives, cost-effectiveness and cost-benefit analyses, and the allocation of funds and other resources in terms of the contributions of various inputs to the final product—in this case the pupils' educational achievement. Performance contracting, particularly with private business firms, has been used and is frequently urged as a necessary or supplemental feature of accountability procedures. Also frequently urged and used are the systematization and focalization of effort achieved by programming and modularizing educational experiences. Voucher plans are occasionally mentioned as an accountability procedure.

Whatever may be the degree of emphasis on management science and educational technologies, it is agreed that too much attention has been paid in the past to inputs—like buildings, salaries, and instructional materials—and too little attention has been paid to the output, the pupils' changed behavior. In order to measure the changes, usually by means of standardized tests, teachers must state precisely the pupil performance goals of instructional units. School personnel, instructional procedures, and other schooling inputs should be evaluated and, if necessary, changed in the light of the objective measurements. Many proponents of accountability believe that compensation and promotion of school personnel should be linked to results. Certainly, detailed accounts of a school's effectiveness should be rendered to the public and to educational authorities. The schools must be watched with greater care and heightened expectations.

Concerning educational objectives, mention may be made, infrequently, of the development of "wit," "creativity," and even "the whole person." But it is almost universally agreed among advocates of accountability—hereinafter usually termed accountabilists—that such objectives are pretty intangible, their development cannot adequately be measured now and, thus, they cannot serve as a basis for accountability. Too, it is felt that there may be little public consensus on educational objectives that go beyond the acquisition of basic skills in reading, writing and mathematics, knowledge of a few basic subjects, and the development of saleable occupational skills. A number of accountabilists point out that, in an economy where less than five percent of jobs fall in the unskilled category, many

ability in Education (New York: Simon and Schuster, 1970); Leon M. Lessinger and Ralph W. Tyler, eds., *Accountability in Education* (Worthington, Ohio: Charles A. Jones, 1971); *Phi Delta Kappan*, Vol. 52 (December 1970), whole issue; *Journal of Research and Development*, Vol. 5 (Fall 1971), whole issue.

young people cannot meet the basic literacy and skill requirements for most civilian jobs or for induction into the armed services. A major share of concern, then, is focused on the development of the basic skills, particularly for children of poor and minority group families. As one educator has remarked, the calls for accountability tend to come from the big cities and not from the Scarsdales of the nation.[2]

Schooling and Education

The accountability movement focuses on schools as the causal agencies of education that *should* be of central concern in improving education. It is the schools that "fail one youngster in four."[3] President Nixon's curious and frightening remark in this connection is this: "Although we do not seem to understand just what it is in one school or school system that produces a different outcome from another, one conclusion is inescapable: *We do not yet have equal educational opportunity in America.*"[4] But there is no need to document this basic fact. The phrase "accountability in education" generally means causal and ethical responsibility of the schools for education.

To be sure, it is often acknowledged that schools in ghettos will not produce "products" comparable to those produced by schools in middle-class communities, and it is often urged that a school's performance be compared with the performance of other schools in similar social conditions. But accountabilists are not primarily concerned about changing the relative conditions of people in ghettos and in wealthy communities. Indeed, like many of our past and present technocratic professionals, accountabilists usually take moral and institutional conditions for granted and work within these frameworks. So, for example, some accountabilists are at work developing new kinds of standardized tests that will facilitate the intercomparability of schools in similar socioeconomic situations.[5]

This focusing of attention and hope on schools is strange. We are aware that, using conventional criteria, it is largely the "good" children—and their families and backgrounds—that make schools good. We are aware of all the interrelations among social class, financial and psychological support of schooling, assignment of educational personnel, achievement scores,

---

[2] Henry M. Levin, "Is Accountability Just a Catchword?," *New York Times,* 6E (January 10, 1972).

[3] Leon Lessinger, *Every Kid a Winner,* op. cit., p. 3.

[4] Leon M. Lessinger and Ralph W. Tyler, eds., *Accountability in Education,* op. cit., p. 16. Emphasis is in the original.

[5] Ralph W. Tyler, "Testing for Accountability," *Nation's Schools,* 86 (December 1970), pp. 37-9. See also Robert E. Stake, "Testing Hazards in Performance Contracting," *Phi Delta Kappan,* 52 (June 1971), pp. 583-588.

and so on. We know that education—in the sense of enculturation or socialization that includes learning in schools—goes on within the interlaced activities and institutions of a society. Histories of schooling here and in other nations clearly indicate that major changes in schooling—reforms, regressions, and revolutions—have been tied to large-scale, pervasive social developments. We know that it is a social system, a socio-educational system, that educates. Yet, in the United States today, we tend to equate education or learning with schooling.

Moreover, the general conclusion that can be drawn from research reports that extend over two generations is that the typical fragmented change in schooling attempted in this or that experiment or reform leaves little if any enduring effect on the typically measured outcomes of schooling.[6] Turning to broader kinds of evidence, we note that the same null effect is found in the great majority of social action programs and experiments. Typically, these efforts are undertaken within some one institution or agency; they rely on some "promising" but restricted approach; and they are not accompanied by major and supportive changes in other institutions. Generally these efforts—directed at improving family conditions, reducing alcoholism, providing psychological or probationary services, and so on—show little or no positive effect in changing behavior.[7]

Turning to matters that bear more directly on the accountability movement, we find that the unusually broad Coleman study[8] indicated that commonly found differences among schools in resources, facilities, class size, and so on, have very little effect on educational achievement in the basic skills and subjects, be the children white or black, or from well-off or poor families. A major reason seems to be that a child's family background, his social class, and the backgrounds of the children he associates with are such powerful determinants of what he learns in school that schooling and intervention programs—so far as we have tried them—are, by comparison, practically powerless. One major finding is significant by way of contrast with most plans for accountability, which usually do not mention the effects on schooling achievement of restructuring social and racial relations. Coleman's study clearly indicated that we could increase significantly the schooling achievement of black children and of white

---

[6] See, for example, John Goodlad et al., "The Future of Learning: Into the Twenty-first Century," in *Report to the President, White House Conference on Children* (Washington, D.C.: U.S. Government Printing Office, 1970), pp. 74-85. See also Martin Levit, "Scientific Method, Social Systems, and Educational Research," *Studies in Philosophy and Education*, Vol. 6 (Spring 1968), pp. 145-167.

[7] Carol H. Weiss, "The Politicalization of Evaluation Research," *Journal of Social Issues*, Vol. 16 (Autumn 1970), pp. 57-68.

[8] James S. Coleman et al., *Equality of Educational Opportunity* (Washington, D.C.: Department of Health, Education and Welfare, Office of Education, 1969).

children from low-income families by sending them to schools where the majority of pupils were white middle-class children—though integration alone is never a sufficient cause of any schooling outcome. Moreover, the study corroborated other findings that indicate that certain racial mixtures under appropriate school-community conditions can help significantly in reducing racial prejudice among youth.

Actually, Coleman's findings should not have been a surprise, as they were to some public figures and educators. His study had some weaknesses, but his results were generally consistent with most of the findings of numerous smaller studies of the relations of social class to educational achievement in various subjects and at various levels, of the influence of class size and other instructional variables on achievement and, more generally, of the influence of social relations on dispositions and abilities. These findings bear not only on educational achievement in the narrow sense used by most accountabilists but also on conjoined cognitive, social, and moral learnings. For example, studies have found repeatedly that children from many minority groups and poor families tend to see themselves as more externally controlled, less capable of determining what will happen to themselves, than do white middle-class children. They tend to believe that luck or the actions of other people or some uncontrollable factors are more important in determining achievement, including educational achievement, than persistent effort or ability. These children often believe that if they try to "get ahead," something will happen to stop them. These tendencies represent appraisals or values, truth-claims about the world, assumptions that guide choice and behavior. These social-personal and cognitive-emotive matters that matter very much, even in just their influence on the limited measures of achievement favored by accountabilists, generally fall outside their range of concern.

Positive evidence in favor of accountabilists' proposals seems to be lacking. As a typical example, we may take the argument of Dr. Leon Lessinger, possibly the foremost advocate of accountability. His most detailed attempt at justifying accountability procedures is an extended fallacy of irrelevant conclusion. He states repeatedly that our schools are not doing their jobs well and then concludes from this that we should introduce accountability procedures that, he promises without evidence, will transform our schools within a decade.[9] This is like arguing that the effectiveness of drug B is assured by the facts that drug A is not working very well and we do need relief from pain. Drug B, of course, may be no better or even worse than drug A. His writings are distinguished by the use of emotive language replete with snarl and purr words, conclusion-loaded terms, and bandwagon and other appeals. He speaks, for example, of "this fact-

---

[9] Lessinger, *Every Kid a Winner*, op. cit., pp. 3-11, 24-37.

generating nation-wide demand for accountability" that promises an over-haul of the schools' "cottage-industry form of organization," and of a "zero reject system" that would "guarantee quality in skill acquisition."[10]

Moreover, early reports on the effects of performance contracting gen-erally have indicated negative or doubtful results. In 1970-71, the Office of Economic Opportunity authorized over seven million dollars for per-formance contracts, with six different educational firms, in 18 school dis-tricts. Although the full report is not available now, the OEO has an-nounced that the results were "a failure."[11]

Many educators believe that the call for accountability has been stimu-lated in some measure by the general failure of compensatory programs to improve the impact of schooling on "disadvantaged" children. One might have hoped that the results of the compensatory education efforts,[12] along with many other cues, would have suggested that education is some-thing much bigger than schooling and that the schools, under present conditions, will find it very difficult to make up for deficiencies in the socio-educational system.

The Ideology of Accountability

It may well be that, given more effort and experience, some significant advances could be made in schools using the means and ends suggested by accountabilists. But such "advances" had far better be left umade— and concerns about expenditures of money or effort are no part of the basic objection to the accountabilists' program. That program seems to bespeak and subserve, however unwittingly, an illiberal ideology.

An ideology is a system of beliefs about man and society that con-stitutes a sociopolitical program. Like other people, educators do have ideologies. To guide their work, educators ought to have clearly defined ideologies relating education to sociopolitical systems. In schools, ideolo-

---

[10] Leon M. Lessinger, "Accountability for Results: A Basic Challenge for America's Schools," in Lessinger and Tyler, eds., *Accountability in Education*, op. cit., pp. 7-9.

[11] *Time*, Vol. 99 (February 14, 1972), p. 42. A preliminary report is contained in OEO Pamphlet 3400-5, published February 1, 1972 by the Office of Planning, Research and Evaluation of the Office of Economic Opportunity. Entitled "An Experiment in Performance Contracting: Summary of Preliminary Results," the report concludes (p. 31) as follows. "The results of the experiment clearly indicate that the firms oper-ating under performance contracts did not perform significantly better than the more traditional school systems. Indeed, both control and experimental students did equally poorly in terms of achievement gains, and this result was remarkably consistent across sites and among children with different degrees of initial capability."

[12] Victor G. Cicirelli et al., *The Impact of Head Start: An Evaluation of the Effects of Head Start on Children's Cognitive and Affective Development* (Westinghouse Learning Corporation and Ohio University, 1969).

gies become suspect when the ideology of a particular teacher—such as the one favored in this paper—works its ways silently or is transmitted without maximum possible opportunity for critical evaluation and comparison. Ideologies should become suspect when they are not based on sound reason and credible beliefs, when they fail to expand the ability of human beings throughout the world to understand themselves and other people, and when they seem to constrict the possibilities of rationally and cooperatively increasing the range of individual and social choices. By and large, as the accountability program speaks up to these criteria, it promises to worsen some of the worst features of schooling and to reduce the bits of enlightenment and liberalization that may be found now in schooling. With its mischievous bustle, it promises to divert attention from the crucial educational task of examining the pressing need for a rational reconstruction of the socio-educational system of institutions, values, and beliefs within which schools operate.

Even within the framework of the schools, undue emphasis is usually placed on dubious ends and means—on the precise specification of objectives in the basic skills and subjects, on packaging and presenting chained or programmed materials in modules of varying length or complexity, on restricting attention to compartmentalized materials or exercises, on the use of extraneous rewards—like radios, games, or free time,[13] and on measuring "educational achievement" by using standardized tests in the basic skills or subjects.

This seems to be an attempt to refine and extend the already too widespread programs of unreflective habit formation. There are many reasons to believe that social and schooling programs that consistently reward success, which is defined in terms of unequivocal responses to items or events within unquestioned contexts, do not develop habits of inquiry. What will be the effect of the accountabilists' thrust on the ability of students to have second thoughts about things? What do these programs do to the drive to go on learning—unlearning and relearning—when such extrinsic rewards are absent? Do these measures promote a self-centered, instrumental conception of learning—the view that "learning is O.K. if it pays off for me?" Do the measures increase our inability to escape bondage to the "programs," that is, the institutionalized reward systems, of our society?

From all present indications, it seems clear that we may never know the answers to such questions if we rely on accountabilists to respond after inquiry. Accountabilists often identify themselves with the scientific enterprise. But unlike a scientific program, the accountability program is not

---

[13] Roger Farr, J. J. Tuinman, and B. E. Blanton, "How to Make a Pile in Performance Contracting," *Phi Delta Kappan*, Vol. 53 (February 1972), pp. 367-369.

concerned with controlling and modifying its procedures and principles by searching for diverse, and in principle, "all" consequences of the interactions or treatments that are proposed. The scientific style uses principles and procedures if and because they promote the ability to inquire, to refine, and expand knowledge. This is not a simple ability. It requires wide and integrated knowledge, and it requires understanding of logic and scientific method. Internally, it requires a host of values implicated in continuing inquiry, and it needs a large array of supportive social conditions. It would be self-destructive for scientific programs to develop efficient procedures for closing minds, though this might well be done by technocrats guided by this aim rather than by scientific criteria.

Accountabilists are not concerned about the many ways in which their program may promote the evaluation—by the public and by all participants in the program, including pupils—of acts and facts in terms of what is accepted and rewarded rather than in terms of scientific criteria of validation. Accountabilists keep their eyes fixed on only a limited set of cues and they use efficiency—the ability to predict certain things or to get certain things done—as *the* criterion of success. If scientists placed such trust in predictability or efficiency in limited domains, we might still have the geocentric theory of the universe, since it could be used to predict the course of the planets just about as well as could the heliocentric theory. Accountability is not a scientific movement. It is a technocratic, and efficiency oriented, one.

Our schools have given occupational skills and knowledge of the basic subjects to many people. Presumably, just about all of the large majority of our middle class and upper-class adults who believed, just a few years ago, that our war in Vietnam was a justifiable war and who, in most cases, changed their minds largely because they felt it was costing *us* too much in the way of lives, resources, and prestige, are people who can read and write, people who took and passed courses in American History, Civics, and General Science. Their problem—and our problem—was not that they did not get through public school successfully. They were otherwise disadvantaged. They did not reason in terms of logic, evidence, and justifiable values. They seemed to accept the official, cultural "definition of the situation." Their schooling certainly did not free them. Schooling probably aided in binding many of them, by pressures and experiences they were not helped to examine, to ways and beliefs they were not helped to evaluate critically.

The most indecently effective aspect of schooling has been the socialization involved in just going through the institution. Schools are more effective in enculturating or domesticating young people than in enlightening them. Young people who have gotten through the public schools have internalized some roles and rules or they have learned to hide their resentments. Unless pressed too much by the increasingly ceremonial and dysfunctional nature of schooling, as it relates to personal and social problems and experiences, they learn to cope. They learn, more or less, the arts of getting satisfactions from, or of foraging and fuming within, existing institutions.

The accountability thrust has not been developed to remedy these defects. Accountability programs are geared to the production of functionaries within a technological society rather than to the development of independent people who are social critics and constructors. The prospect is intensified development of modularized man, increasingly conditioned to being conditioned and to having "the changing times and new social needs" replace bits and pieces of himself with other skills and beliefs and values, but lacking in the virtues necessary to help control his society and his commitments. The approach is likely to intensify some of the worst features of American life—competition for personal gain; domination of efficiency over moral and rational values; confusion of fad and technology with science. Possibly the most worrisome aspect of the movement is that its proponents are sincere and well-intentioned people. They are concerned about unemployment, "disadvantaged" children, and a "sound basic education" for all children. But they have little or no realization that the accountability program probably represents an illiberal ideology of a society that in many ways is a disadvantaged society.

Undoubtedly, most accountabilists will believe that the objections presented here display little sense of reality, of what is practical and possible. An accountabilist might argue, for example, that children from poor and minority group families often will have great difficulties in learning the basic skills, and that they must first learn to read and learn some "content" before they can begin to reason, evaluate, and integrate one idea with another idea.

There are many possible responses to such arguments. Some directly and indirectly relevant data and reasons might be mentioned for believing that critical thinking skills can be taught to very young children from varied backgrounds. Cases might be cited of teachers, here and there, who analyzed with first or second graders in various urban schools the "games people play," some of our phony "be-sincere-even-if-you-don't-mean-it" kinds of behavior, and whether art could refer not only to throw-away copyism or expressionism but also to the styles and qualities of their lives and social experiences—and did such things while teaching basic skills, and developing interests in learning and in relating personal and social aspects of life. Now all of this is true, and it is good and it is beautiful. But it is just as irrelevant to the main point as are the arguments and counterarguments of the accountabilist.

The main point is that the aims here claimed to be the valuable ones cannot be widely or adequately realized under the present conditions of schooling and society. It would take something like a peaceful but pretty thorough revolution in both society and the schools to attract and hold teachers who have the ability and freedom to help children critically examine the intellectual and moral foundations of alternative social structures and personal choices. At present, our society does not develop support, or tolerate very many teachers like that. Nor can our society now generate the host of other reforms needed in schools. Though there are bright spots, by and large our present social institutions and values miseducate too much for us to want better schools than we have. For this, society, including the schools, should be held accountable.

Toward an Accountable Socio-Educational System

We have tinkered long enough with the more manifest and generally weaker causes of education. The strengthening of the school—or something like the school—as a liberalizing institution depends greatly on the reconstruction of the culture, the social institutions and values, within which all education, including schooling, takes place. We may be able to move fairly rapidly toward a major turning point in human history if we realize the powerful and shaping pressures of largely unconscious enculturation on the somewhat more conscious schooling process and then exert a more conscious control of our socio-educational system. This would be a great advance in what might be called Social Freudianism.

'The basic grounds for hope of improvement in our schooling lie in many of the same pervasive social conditions that afford great possibilities not only of deterioration in the quality of life and schooling but also of world-shaking catastrophes. The quickened parade of social orders and powers over time and space, and the mutability of our own society, have bred fears and anxieties, international and domestic conflicts, apathy in the face of complexity, and other dread ailments. But they also have helped generate an increasing awareness of the "metaphysical pathos"[14] that lies in attributing absolute reality or compelling necessity to the needs of established institutions, to the determination of importance and possibility by the demands for improving national power, however used, and national affluence, however distributed and used.

At the same time that many give way—in very many forms—to the claims of what is personal and immediate, there is increasing awareness

---

[14] Alvin Gouldner, "Metaphysical Pathos and the Theory of Bureaucracy," *American Political Science Review*, Vol. 49 (June 1955), pp. 496-507. A significant work by Professor Gouldner that bears directly on some of the basic ideas in this paper is *The Coming Crisis of Western Sociology: The Social Origins of Social Theory* (New York: Basic Books, 1970).

that perception and choice, modes of thought and of passion, emerge from the intersections of complex bio-social contexts that include, but far transcend, the individual. To turn away from the study of man in society and nature over time and space is to turn away from possibilities of increasing freedom and control of self and society. The ability to produce knowledge is now and increasingly will be the major source of power. Today there is a growing recognition of the fact that the uses of science and reason in the interests of national power and economic power very often conflict with their uses in the interests of freeing and enlightening man.

More and more, we are a society of culturally marginal people caught between old and new roles, perspectives, and loyalties. Lack of commitment and other ills may arise in this connection, but so may an openness of mind and an increased capacity to reflect on different styles of life.

More generally, our society is now characterized by rather minimal social consensus and cohesion, by an increasing number and variety of subcultural groups that attack or desert core institutions, and by the absence of any single dominant reactionary group or revolutionary group. Of course, this crisis in legitimacy is but another name for our time of troubles. We know the many faces of misery, chaos, and evil of this time. But we know, too, that many people now see complexity and problems where formerly all was clear. We know that in varied ways many people are questioning and seeking to transform basic institutions and values. Moreover, structural transformations are occurring—even in such nodal principles as compensation in terms of production rather than in terms of need.

There is no assured future for these currents or for the many, and quite possibly stronger, contrary currents. But these are social forces—many people in government, business, labor, education, and other professions, the many publics—that may support and guide the development of socio-educational conditions that are favorable to the program recommended here. Essentially, the recommendation is that, while performing other necessary tasks, the schooling parts of education should increasingly adopt as their architectonic aim of basic and liberal education the development of the intellectual, social, and moral qualities required for cooperative, critical, and comprehensive and comparative evaluation of socio-educational systems, of the life we lead and the lives we might lead. In this process, the specific conclusions of any particular teacher should be but material for this program, as should the program itself and all of its assumptions.

Something of the immensity of the task and of possible general directions of effort must at least be suggested.

In order to give new orientations to schools (or alternative agencies) and to increase their educational influence, we will need massive and integrated reconstruction of the institution of schooling. Here the term "institution" is to be understood in the sociological sense that refers to an organized pattern of relations among people involving values and purposes, technologies and resources or materials, role-systems and communication networks, decision-making procedures and allocations of power, characteristic evaluative criteria and modes of thought, and relations with other institutions. What are known as techniques, tests and measurements, classroom organization, and so on are vitally important—as this analysis of accountability has tried to show—but they will have to be selected, changed, and organized in terms of other and broader contexts, understandings, and purposes than are now commonly used in schools.

Clearly, the social position of teachers and the selection, general and professional education, and work of teachers will have to be changed, radically. Contrary to the views of a number of accountabilists,[15] something like college-level schooling would be seen as an integral part of the general education of almost all youth, and not as primarily occupational training for some youth. It is almost universally agreed that preschool years are the most influential years of our lives. Coordinated child-care, educational, family, housing, and community resources and services will have to be developed and extended in at least this connection. We need varied socio educational reform experiments[16] that embrace as yet untried ranges, intensities, and integrated sets of significant variables in schools, prospectively reasonable alternatives to schools, relations among formal and informal modes of education, and community or social settings.

Professional educational organizations are now divided largely according to specializations within the present structure of schooling. In most organizations, attention is focused largely on problems of efficiency and of objectives within the framework of largely unquestioned values and social institutions. We need a professional organization, perhaps something like the defunct Progressive Education Association, that unites and strengthens the minds and hearts of all educators and laymen who are concerned about socio-educational reforms. We need a strong organization that, speaking regularly to and with the public, could raise schooling issues from the level of technique-talk or discussion about fragmented problems to the level of socio-educational policy debates—a level that pulls schooling into discussions of national priorities and social institutions, discussions of what we want to be, do, and know.

A final comment. As noted earlier, many people would label this an unrealistic program, one that offers no guidance in solving the pressing,

---

[15] See, for example, Lessinger and Tyler, eds., *Accountability in Education*, op. cit., p. 43.

[16] Lee J. Cronbach and Patrick Suppes, eds., *Research for Tomorrow's Schools* (New York: Macmillan, 1969)', pp. 141-148.

daily problems of schooling. But this view from the side of "hard-headed realism" may be precisely the niche-filling, efficiency-oriented disposition that has been cultivated in the long history of our technological society. The basic moral and rational question is whether the institutions developed by Western man as he spread out over the face of the earth after the Medieval Period represent and maximize reason, freedom, and justice.

Moreover, these institutions and policies—nationalism and the state as the commander of war; private enterprise and the managed economy devoted primarily to production and profit, and not to improving the quality of lives; the social class system and the dominance of whites, males, older and conforming or socially aggressive people; the exploitation of science and of natural resources; and an emaciated participatory democracy and the use of people by institutions and customs they generally are not educated to evaluate—these and other structural features of our lives are increasingly maladaptive and malignant. They pollute mind and environment. In psychological, domestic and international arenas, they heighten probabilities of conflicts and explosions that rock or destroy an increasing number of lives. For those who value peace, security, and happiness—even if just for themselves—the program sketched here is a realistic one.

11. *The Dominion of Economic Accountability*

Ernest R. House

While recognizing that accountability may be a passing fad, and that some manifestations are as ephemeral as this paper, I believe that the idea is going to be around for a while. If for no other reason, it is a way of lassoing the wild stallion of educational spending. Groups competing for funds at the federal, state, and local levels insure that educational spending will not continue to climb as rapidly as it has in the past. So whatever else accountability may be, it is a way of holding down spending. And although some good may come from it, I am disturbed at the form it is taking.

It has been said in support of accountability that it will result in favorable changes in professional performance "and these will be reflected in higher academic achievement, improvement in pupil attitudes, and generally better educational results."[1] I would contend that accountability will not automatically do good things, that we are already accountable for many things that we do, that being accountable, in fact, makes our lives miserable in certain ways, and often actually prohibits favorable changes in professional performance and better educational results. For example, college professors are quite accountable for publishing articles, yet one would be hard pressed to show how this arrangement helps, say, the public schools. Similarly public school teachers are accountable for keeping their class-

Source. Reprinted from *The Educational Forum*, Vol. 37, No. 1 (November 1972), pp. 13-24, with the permission of the author and Kappa Delta Pi, An Honor Society in Education.

[1] Stephen M. Barro, "An Approach to Developing Accountability Measures for the Public Schools," *Phi Delta Kappan*, **52**, 4 (1970).

rooms quiet, and I have heard it said that this is an impediment to good teaching.

So when one hears talk about accountability as if it did not now exist and about all the good things that are going to happen when we get it, one must regard this argument as too simplistic and look more squarely at what is being proposed. It is safe to assume that somebody wants something he is not now getting.

Economic Accountability

Not long into any discussion on accountability, someone always raises the question "Who is accountable to whom?" Almost invariably the response is that one is accountable to his superior. In fact, most people apparently perceive the society as being a vast hierarchy in which each person is accountable to his boss and his boss is accountable to someone else and so on. In this conception the school district, the society, the world is perceived as being organized like a vast bureaucracy, a gigantic corporation. Accountability is upward. Each person is accountable to the institution.

Nowhere is this better illustrated than in a recent issue of the *Phi Delta Kappan* (December 1970) devoted to the theme of accountability. Explicitly or implicitly several articles in the magazine harbor this view, but the apotheosis of it is the lead article written by a Rand Corporation economist. He proposes that pupil performance measures be given to all the students in a school district. Then, through a series of multiple regression equations, each teacher, each principal, and the superintendent be held accountable for that bit of pupil performance that the analysis attributes to him. Mrs. Smith, for example, is responsible for three percent of verbal reasoning while Mr. Jones only managed to get in one percent. Presumably Mrs. Smith and Mr. Jones will be differentially rewarded for those contributions. Good girl, Mrs. Smith. Bad boy, Mr. Jones.

The technical and political problems that this approach would encounter are insurmountable. Technically the conditions necessary for employing the statistical analysis cannot be met: none of the current measures are adequate indices of the relevant variables; the variables cannot be made independent of one another; and there is no way of specifying all the critical variables that should be included. The political problems are even more formidable. If the teacher organizations are anything like the rascals I know them to be, they would never allow such a thing.

But I must confess I am intrigued by the prospects of Mr. Jones sabotaging Mrs. Smith's lesson plans so he can pick up a few points on her. Or the kids in eleventh grade algebra organizing to throw the math test and send the despised Mr. Harms into bankruptcy. My mind slips back to those exciting days of comparative anatomy practical exams when the desperately competitive premeds would pull the numbered pins from one part of the cat's brain and stick it into another in order to fool their rivals.

Although this particular scheme is not going to be widely employed, this concept of accountability is so widely accepted that I would not be surprised to read in an education newsletter that the superintendent in Lockjaw, California, or Bone Gap, Illinois, having secured a batch of army surplus tests and a slide rule for the business manager to work the regression equations on, has decided to institute the system.

The point I'm trying to make is that discussions of accountability always lead us down this dismal road. In fact, we are so far down the road that it is impossible for many people even to imagine another type of accountability. For the dominant theme today is economic efficiency and its purpose is control—control over pupil behavior, control over staff behavior, control over schooling.

At the risk of oversimplification let me outline this mode of economic accountability. It is an economist's view of the world. Basically it assumes that the purpose of education is to supply manpower to other institutions of the society, particularly the economic ones. The skills needed to run the societal machinery can be formulated in specific terms, so educational goals are mandated by technological demands. The goals being specific and set, the job of educators is to maximize these goals, (usually forms of student achievement) with the greatest efficiency possible. Ultimately, then, the goals of education become economic, and the attendant accountability system is economic.

Economic analysis always has to do with maximization of *known* objectives.[2] It provides a descriptive theory of how maximization will happen or a prescriptive analysis of how to get it to happen. Thus we get analytic tools like systems analysis, cost/benefit analysis, PPBS, and performance contracting. Perhaps the technique *par excellence* is regression analysis against a production function, in which the most efficient combination of inputs is related to output.

There are serious problems in applying economic analysis to education in a pluralistic society. Where objectives or outcomes are not known, economic theory offers no way of determining them. And where there are competing viewpoints of what education should be doing, the maximizing solution does not even apply. In a pluralistic society like ours, there are irreconcilable differences as to what the outputs of education should be. At best one can compile a great list of possible outputs and try to relate inputs to them, thus assembling a collage. But this solution does not have

---

[2] John E. Brandl, "Public Service Outputs of Higher Education: An Exploratory Essay," in *The Outputs of Higher Education: Their Identification, Measurement, and Evaluation* (Boulder: Western Interstate Commission for Higher Education, 1970).

much practical appeal to administrators who want to make decisions. For example, it would not tell them what would happen if an attempt were made to increase a particular output.

The alternative is to reconcile these differences into a few set goals, which is what I believe the demands for economic accountability are attempting to do. The ultimate form of accountability then is to tighten the system to the point that each person is held personally accountable for his contribution to those few goals—just as the Rand economist suggested. In this scheme students are shaped to prespecified ends, educators are efficient at producing those ends, and education is more closely wired to the economic institutions of the society. The whole social system is more efficient, but the cost is terribly high: it is our cultural pluralism and our humanity. For this mode of accountability reduces to simply this: the individual is accountable to the institutions, but the institutions are not accountable to the individual.

Dominance of Managerial Education

Inextricably bound to economic accountability is what Thomas Green[3] calls "managerial" education. The same principle of economic efficiency shapes both the accountability system and the nature of education. Managerial education dominates when the schools are assessed by the utility of their "product" to the dominant institutions of the society. In our society this means that the schools are held accountable for effectively and efficiently meeting the demands for educated manpower. To the extent that the economic institutions maintain their voracious appetite for technical skills and to the extent that school credentials become the primary means of placing people in the structure, managerial education will predominate.

Contrast this with "humanistic" education in which schools are assessed in terms of what they do for people—independently of their contribution to other institutions. The humanistic credo, often expressed as the impossible goal of "developing each individual to his fullest," is the official ideology of most educators. It seeks not to shape the individual to a predetermined end, to some criterion of external utility, but to cultivate independence and individualism.

Yet, according to Green, in spite of this credo, managerial concerns now shape the schools and will increase their dominance substantially over the next two decades. One reason is that each lower educational level must at a minimum prepare its students for the next higher level, and at the

---

[3] Thomas F. Green, "Schools and Communities: A Look Forward," *Community and the Schools* (Cambridge, Mass.: Harvard Educational Review Reprint No. 3, 1969).

top of the pyramid are the graduate and professional schools, which feed into the economic institutions.

Down this road a few decades, Green foresees a very high level of managerial education for an elite and a lower level for the majority of people. To a certain extent this has already happened. As we investigated gifted programs across Illinois we found gifted children being educated toward some kind of vocational marketability. In shaping the child toward these distant and prespecified goals the classes tended to be dull and repressive, often requiring that both teachers and parents exert great pressures on the child in order to get him to perform. The rationale underlying these classes was usually "This may be painful now but it will help the child when he wants to get ahead."

Here are some excepts from one of our case studies. First, here are excerpts from an interview with the teacher Mr. Harms.

Q: What would you say your major goal is for this particular class?

Mr. Harms: I'd say the major goal is to prepare them for advanced math. Most of the students will probably go ahead and take college work in math as either a science, math, or engineering major.

Q. What do the students do that is especially appropriate for the gifted?

Mr. Harms: It's primarily a matter of acceleration and an enrichment of mathematics. Projects are good but I feel that in math there really is no substitute for hard work; there just isn't any royal road to mathematics. I'm afraid I probably assign more problems than some teachers do, but even the good students need practice.

Q· How would you describe a successful student in this class?

Mr. Harms: A successful student would be one that studies regularly every day, pays attention in class, does well in his tests, and does his homework pretty regularly. I have some students that ask questions and others that don't. I believe that I like to have them ask questions but some students have gotten to the place where they get it pretty much on their own and they don't have to ask questions. Others don't ask questions because they're . . . well, they don't.

Q: What does it take to get an 'A'?

Mr. Harms: Well, my feeling is you have to be pretty good to get an 'A'. You have to be an outstanding student, have to almost have an A on every test. It depends somewhat on how many tests we have during the quarter but unfortunately with an A, you don't have a grade above the A to average with one below to bring it up, and so it's a little tough.

The student enthusiasm is extremely low, and, what is rare for a gifted group, there is no humor in the class. Here is a brief excerpt from an interview with Donna, the best student in the class:

Q: What kind of things do you do in this class?

Donna: Mr. Harms will ask us if we have any questions over the problems we did, and if we do, he'll discuss them and write them on the board. He'll also give us at least one proof a day. And he kind of yells at us a little because we don't like them. But he keeps saying that we should like them, and we should like them because that's all we're going to do in college.

Q: What kinds of things are you supposed to learn in this class?

Donna: I think we're supposed to learn the generalities with proofs and just learn the technique of proving. He doesn't give us too much busy work, like some teachers do. He is concerned about us knowing proofs because he keeps saying we have to know this for college.
We have to learn how to do the proofs; we are going to have to realize that we can't skip over them. Some of us work the problems and don't have enough time to get to all of them so we'll do the rest of the problems and skip the proofs. And say we didn't get them because we probably wouldn't get them anyway.

Q: Do you get graded in this class?

Donna: Yes, and I need to be graded so that I have some drive to get me going. It makes me feel real good when I can bring home an A and my Dad is real proud of me.

Mr. Harm's class is the stereotypical math class that students through the years have come to dislike intensely. Of more than 100 classes examined, this one is lowest on student enthusiasm. The unremitting aim of the teacher is to ingrain the subject matter into the heads of his students so that they can "get ahead" vocationally. The future orientation of the teacher and the degree to which he impresses it on the students is a significant feature of the class. The rationale for the future utility of the subject attempts to mitigate current unpleasantness.

To the teacher's credit he does manage to teach for the higher thought process of "analysis." This emphasis occurs in all math classes we have studied. In all probability, the students will perform well on the Advanced Placement tests he keeps reminding them about. Since this is the main goal, the class may be a success in that regard. The cost is high, however. The strict humorless classroom atmosphere and total domination of the class by the teacher results in a particularly uninspiring class. There is no joking, no questioning—only the grimmest pursuit of subject matter. When he wishes to "enrich" the class he does so by showing the students other ways of solving quotations. His pathetic attempts at "making the students independent" consist of occasionally not giving them any help on their homework.

When Mr. Harms tries to start a discussion in class, he asks recall questions that leave nothing to discuss and that no one cares to answer. In addition, he is a very hard grader. The extreme emphasis on grades is strong in the entire school—quite typical of all the middle-class suburbs studied—and the teacher manifests these pressures. The severe competitive environment is very real to the students. There is one thing that the students like about his class—he does not collect and check their homework. However, unknown to them, he does check on them covertly.

Even the best student stresses the dullness of the class and claims that the only thing that keeps her going is pressure from her father to make good grades. At best the other students are resigned. As a helpful crutch, Mr. Harms relies on his ultimate rationale—that learning math is unenjoyable ("There is no royal road") but one must do it in order to get ahead in college and eventually gain a competitive advantage in the job market. The philosophy of the community is embodied in the classroom of the teacher—learning is not intrinsically worthwhile but is unpleasantly necessary to "success." The honors classes reveal a considerable trace of elitism. Parents and students see the classes as quite a status symbol.

In summary, strong community pressure for competition and success, a subject difficult to teach enjoyably, and a teacher who has little flexibility, humor, or ability to enliven the class combine for an unhappy learning experience and a negative feeling toward the subject. As one of Mr. Harm's students says, "Math is a lot more 'cut and dried' than most subjects. I'm sorry to say it seems mostly dried, and I don't think anything can help."[4]

Atkin[5] has called attention to the paradigm of this type of education in which educational services are perceived as "products" to be mass pro-

---

[4] Joe Milan Steele, Ernest R. House, Stephen Lapan, and Thomas Kerins, *Instructional Climate in Illinois Gifted Classes* (Urbana, Ill.: Center for Instructional Research and Curriculum Evaluation, University of Illinois, August, 1970). 55 pp.

[5] J. Myron Atkin, "Curriculum Design: The Central Development Group and the Local Teacher," prepared for *Institute für die Pädagogik der Naturwissenschaften,* Invitational Symposium (Kiel, West Germany, October 14, 1970).

duced. This production-line model calls for elaborate prespecification and quality control. Emphasis is placed on that which is replicable, easily quantifiable, readily discernible, and unambiguous. Education becomes engineering and finally industrial production. Evaluation becomes greatly simplified: one need only compare the prespecification to the final product.

PPBS—An Accountant's Dream

Thus we get simple business management tools applied to education—like the PPB system California is implementing soon. The system promises no less than providing "information necessary (1) for planning educational programs that will meet the needs of the community; and (2) for choosing among the alternative ways in which a school district can allocate resources to achieve its goals and objectives."[6] According to the State's lucid and well-written manual here is how the system works.

The school arrives at a set of *goals* that are the cornerstone of the system. From the goals is derived a set of objectives that must be measurable. Based on these objectives the *program* is developed, which is a group of activities to accomplish the objectives including attendant resources and schedules. This completes the program development. Then the *program description package* is drawn up that includes the course content, objectives, and method of evaluation. Then the *program structure* is set up which is a hierarchial arrangement of programs. (The system is very big on hierarchies; about 15 of the 18 charts in the book are some kind of hierarchy.)

Finally the *program code* is built, which means each program is assigned a number; the *program budget* is completed; and the *multiyear financial plan*, a five-year cost projection, is constructed. All neatly rational and internally consistent—if you believe in an abstract "economic man." Actually, any relation between the PPB *system* and reality will be purely coincidental.

First the problem of defining goals in a pluralistic society has already been noted. The PPBS manual spends no time on how to arrive at goals, and with good reason. Defining goals is a political, not an economic process. Empirical studies of business organizations have shown that their goals are changing, multiple, inconsistent—and the organizations survive quite nicely.[7] Upon close inspection, even the profit goal in business organizations turns out to be quite elusive.

---

[6] California State Department of Education, *Conceptual Design for a Planning, Programming, Budgeting System for California School Districts* (1969).

[7] James G. March, "Organizational Factors in Supervision," in *The Supervisor: Agent for Change in Teaching* (Washington, D.C.: NEA, Association for Supervision and Curriculum Development, 1966).

Assuming that the goal problem is overcome, one must then develop a set of objectives that are measurable—the old behavioral objectives problem. Here is a behavioral objective for students from *Educational Technology*.

The student will be given a problem which is totally unfamiliar to him. He will be able to respond by stating ideas or solutions to the problem. The responses (as measured by a choice of checklists, teacher observations, teacher-made exercises) will be rated on the basis of newness and uniqueness.[8]

How many of these would one have to write to cover fully what a child should be doing? One Office of Education project set out to compile a complete set of behavioral objectives for the high school. Before it was abandoned, they had 20,000. Teachers must teach and measure each one. No wonder they want a raise.

There are many other objections to behavioral objectives, most of which revolve around the impossibility of specifying a complete set for anyone and the difficulty of specifying any but the most trivial tasks. I might add that of all the gifted programs we investigated in Illinois, not one employed a set of behavioral objectives.

The program description package is prepared after the program has been "developed." (See page 21.) If you compare the simplicity of this program description with even the brief excerpts from our case study example, you will see how something as complex as a classroom cannot be reduced to a ledger sheet. I submit that with this form completed you would know almost nothing worthwhile about any program. Here is also implicit the interesting idea that "program development" is completed when these activities are specified. This is not how good programs develop. Our own data indicate that program development is a complicated process that occurs when an "advocate," perhaps a parent or teacher, becomes interested in developing a program for pupils. This advocate organizes a group of people, secures resources, and proceeds to build a program. The development of the program is never complete.[9]

Finally these artifacts are coded and related to the budget—which I suspect was the purpose all along. The code numbers can then be manipulated as if they meant something—which they clearly do not. The manual is peppered with statements like "Assessment of results is essential" and other exhortations to evaluate these programs, do cost/benefit analyses,

---

[8] Miriam B. Kapfer, "Behavioral Objectives and the Gifted," *Educational Technology* (June 15, 1968).

[9] Ernest R. House, Joe M. Steele, and Thomas Kerins, *The Development of Educational Programs: Advocacy in a Non-Rational System* (Urbana, Ill.: Center for Instructional Research and Curriculum Evaluation, University of Illinois), 30 pp.

and so on. But actual procedures for doing so are glossed over at great speed, and well they might be, for there is absolutely no legitimate way to collect the measures and make the comparisons the system demands.

The end result is what I always find in dealing with systems analysis—a lot of hazy generalizations that seem reasonable on the surface but are actually impossible to implement. All the objections to this system that I have raised are based on either empirical evidence or experience. But I have found that systems people are never disturbed by data. They simply say "You aren't doing it right," which means that people are not behaving in accordance with the rationalistic—economic model that underlies the system. If they did behave properly the model would work—a brilliant piece of circular logic.

In short this system seems to be an accountant's dream of how the world should work. Its implicit message is economic efficiency, promoting economic rationality at the expense of other human characteristics such as political rationality.[10] Significantly, the California system was drawn up by an accounting and budgeting commission and almost all the examples used are in business education.

My prognosis is something like this. My worst fears are that the system will actually succeed in doing what I see as its real design. In that case, we will have a very high level of managerial education. The repression and dullness of the classroom will increase and we will have succeeded in crucifying our kids on the cross of economic efficiency. My most hopeful prediction is that people will realize the restrictiveness of this system and subvert it into an information system that attends to the needs of the pupils instead of simply shaping them to the needs of the institutions.

PPBS ELEMENT FORM

GOAL STATEMENT

To provide all students the opportunity to develop skills in typing, shorthand, bookkeeping, and office machine operation.

DEVELOPED BY _____

---

[10] Aaron Wildavsky, "The Political Economy of Efficiency: Cost-Benefit Analysis, Systems Analysis, and Program Budgeting," in Fremont J. Lyden and Ernest R. Miller, (eds.), *Planning, Programming, Budgeting: A Systems Approach to Management* (Chicago: Markham, 1968).

OBJECTIVE STATEMENT AND EVALUATIVE CRITERIA

Ninety percent of graduating Business Curriculum students shall meet the following standards:

Typing—70 words per minute as measured by the IBM Test with 90% accuracy

Shorthand—100 words per minute as measured by the Gregg test.

Bookkeeping—Demonstrate understanding of journals, income statements, and balance sheets as determined by decision tests.

Office Management Operation—Mean score equal to national average on NCR test

DEVELOPED BY _____

PROGRAM DESCRIPTION SUMMARY

This program is designed to allow students to develop skills in the areas of typing, shorthand, bookkeeping, and office machine operation sufficient to gain employment using these skills. This program will include practice with typical problems and situations found in actual employment situations. Contacts will be maintained with the local business community to aid students in obtaining employment.

DEVELOPED BY _____

PROGRAM TITLE _____

PROGRAM ID NO. _____PROGRAM NO. __PROGRAM LEVEL __

SUPPORTED PROGRAMS _____

SUPPORTING PROGRAMS _____

But neither of these projections is likely in the near future. Schools will stay pretty much as they are now. Schoolmen will get by just as they got through chemistry lab—by filling out forms regardless of what is happening in reality. In California the PPB system will take more people to fill out the forms, more destroyed trees to provide the paper, and more people in Sacramento to shuffle them around. As one economist says, most PPB systems have culminated in "sterile accounting schemes."[11] But one can see the public and certain government leaders providing more money for the schools now that "sound business procedures" have been adopted. The end result will be a slightly less efficient system that looks more efficient. But even that is preferable to the first choice.

Institutional Accountability

Here is a newspaper clipping from *The Wall Street Journal* dated June 24, 1970, datelined San Francisco. The headlines read:

EDUCATED DROPOUTS
COLLEGE-TRAINED YOUTHS
SHUN THE PROFESSIONS
FOR A FREE-FORM LIFE
John Spitzer of Harvard Is
Cabbie; Clara Perkinson,
Smith, Carries the Mail
OPTING OUT OF "THE SYSTEM"

The article goes on to say that increasing numbers of highly talented and educated young people do not want to join the system. John Spitzer says, "When I was a senior, Dylan's 'Subterranean Homesick Blues' came out. Remember that's the one when he says 'twenty years in school and then they put you on the day shift.' That touched so many nerves for so many people; that said it all." Although we might not agree on whether those young people are refuse or martyrs, saboteurs or saviors, we would agree that PPBS is not going to solve the problem. In fact, it would make the situation worse.

I wish I had a well worked out alternative to economic accountability that would solve all our problems. I do not. But let me suggest a different mode of accountability in which institutions are accountable to persons rather than persons being accountable to the institution. Such an accountability scheme would provide feedback on the clients' well-being instead of just how well they are "shaping up." Teachers might be responsible to students and administrators to teachers. The information system attendant to this mode of accountability would revolve around the question, "Is this information going to help the institution adjust to characteristics of the student or will it result in shaping the student to the demands of the institution?"

---

[11] Brandl, op. cit.

With this in mind here are some recommendations for dealing with any kind of information system.

1. *Examine the function of the system, not just its rationale.* The true nature of the system is revealed by how it works, not what it promises.

2. *Try to respect the complexity of reality.* Good programs do not result from establishing a few objectives and selecting appropriate activities. Establishing any program successfully necessitates complex political processes. Any model of development that denies this is dysfunctional.

3. *Insist on multiple outcomes.* No educational program should be judged on the basis of one or two measures. Resist attempts to reduce educational output to simple achievement scores.

4. *Look at classroom transactions.* Regardless of outcomes, the atmosphere in which a child spends a good portion of his life is important. Many instruments for doing this are available.

5. *Collect many different kinds of data.* In light of all the above, the more kinds of data the better. Testimonials, interviews, classroom interaction analysis, objective tests—almost any data are appropriate. They provide a picture of the richness of classroom life and mitigate against making decisions based on highly abstract information. One thing we did in a recent evaluation was combine 25 different kinds of information to produce a case study of the class. The resulting image of the class was much superior to combining just a few kinds of data.

6. *Collect data from different sources.* It is especially important to find out what students are thinking, even if one asks only "What are the three things in this class you would like to change most?" Students can give as good a reading of what is going on as anyone else. Information should also be collected from parents and other groups.

7. *Report to different audiences.* For example, parents have a right to know something about what's going on in class. So do many other people.

8. *Rely on intuition and professional judgments.* Many experts on PPBS emphasize that analytic tools should only provide assistance to intuition. There is no substitute for human judgment.

9. *Promote diversity within the system.* The most difficult task for organizations is to generate alternative ways of doing things.[12] An infor-

---

[12] March, op. cit.

mation system should promote the development of divergent ideas, not inhibit them. There are many places where even economic efficiency should be the criterion. For example, recently we did a cost/benefit analysis comparing the efficacy of demonstration centers and summer training institutes. But the circumstances were proper—a few short-range goals were at stake. Ordinarily, life is not that simple.

Breaking the exclusive hold of economic accountability is not easy to do. I hope that economists and those who control our economic institutions will stop maximizing economic gains long enough to assess the long-range consequences of doing so. There is some hope. Even an economist has remarked "When my son Christopher got all A's in first grade but found school repressive and dull, the arguments that his grades indicated a successful and lucrative future was little consolation to him or to me."[13]

---

[13] Brandl, op. cit.

12. *Accountability—What Does Not Go Without Saying**

Harry S. Broudy

A major difficulty in presenting a paper on educational accountability before a meeting of philosophers is to decide what does or does not go without saying. For example, there seems to be no point in reviewing the standard arguments and controversies about moral responsibility. Nor is it necessary to affirm the principle of accountability of schools to parents, pupils, and citizens. From the very beginning, mechanisms for overseeing instruction were built into our schools, partly, because of the Americans' distrust of institutional tendencies to authoritarianism, and partly, because they have traditionally expected schools to yield demonstrable economic gains. But colonial schools also were held accountable for maintaining community standards of social behavior and doctrinal purity. Questions arise, therefore, not so much with regard to the validity of the principle, but rather as to accountability for what, to whom, and by what criteria.

Even when demands for accountability are challenged, the challenges are very diverse, and not all of them are of equal theoretical interest. For example, universities—especially public ones—are being called upon to assign dollar values to costs of individual programs. The university demurs because it has no really workable way of calculating such costs, and not because it rejects the principle of accountability. On the other hand, the decision of a board of trustees not to expel a professor of political science because that professor refuses to teach his courses in accordance with an edict of a legislative committee represents a challenge to accountability

This article is published here for the first time.

* Symposium address on Accountability, Western Division, American Philosophical Association Annual Meeting, St. Louis, May 4, 1972.

in principle. Should school authorities be held accountable for the sale of drugs in the vicinity of the school? This demand for accountability might be challenged on at least two grounds: the difficulty of preventing such sales and the responsibility for preventing them. Because possibility is a necessary condition for moral responsibility, challenges to accountability made in the name of practical difficulties may not be irrelevant to accountability in principle. Nevertheless, possibility is not a sufficient condition for obligation, and so it might not be the proper responsibility of the school to devote its resources to the prevention of drug sales, even if it were possible for it to undertake such measures. Indeed, some of the most vexing problems of school accountability arise when it is not impossible—and it may even be convenient—for the school to perform worthwhile tasks that have little logical connection with instruction. Administration of dental examinations in school time on school property is one example. Student housing and feeding are others. With a little imagination, one can include virtually anything as a condition of learning something or other; it is difficult, therefore, for the school to resist taking on almost any task that some insistent group regards as beneficial to pupils as pupils or as persons.

In this paper I shall confine my remarks to situations in which educational institutions believe that they are justified in resisting demands for accountability and the reasons that are, or might be, presented as justification for the resistance.

The paper falls roughly into three sections, the first of which will take up some general disclaimers of responsibility for the policies and results of institutional behavior; the second deals with disclaimers based on disagreements on objectives of schooling and the criteria for estimating success in achieving objectives. Finally, there is the disclaimer of responsibility on grounds of lack of power to achieve imputed objectives.

I.   General Disclaimers

The difficulty in determining what does and does not go without saying is illustrated by the problem of collective responsibility. One moves into the general area of the problem when it is asked under what circumstances it is morally allowable to disobey a law, and when an individual is to be held responsible for performing morally reprehensible acts under the command of the law or of some lawfully authorized person. Thus Thomas Hobbs argued (*Leviathan*, Chapter XVI) that refusal to obey a lawful command to do something against the law of nature is not permissible, but rather that to refuse to obey such a command is "against the law of nature that forbiddeth breach of covenant."

There is also the problem of relating positive law to moral considerations, and whether under certain circumstances moral considerations prevent a law from being a law, for instance, some of the laws enacted by the Nazis regarding the duty of citizens to inform on persons suspected of opposition to the government.[1]

Still another philosophical problem might be relevant in the matter of accountability in education. Suppose one holds to the Marxian doctrine that moral arguments are part of the ideology used by social classes in their struggle for economic dominance. Suppose that the demand for accountability is interpreted as a ploy or weapon used by one social class to embarrass the other. One could, of course, still try to determine whether schools in fact were or were not doing what one had a right to expect from them, but conceivably one might challenge the demand by branding it a political red herring and refuse to play the game, or at least object to playing the game. As there will be occasion to note, there may be some justifiable resistance to accountability in principle on these grounds.

The collective responsibility issue can arise in two forms. First is the demurrer based on the complexity of large institutions. It is argued that such organizations are forced into bureaucratic structures in which it is difficult to identify the decision-makers and the decision-implementers. Hence the blame for an undesirable result cannot be fixed. The buck is passed around and around, and even when the president of the corporation or the university announces that the buck stops with him, we are supposed to understand that this is a ritualistic affirmation of a pro forma assumption of responsibility; that he is a victim of circumstances for which he is really not responsible. In other words, bureaucracy transmutes voluntarism into determinism; individual actions into institutional behaviors, and so cancels out moral responsibility.

The second form of the argument relies on the denial of the possibility of a collective mind or will that alone would be the proper source for an institutional decision. If, strictly speaking, an institution cannot make decisions, it cannot be held responsible for any. Hence all responsibility would be individual, but—to come back to the complexity of the argument—if no individual responsibility can be fixed, then neither the individual nor the institution can be held accountable; all demands for accountability from educational institutions would be misuses of language. To avoid short circuiting the whole accountability problem in this fashion, and without arguing the metaphysical status of group minds or the legal status of persons, I would suggest that taking into account both the arguments from complexity and from nominalistic metaphysics, there are still grounds for holding individuals responsible for participation in the making and implementing of institutional policy.

Individuals in an educational or other collective human enterprise can-

---

[1] See for example the discussion of H. L. A. Hart and Ron Fuller in the *Harvard Law Review* (1958).

not completely escape blame for institutional behaviors. The individual, as a moral agent, can acquiesce or refuse to acquiesce in institutional action. The price, to be sure, might be high, and a person might justify acquiescence in an act that he disapproves of on moral grounds, viz., by pointing to overriding considerations that could have created more evil than acquiescence. These judgments have to be assessed in particular cases, as in the Nuremberg and the My Lai trials. In principle, however, the operations of a school system or a university can be laid at the door of the individuals who carry on the functions of these institutions—not, to be sure, in the sense that they could have prevented the result or achieved a better one, but in the sense that they can acquiesce or refuse to acquiesce in a line of action. Thus the professors who denounce the immorality of a university's collaboration with the industrial-military complex and yet retain positions in that university are morally obliged to give excuses for doing so or be liable to the charge of insincerity or cowardice. Nor is the excuse that one remains within the disapproved institution in order to reform it to be taken at face value; it too needs evidence of sincerity.

Another common challenge to the demand for accountability that is liable to be abused is the contention that the school depends on other institutions and on noneducational factors to do its own job. Thus whether a child learns to read is held to be dependent on whether or not the child has had the proper nutrition, psychical and physical; whether he has been nurtured in a reading-prone family; and whether the government allots sufficient funds for equipment, and the like. Not having control of these causal factors, the institution argues, it cannot be held responsible for the failure of its mission.

This argument from interdependence can take at least two forms: it can be argued that various institutions contribute special components to the final result, but that all factors have to collaborate for the result to accrue. However, if we can determine which institutions did or did not do their jobs, then we can apportion responsibility and thereby meet the challenge to accountability.

The second form of the interdependence argument does not assign special functions to the several institutions; it insists rather that governments educate as well as rule; that families are economic units as well as child rearing agencies; and that schools have political functions as well as instructional, and that to try to isolate these is to distort the social reality. On such a view of interdependence the demand for accountability from any particular institution raises the problem as to whether it could be answered at all, so that it is a mistake to raise it in the first place.

However, if this view of the way institutions operate is correct, then why different kinds of institutions are necessary becomes a relevant question. If all institutions educate, why do we need schools? If all institutions are production agencies, why industry or business? As the social order enlarges, one might need larger institutions, but why institutions of different kinds? Lest this be dismissed as a straw man, I urge the examination of the acres of literature that proclaim that schools must minister to the whole child in all aspects of his life, or that professors—all of them—must do teaching, research, and service, or that there shall be no ivory towers. Conversely, it is argued that home, government, church, the media, labor unions, and industry have educational functions—in short, that school and community are one, that schools can have no walls. To which one might retort that institutions that cannot identify the differences they make may not be making any difference. If they can identify their impacts, they are in some way responsible for them; if not, they may have no reason for being.

Is there any evidence that the demands for accountability are not always what they purport to be, viz., a request for an accounting of achievement of a set of goals or the fulfilments of contracts or implied promises? Are some demands punitive in intent? Are they masks for pressures on schools to change their goals? Are some demands for accountability intended to change the social system? Are some of the demands a phase of the class struggle?

Consider, for example, the recent remarks of U. S. Commissioner of Education, Sidney P. Marland, Jr., to the effect that "management by objective has been recognized as an important key to the smooth operation of our contemporary educational institutions."[2] He then goes on to announce that objectives for fiscal year 1972 included career education, racial integration, innovation, education for the handicapped and the disadvantaged, the right to read, special revenue sharing, and improved management. Funds would be given to institutions that could show they were achieving these objectives and presumably denied to those that were not.

Leaving aside the merits of the objectives, it is clear that for Commissioner Marland they are a way of persuading schools by means of bribes to move in certain directions. It would seem, therefore, that schools are accountable for the achievement of the objectives only if they take the bribes. Other schools would not be accountable for these objectives. But later in the article, accountability is taken to mean "a nationwide accounting process or institution which would act like a certified public accountant in business, objectively assessing the success and failure of the schools and reporting the findings to the public" (p. 344). Now if this were done, every school would be made accountable for Commissioner Marland's objectives whether it took federal funds or not. The matter is straightened out a few paragraphs later when it is noted that ". . . we must weigh edu-

---

[2] "Accountability in Education," *Teachers College Record*, Vol. 73, No. 3 (February 1972), p. 339.

cational goals against the needs and goals of all our country's people" (p. 345). Surely, if all the people are for the given objectives, or the objectives are assumed to be valid for all the people, then no school can disclaim accountability. In other words, HEW's objectives are really the peoples' objectives—a doubtful conclusion, to say the least.

Advocates of open schooling, decentralized schooling for ethnic minorities, free universities, and open admissions to the universities and of the politicization of educational institutions all exploit the virtual synonymity of accountability and morality as an ideological weapon. Paulo Freire wants the schools to be accountable to the oppressed people of the world.[3] Another writer says that schools emphasize a philosophy of competition, which he regards as deplorable, and one anthropologist has warned that schools must stop serving the narrow interests of the economic system and concentrate on love, kindness, honesty, and simplicity or we are courting disaster.[4]

Similar comments can be made about the proposed voucher system. The scheme whereby in one form or another parents and students would be allowed to use public funds to choose their schools is defended not only because it gives freedom of choice, but also because it would force schools to become accountable to their clients. Thus the Citizens for Educational Freedom, a predominantly Catholic lay organization, could make sure that schools patronized by their vouchers would serve their interests.[5] Milton Friedman would use the vouchers to force public education into the private sector, where he believes most enterprises ought to be anyway.[6] Some want to use vouchers to preserve segregated schools, and still others want to promote integrated ones. But generally the voucher system, whatever its merits or demerits, is primarily a way of politically undermining the public school concept, and one of the most voluble exponents of the voucher scheme admits it.[7]

Is a demand for accountability when motivated by such political considerations validly resisted? It occurs to me that there are situations in which they could be. One would be when there is reason to believe that the political considerations are overriding, even though nonpolitical motives may also be operating. Suppose that A proposes that school X be held accountable for improving reading skills in ethnic minority children,

---

[3] Paulo Freire, *Pedagogy of the Oppressed* (New York: Herder and Herder, 1970).

[4] Jules Henry, *Culture Against Men* (New York: Vintage Books, 1965), pp. 13-15.

[5] Virgil C. Blum, *Freedom of Choice in Education* (New York: Macmillan, 1958).

[6] Milton Friedman, *Capitalism and Freedom* (Chicago: The University of Chicago Press, 1962).

[7] Christopher Jencks, "Is the Public School Obsolete?" *The Public Interest* (Winter 1965), p. 27, where he notes that the voucher system in one form or another would "destroy the public school system as we know it."

and suppose that A hopes to displace B, the superintendent of school X, if it shows up badly in the accounting. If both A and B agree that improving the reading ability of ethnic minorities is a worthy goal and that it is reasonable to expect a school to achieve it, then the overriding issue is the achievement of the reading goal and the political motivation, although present, can be dismissed as a ground for a challenge to accountability. But suppose A is the proponent of a voucher system, and suppose that it is known by examination of his speeches and writings that A's motivation is ideological or political. To urge that B make an accounting of his school's success in teaching children to read does not reduce the political motive to irrelevance, even though all agree on the importance of children learning to read. If the control of the schools is the real issue, a demand for accountability in terms of criteria that have little or no relation to the issue of control does not automatically obligate the school to make the accounting. B may suspect that, even if his school shows up well in reading, it will not prevent A from making further demands. Furthermore, it is conceivable that the school may not have taught reading successfully, yet this would not justify change of control; B may want to make sure that A's inference that it does will not be drawn. For example, if B is convinced that an accounting, by shifting control, would be more detrimental to the school's work on reading than continuing on its present course, B might be justified in refusing to acknowledge accountability. A's ploy here reminds us of the police who respond to a protest march by charging the marchers with obstructing traffic. This reveals nothing about the merits of the march, but it does stop it.

The injection of an overriding political motivation complicates an already complicated situation, which I do not presume to be able to unravel. The point I wish to raise is that the general assent to the accountability principle is compatible with an expectation that the demander come into a court of equity with clean hands; that when this is in doubt, it is proper to question the motives for accountability demands.

II. Disagreements on Objectives and Criteria

The demand for accountability is generally urged and resisted in the language of contractual relationships. Schools ordinarily do not enter into formal contracts with their clients, although there is no lack of stipulations and conditions about fees, rules for attendance, dismissal, and the like. Explicit contracts with school employees deal more with conditions of tenure and remuneration than with their professional duties. As to results, the covenant between school and client is implicit, and the stated objectives of the school rarely descend in generality from what might be called broad life outcomes. Good character and citizenship and the ability to think and judge are typical of the implied promises and expectations of elementary and secondary schools, and of general education at any level. To be sure, vocational preparation is also implied in the covenant, as well as the preparation for more schooling. Underlying everything else is a tacit agreement that public schools, at any rate, should profess the ideals of the social order. When no consensus exists as to how these ideals shall be interpreted, controversy arises over such criteria as "truly democratic," "truly humane" schools, and "really equal educational opportunity."

Differences in objectives tend to fall into three types: first is the disagreement that occurs when objectives are stated at different levels of generality. Vocational versus liberal goals; skills versus generic habits of mind (e.g., critical thinking); and attitudes toward specific values versus large outlooks on life—all illustrate this type of conflict. Evaluating an institution in terms of one set of goals may earn high marks for it, but it may be downgraded by those who hold to the values represented by the other term in the dichotomy.

This vagueness of objectives in the tacit covenant, the advocates of accountability argue, permits schools to evade accountability. Hence, Commissioner Marland and Leon Lessinger insist on making the contract explicit and the objectives definite, identifiable, and accessible (preferably measurable).[8] Without such definiteness, management-by-objectives, cost-effectiveness, and cost-benefit analyses will not work. Much of the pressure for accountability comes from minority groups whose children, it is charged, are not learning skills that are measurable—reading, writing, computation, and knowledge of a few basic subjects. Understandably, schools that differ about objectives will not willingly be accountable for heteronomous goals.

The insistence on identifiable objectives has led to the slogan "Down with nonbehavioral objectives." This enthusiastic neo-positivism is buttressed by educational industries that produce packages of behavioral objectives and legislation at the state level that puts pressure on schools to use them or contrive their own versions of them. This movement is well on the way to undercutting more generic personal and societal objectives of schooling.

A special problem is created when the outcomes of schooling are stated in neohumanistic terms: self-identity, caring, expansion of consciousness, freedom, creativeness, and the like. These can be stated in the language of life-styles, but not as specific behaviors, knowledge, or skills. The difficulty with objectives of this sort lies in their dissonance, if not incommensurability, with the cognitive outcomes of studying certain bodies of knowl-

---

[8] Leon M. Lessinger, *Every Kid a Winner: Accountability in Education* (New York: Simon and Schuster, 1970).

edge or acquiring certain scholastic skills. Encounter groups, role playing, and sensitivity training are not assimilable to such study, hence conventional schools, at any level, are baffled by demands for neohumanistic demands for accountability.

Such dissonance in aims has led to the establishing of free schools and universities, quite unlike the standard ones, the chief difference being that a mode of life rather than study of a logically-organized subject matter is the dominant activity of the student. No doubt, students, parents, and perhaps the general public want to hold the school responsible for helping the student mature into a healthy, wholesome, and responsible self. A school, however, that makes formal studies paramount is not a good aging vat. Logically-organized subjects have little immediate relevance for existential predicaments, and the young are not excited by remote relevance.

Furthermore, the concern for the "soul" of the student, characteristic of Socrates in the early dialogues, and the efforts to elicit a like concern from the student for his soul, for example, in the opening remarks of the *Protagoras*, are not the distinguishing features of the academic guilds in this country. Accordingly, when the demand for accountability is couched in neohumanistic terms, the professoriate is understandably unready and often unwilling to render such an account or to be held responsible for such an accounting.

At all levels of instruction, it is difficult to fix responsibility for the proper personal relationship between the student and the teacher. It is a truism that teachers of the very young ought to love their pupils, and in general, the teacher is supposed to be concerned about students as persons. This relationship is stressed in the neohumanistic versions of schooling, and the word "relating" is used to cover all satisfactory instances of personal interactions.

However, it is doubtful that ordinary love, friendship, and companionship can be assimilated simply with the pupil-teacher relationship. Aside from disparity in ages, common school practice gives the teacher the powers of a judge and policeman, and this makes it awkward to play out the role of friend or parent or lover surrogate. If the teacher is to be *in loco parentis*, then he must be an ideal parent who can love without the bias of a natural parent. If the teacher is in some sense to serve also *in loco communitatis* and *in loco humanitatis*, then again he cannot easily enter into personal relationships as ordinarily conceived. Like Christian love, pedagogical love may or may not have much resemblance to the more familiar and everyday forms of that passion. Accordingly, when teachers and schools are held accountable for loving their pupils, there will be a wide range of interpretation that will make it virtually impossible to determine which criterion to apply and to know when it has or has not been met. As but one of many possible examples, consider the appropriate behavior for the requirement that the pupil be accorded the dignity of a person. Does this mean to be lenient with the pupil or strict? It probably means not demanding what he cannot reasonably be expected to accomplish, but does it not also mean paying him the respect that comes with not letting him perform at a level lower than that of which he is capable? Does it make sense to say that a demanding, strict, even harsh teacher loves pupils more than an easy going affectionate one?

The second type of disagreement on objectives may be called ideological, to which allusion has already been made. The establishment versus the counter–culture, Puritan ethics versus libertarianism, and Washington versus Peking are polarizing in their effect and influence the judgments about the school and demands for accountability.

The third type of disagreement over objectives is jurisdictional or functional. What is the role of the university is a question that is inevitably raised when disputes over teaching versus research, military contracts, student governance, and the curriculum have reached an impasse. There is no dearth of attempts to define the peculiar role of the university and other educational institutions. But settling of jurisdictional disputes by definition is precisely what is being contested; each of the contending parties wants a definition that legitimates its own view of what education is to accomplish.

For example, much of the criticism of the accountability drive charges that under the slogan of accountability, narrow objectives are *forced* upon schools by funding agencies such as HEW, philanthropic foundations, and sundry legislative bodies. However, even when school officials agree freely and even eagerly to enter into performanc contracts or universities freely accept objectives stipulated by funding agencies, some people feel protests should be made against activities that contravene the "true" mission of the university or the school. Such a protest, they say, is especially justified if the institution has announced a true mission that is at odds with some of its activities.

Universities and other educational establishments under such circumstances could be said to have an implicit covenant with the community to carry out the mission. But what is the true mission? Historically it has been centered on knowledge and wisdom, that is, knowledge as applied to conduct. The difficulty arises when the institution goes in for applying knowledge to serve the military-industrial complex or to fomenting social change. Some faculty say that such activities subvert the true mission of the school's devotion to knowledge as such.

If the knowledge mission of the school is taken as its true mission, accountability can be given a fairly clear meaning. For one thing, we have the institutional apparatus for defining knowledge. Institutionally, the truth in physics at a given time is what the credentialled guild of physicists say it is. This is an institutional not a philosophical criterion of truth. The credentialling process involving methods of inquiry and apprenticeship with credentialled masters generates authority for the guild despite disagreements among the guild members. On this view the schools are accountable to the consensus of the learned in all disciplines.

However, some accountabilists[9] challenge the academic credentialling system itself in the name of a higher (or lower) humanity, social activism, or some ideology. Open admissions, the attacks on grades, degrees, examinations, curriculum requirements, and the academic reward system are examples of such challenges to the system. Demands that academic inputs be made accountable for producing life outcomes such as good income, a just society, and personal happiness embarrass the academic guilds, because the evidence is far from conclusive that the study of logically organized disciplines does in fact produce these goods.

Although this is a predicament for educational institutions, it does sharpen the alternatives open to them. If schools claim to produce certain desirable life outcomes, then they must explain why and how the *formal* study of science, history, and the like, can produce superior citizens, even though academic achievement seems to correlate indifferently with vocational success and other life outcomes.[10] The organization of the intellectual or academic disciplines is not parallel with the organization of knowledge for professional training, on the one hand, or with the way we use knowledge in coping with life situations, on the other.

I have written elsewhere how such a rationale might be constructed by exploiting Michael Polanyi's notion of tacit knowing and distinguishing various uses of schooling.[11] Perhaps a better rationale can be constructed, and I can think of no more important contribution philosophers can make to education than to work on providing one. Until a credible rationale is produced, the demand for accountability in terms of objectives defined in terms of observable behaviors will threaten the more global claims made for formal schooling and especially for general and liberal studies. Indeed, even the theoretical components of professional curricula are now under suspicion.

Another alternative is for the school to disclaim responsibility for life

---

[9] A term I picked up from a paper on accountability by Martin Levit entitled "The Ideology of Accountability in Schooling." Reprinted in this volume.

[10] The de-schooling proposals of Ivan Illich are merely an extreme variant of the general argument against formal schooling as found in Ivar Berg's *Education and Jobs: The Great Training Robbery* (New York: Praeger, 1970); the *Harvard Business Review* articles by Sterling Livingston on success in management, and the plethora of proposals to de-formalize and de-theorize general and professional education.

[11] "On 'Knowing With,'" *Proceedings of the Philosophy of Education Society 26th Annual Meeting*, 1970.

outcomes in any global sense. The stance can be uncomfortable because it will involve some isolation, ivory towerism, apparent irrelevance, and a dull life for students and for some academicians. It may also mean regressing to living standards somewhat below those to which academics became accustomed in the affluent 60s. Universities are reluctant to give up either intellectual autonomy or social involvement, but accountabilists may force a choice or give them far less of each than they would like.

The authority of the academic guild also enters into the problem of accountability through the question of faculty tenure. This occurs because one of the arguments against tenure is that it shields the tenured professor from accountability. It is argued that:

> Since no one else in American society can escape the intolerable pressures of a complex technological culture, and since few in the world are free from economic, social, or political "repression," why should professors be so protected, or enjoy such freedom?[12]

To these and kindred attacks on faculty tenure, the Harvard report replied in many ways, but for our purpose the basic justification of that tenure is ". . . that society may have the benefit of honest judgment and independent criticism which otherwise might be withheld because of fear of offending a dominant social group or a transient social attitude.[13]

No tenure arrangement justifies everything a professor might wish to do, but the most important cause for dismissal is the judgment of his peers that he is incompetent, that is, his failure to come up to the scholarly standards of the guild and to live up to whatever code of behavior the guild regards as appropriate for its members.

An obverse case arises when a professor is given low scores by his students on a rating scale such as is now being so widely used on college campuses. The argument for the use of these scales is that the student (the client) is in the best position to know whether or not the teacher has rendered satisfactory service.

Although many professors are not unduly disturbed by the judgments passed upon their teaching by students, some instructors are almost pathologically opposed to it. Discounting all self-serving motives that might account for opposition to what seems, on the face of it, to be an eminently plausible procedure, there remains some reasonable ground for the opposition.

I have in mind the fact that in law, medicine, and other well-established

---

[12] "Academic Tenure at Harvard University," *AAUP Bulletin* (Spring 1972), p. 63.
[13] Quoted in the article cited above from Byse and Joughin, *Tenure in American Higher Education* (1959).

professions it makes sense to say, "The case was well argued, although the client is now in jail." Or, "The surgery was successful, but the patient died." In these instances client dissatisfaction is not taken as the sole or final criterion of the service. What, then, does it mean to say that the surgery was good, but that the patient expired? No more than that, as judged by his credentialled peers, the surgeon carried out conscientiously a correct, reasonable procedure. The accountability of the surgeon to the patient is to do the best he can to save his life, but his culpability, if things go wrong, is limited by the correctness of procedure. For this he is accountable to the profession. I believe that it is to this sort of procedural defense that some professors are appealing when they oppose making the student judgment on their teaching final. However, in teaching, such defense is not routinely available. In higher education, professors rarely see their colleagues teach; at lower levels it would be difficult to secure consensus as to what constitutes correct procedure.

The possbility of denying accountability to X because of accountability to a prior or higher claim is perhaps even more important in the public schools than in institutions of higher learning, because the former lacks a strong academic guild to protect it from lay pressures. Indeed, in the name of democracy and freedom of choice, many lay groups demand the right to participate in the fashioning of the curriculum, the organization of the school system, staff appointments, and all matters educational. In part, this situation arises from lack of agreement on what constitutes educational expertise; in part, it is the result of educationists making a virtue out of consulting with their clients in decision–making. Having disclaimed authority based on superior knowledge in matters of curriculum, school organization, and even in methods of teaching, school administrators cannot in good grace oppose the voice of the people when they insist on being consulted on what is "good" literature, good history, and good social science. This leaves the school with no intellectual defense against popular assaults on the freedom of teaching. There is no "higher" target of obligation and accountability than the wishes of the electorate, and there is, therefore, no way of refusing to be accountable to any pressure group on principle even in matters that are clearly educational. That in the current literature of accountability of the public schools there is little about their primary accountability to the intellectual disciplines is something for which one might try to hold somebody accountable.

To summarize: school people and accountabilists do not always, or even for the most part, agree on the proper objectives of schooling or on the criteria by which achievement of all but the simplest objectives are to be judged. Under such circumstances the conditions for a voluntary covenant explicit or implicit are not fulfilled; accountability is not an unqualified imperative and challenges to it not necessarily illegitimate.

III. Disagreements as to Causal Efficacy

So far, challenges to demands for accountability have been justified by proper disclaims of moral responsibility for results demanded by the accountabilist. Another sort of disclaimer argues that the school could not achieve certain results even if it acknowledged them as desirable.

For example, suppose it is agreed that schools ought to contribute to the reduction of alcoholism, crime, divorce, and pollution. However, the general conclusions from studies on the effects of schooling on social conditions are not encouraging.[14] Further, commonly found differences in school facilities, class size, and resources have little effect on educational achievement in basic skills and school subjects for which schools would want to be responsible. The major factor seems to be the pupil's socioeconomic environment and the backgrounds of his play-peers.[15]

Nor are the reports from the performance–contracting experiments uniformly or even generally optimistic. In 1970-71 the Office of Economic Opportunity authorized seven million dollars for performance contracts with six educational companies in 18 school districts, but early in 1972, OEO announced the results to be a failure.[16]

It has been argued by one study that the usual criteria for a quality college have little to do with the student's learning. On the contrary, good schools are peopled by good students; so the "better" the school, the less it does, relatively, for the student.[17]

If these are indeed warranted assertions about what schools can and cannot do, then it is a mistake to hold them accountable for certain results. At worst, the schools and their critics are guilty of ignorance about the efficacy of schooling.

Are educational institutions to be held accountable for their ignorance? Is anybody to be held accountable for it? The answers must be mixed. There are lessons from history that one might reasonably expect "professionals" in education to be familiar with. The redemptive power of education for the "wretched" poor has been tested or at least experimented with since the time of the charity schools of Europe. That schools are not necessarily or even usually pleasure houses for the young is also an old story, so are the attempts of Rousseau and dozens of others to make schooling easy, pleasant, and natural. That schooling has always been a vehicle

---

[14] Carol H. Weiss, "The Politicalization of Evaluation Research," *Journal of Social Issues*, Vol. 16 (Autumn 1970), pp. 57-68.

[15] James S. Coleman, et al., *Equality and Educational Opportunity* (Washington, D.C.: HEW, Office of Education, 1969).

[16] *Time*, Vol. 99 (February 14, 1972), p. 42.

[17] Alexander W. Astin, "Undergraduate Achievement and Institutional Excellence," *Science* (August 16, 1968), pp. 661-668.

for the dominant social class to perpetuate its values and to secure its dominance likewise is not a recent discovery. That the conglomerate of nearly 45 million pupils and two million teachers, which we call the public elementary and secondary school system, cannot implement innovations that reverse its direction every five years should have been known to responsible school reformers. Responsible critics, it seems to me, should be held accountable for such knowledge or ignorance, as the case may be. The U. S. Office of Education and other well meaning instigators of reform have not always been sufficiently responsible in this regard.

But there are other situations on which history throws little light. No country has had to cope with the problems of making good on its promise of equal educational opportunity on the scale attempted in the United States. We do not know whether integration of the races is essential to equality of educational opportunity, just as we do not know how formal studies of the academic disciplines work themselves out in the quality of adult life. The academic guild system that works so well with graduate students, who themselves aspire to membership in the guild, does not work well at all with undergraduates who have no such aspirations, and indeed may have no academic aspirations. We do not yet know how to make a large university into a suitable place for late adolescents to become young adults. Trying to hold the faculty of such a university accountable for knowing how to cope with demands for relevance, freedom from dormitory regulations, and resistance to the draft is simply to ask what the guild member—regardless of his discipline—is occupationally unfit to do.

We know very imperfectly the educative and miseducative effects of the electronic media, of instant communication. We have not fully realized the effect of the disappearance of community supervision of the young upon which so much of the social controls of the past depended. We have only the faintest intimations of the effects of drugs and neurosurgery on learning and possibly on schooling. These are only a few of the questions to which we can respond with little more than shrewd conjectures and common sense. In many areas, therefore, the domain of accountability is far from being clear.

Summary

The problem of accountability of educational institutions may be rephrased by asking whether they are in fact fulfilling their roles *in loco parentis, in loco communitatis,* and *in loco humanitatis.* I think it is clear that unless the conditions for defining these roles and for playing them are agreed upon by the parties to the covenant, demands for accountability —except in the sense that one is accountable to God or one's conscience —are not only meaningless but may even be mischievous. No such agreement as to definitions exists, and if we adopt traditional meanings for *in loco parentis, communitatis,* and *humanitatis,* then it is doubtful that the conditions for playing these roles now exist. For example, the family, the school, and the community no longer have the power to supervise the young, if the young are determined to evade supervision. Family and community supervision of the young has broken down wherever the automobile makes it easy to escape the scrutiny of neighbors and friends; the powers of school supervision are strictly limited and have been subjected to a severe strain in recent years.

The school, in summary, does not know what sort of family, community, or version of the good life it represents, and it hesitates to be dogmatic about what it ought to represent. If it makes attention to cultural diversity and individual interests its sovereign policy, then its accountability is limited to demonstrating that it has not knowingly prevented any pupil, any family, or any group of them from using the schools in their own interests.

All of the foregoing siftings through the complexities of accountability lead to the conclusion that where schools are concerned, the demand for accountability is valid only under certain limited conditions.

1. A special function of the school or college is identifiable and its nature agreed upon by the parties to the social covenant.
2. The outcomes for which the school is held responsible by virtue of its function are identifiable and within its control.
3. The standards for quality of schooling are agreed upon by the contracting parties.
4. There exists a body of expert judgment that will be acceptable to parties to the contract on such topics as curriculum and conditions and methods of instruction.

Even then, schools cannot be held accountable for a product, because the product continues to develop long after schooling ceases. But given the conditions listed above, schools should be able to give an account and rationale of their processes of instruction, for instance, the degree to which they have fulfilled their special function. Insofar as the conditions are not met—and today they are largely unmet—even the demand for accountability for process may in many instances be properly challenged.

13. *PBTE and Measurement: A Program Based on a Mistake*

Donald Arnstine

I. Introduction

Performance-based teacher education (PBTE) is the name given to a series of efforts to improve the training of teachers. These efforts focus on the explicit, observable acts which teachers perform and for which prospective teachers need to be trained. Because it is focused on behavior, it is believed that PBTE need not depend solely on commitments to ideals of "good" teaching, and that it can free itself from any hint of vagueness in its references to the worthwhile things that teachers do.

PBTE is based on a technique of measuring behavior. In dealing only with whatever can be observed, it seeks to achieve a maximum of clarity and precision in its results. Not only is the success of PBTE to be evaluated in terms of these measurements, but the aims and objectives of PBTE programs are formulated in terms of the behaviors that are amenable to these measurements. Thus measurement is at the heart of PBTE, from the initial conception of particular programs to the evaluation of the teachers who are trained in them.

In this essay I will show how the measurement procedures on which PBTE is based fail to provide the kind of information and guidance that would make possible either the construction of a defensible teacher–education program or the evaluation of the teachers in it. The reason for this is that the concept of measurement underlying PBTE is based on a fundamental misunderstanding of the ways in which people judge one another's behavior. In the course of explicating this misunderstanding, I will

This article was prepared especially for this volume.

indicate what alternative procedures might be appropriate for measuring effectiveness in teaching. I will also indicate how such an alternative approach to measurement is related to the ways in which we formulate goals for teacher education.

II.   The Development of PBTE: A Marriage of Politics and Psychology

The impetus for the development of PBTE did not come from schoolteachers, nor did it come from those whose primary business is the preparation of teachers. On the contrary, it appears to have emerged from the union of two distinct and separate concerns: on the one hand, from representatives of a public that wanted to know whether its taxes were well spent on education and, on the other hand, from educational research workers concerned with developing more precise modes of controlling, analyzing, and measuring human behavior.

The man in the street has probably always been interested in how his tax dollars were spent, but only lately has this concern begun to change the focus of public education. In the increasingly conservative political climate of the late 1960s and 1970s, a dominant thrust of government at the national and at many state levels has been to reduce spending in the public sector. Education has been a primary target for this economic contraction. But no administration can maintain itself in office simply by cutting funds for needed public services. Thus the political posture toward the support of education has been one of appearing to "protect" the public by reducing funds for "wasteful" enterprises.

Public schools have long been recognized as a potentially wasteful enterprise, because teaching has typically escaped careful, public assessment, and because many obviously incompetent school personnel have lifetime tenure. Economy-minded politicians could thus at one and the same time aim at reduced spending (and correlatively promise lower taxes) *and* at better education. All they needed was some reliable means of measuring and evaluating the effectiveness of teachers. Backed by such measurements, they could justify both the expulsion of ineffective school personnel and the more efficient preparation of those who might replace them.

Fortunately for many people with political ambitions, the necessary modes of measurement appeared to be at hand. For more than a generation, psychologists in the United States had been developing modes of explaining animal and human behavior on the basis of observing and measuring discrete, precisely describable movements. These behavioral scientists could correlate the movements of the organisms under investigation with other related events ("contingencies") in such a way as to explain why one rather than another movement was observed, and why a particular rate of movement was observed. Thus supplied with mathematically precise contingencies of reinforcement, behaviorists were able not only to *measure* the rate and direction of change in behavior, but they could also *produce* certain predictable changes in behavior—in lower organisms, at least.

It was not long before psychologists came to believe that their success in training rats and pigeons to acquire simple movements (e.g., maze-running and bar-pressing) could be reproduced with children in school classrooms. Critics were aghast at such claims, and denied that it was possible to measure and then produce at will such intangibles as a love of poetry, a sense of history, or the ability to read critically. But to every objection the behaviorists had a similar answer: whatever it is that you might wish to teach, it must result in some sort of observable behavior. And no matter how complex that behavior might be, it is always possible —at least in principle—to analyze it into a series of discrete, describable movements. Any child, they claimed, could be taught to acquire these movements if the appropriate contingencies of reinforcement were provided.

Contemporary discussions in education about the need for behavioral objectives has its origin in these theorists' claims about the acquisition of behavior (movements or utterances). We are cautioned that before any teaching is undertaken, we must first establish our objectives in terms of discrete, observable behaviors. Then we will understand just what it is we hope our pupils will be able to *do* as a result of our instruction, and we will be able to organize our teaching methods with these objectives in view. Just as important, we will have a foolproof way of telling whether we have succeeded in our instruction, since success is indicated by the appearance of the aimed-at behaviors. Since these objectives are cast in a form that permits unambiguous observation, it is possible to measure, in a precise way, the *degree* to which the objectives have been met.

In a short while I will show why the behaviorists were mistaken in drawing careless analogies from the acquisition of movements in pigeons to what we ordinarily mean by learning in children. But for the moment we can see how propitious was the development of behavioral psychology for economy-minded politicians and administrators who were interested in measuring the effectiveness of teaching. Because if the behavior of children could with precision be measured, then why not measure the behavior of teachers in similar ways? All one needed to do was to specify *which* behaviors teachers should engage in. Those whose measured performance matched the specifications—for example, the behavioral objectives for teachers—could be retained or even promoted in their jobs. Those whose performance did not measure up could, with a clear conscience, be let go. (This reasoning has been turned into law in California's notorious Stull Act, which calls for the promotion and termination of teachers on the basis of the extent to which their students fulfill preestablished behavioral objectives.)

PBTE is but a logical extension of this reasoning. If it is possible to identify an appropriate set of teaching behaviors and measure against them the perfomances of teachers, then it is possible to establish these criterion behaviors as objectives in programs of teacher education. Thus the efforts of teacher educators can be directed toward helping prospective teachers acquire whatever set of behaviors has been identified as the one possessed by competent teachers.

III.   Measuring Behavior as a Means of Determining Teacher Effectiveness

It is important to be clear about *what* it is that is to be measured in the PBTE approach. It is said that we cannot directly measure a teacher's sensitivity to differences among children, or his ability to stimulate their interest. We cannot measure these qualities because they simply cannot be *seen*. What we *do* measure is a behavior or, in contemporary parlance, a performance. It must be remembered that, since we are dealing with observables, the terms "performance" and "behavior" can be reduced without residue to the terms "movement(s)" and "utterance(s)."

It might seem a little strange, if not pernicious, to talk about "movement-and-utterance based teacher education." But if we do not keep in mind just what is meant by the more customary and acceptable term "performance," we may come to think that a performance is something qualitatively different from, or more than, a mere movement or series of movements (or utterances). But according to behavioral psychology, this would be a mistake. If we cannot analyze a performance (e.g., providing a child with written exercises appropriate to the mastery of ten irregular verbs) into a set of movements or utterances, then our conception of the performance must have been cloudy and vague. As such, it would not lend itself to precise measurement and we could not tell whether we had been successful or not.

It is at this point that a fundamental question must be raised: Is it possible to conceive of what it would *mean* to be a good (i.e., effective, competent, successful, and so on) teacher *wholly* in terms of some set of performances (movements) that such a teacher might undertake? Generations of educational research failed to reach a consensus on a set of qualities, characteristics, or personality traits that distinguished better teachers from worse ones.[1] But can we now abandon matters as intangible

---

[1] After an extensive review of research in this field, Getzels and Jackson concluded, "Despite the critical importance of the problem and a half-century of prodigious research effort, very little is known for certain about the nature and measurement of teacher personality and teaching effectiveness." J. W. Getzels and P. W. Jackson, "The Teacher's Personality and Characteristics," in N. L. Gage, ed., *Handbook of Research on Teaching* (Chicago: Rand McNally 1963), p. 574.

as personality traits, and find instead a list of behaviors that might distinguish the better teachers from the worse?

It is worth noting that as of this writing, no such agreed-upon list has appeared, nor does one appear to be forthcoming. This is an ominous—although not unexpected—turn of affairs, for *without an agreed-upon set of teacher behaviors, there is apparently nothing reliable on which to base any PBTE program!* And without some widely desired set of behaviors, there is no firm criterion against which to measure the performances of teachers and prospective teachers.

But the absence of any widely accepted list of desirable teacher behaviors does not mean that such a list will never be produced. Given time and continued effort, we might someday agree on the behaviors that all good teachers should engage in. Or so it is believed by many hopeful psychologists, test constructors, teacher educators, administrators, and politicians. Yet there are no firm grounds for this belief. Let us see why.

From the perspective of human investigators, the life of a laboratory pigeon is relatively simple. It eats, sleeps, and eliminates its waste. It moves about in random but describable ways, and it pecks at food at rates that can be measured with great precision. We do not worry about the hopes and aspirations of laboratory pigeons. We do not worry about their maturity or their creativity, their sense of belonging to a group or their commitments to ideals. When we have measured their movements, *there is nothing about them* (save their physical properties) *left to measure*. And if we are able to train them to adopt different types or rates of movement, *there is nothing else in which we can train them*. Were we to establish a program to produce pigeon trainers, we might justifiably call it performance—based teacher (or trainer) education.

But no one would claim of children and teachers that only their movements are of any interest. We do care a great deal about their hopes and aspirations, their maturity and their creativity, and the extent to which they might become committed to ideals. The question that must be raised is: *Can we measure the growth of these typically human characteristics by measuring only the movements of teachers and children?* This is not an easy question, since it implies that traits like maturity, for example, can be analyzed into a series of discrete, measurable movements (which distinguish it from immaturity).

I submit that the answer to this question is negative, for at least one conclusive reason: human development from immaturity to maturity (or from imitativeness to creativity, from apathy to idealism, or whatever) is a relational matter, and to recognize its appearance one must *compare* a lengthy and varied series of behaviors to each other. Hence it follows that *no single set of movements could ever be taken as characteristic of some ideal, abstract concept of maturity (or creativity, etc.)*. Thus the conceptually easy shift from measuring and producing movements in pigeons to measuring and producing movements in people leaves us with a conception of education in no way distinguishable from sophisticated animal training programs. As noted earlier, when we have talked about a pigeon's movements, there is little left to be said. But when we have described the movements—including serial movements called performances—of children and teachers, there is virtually everything left to be said. Imagine evaluating a violinist, or measuring his growth as a musician, by measuring the movements of his bow.

To say that it is a mistake to focus educational measurement exclusively on the movements of teachers and children is not to reject the utility of measurement in education. It is, rather, to suggest that there are other things more worth measuring. It is to these other things that we must now turn, in order to get clear about an appropriate focus for teacher education, and to better understand the extent to which PBTE is misguided.

IV.   Measuring Dispositions as a Means of Determining Teacher Effectiveness

If we want to assess the effectiveness or competence of teachers, there is not much point in measuring a performance unless it can be unambiguously related to what we think is a goal worth striving for. A teacher's smile, for example, and her utterance of the phrase, "that's right," are performances. We can with considerable accuracy measure how frequently she undertakes those performances in response to students who offer correct answers to her questions. But what we really want to know is not some abstract frequency count, but whether the teacher offers appropriate encouragement and reinforcement to students who perform well in her class. Yet it is tempting to give up trying to find out what is worth knowing for the sake of achieving precision about what may in fact be trivial. In a given period of time we may count the number of words uttered by teacher and pupil, and we can, with a little more effort, put the words and sentences into categories (e.g., structuring, soliciting, responding; defining, describing, designating; accepting, praising, questioning; and so on) and find out whose utterances fall into which categories. But to do so gives us no direct clue about the *effectiveness* of the teaching thus measured, since there is no manual for translating different categories or word counts into different degrees of goodness in teaching.

This is not to disparage the analysis of classroom discourse, or such measuring techniques as interaction analysis. Those who have worked out procedures for counting and classifying the utterances heard in teacher-pupil interactions have provided teacher educators with a powerful means of helping students to become sensitive to the patterns of language used in their own and others' classrooms. Without knowing *what* is going on, any attempt at evaluation is likely to go astray. But what is being emphasized here is the difference between measuring utterances and judging teacher effectiveness. Two observers may be in perfect agreement about what they saw and heard, yet still disagree sharply on whether the teacher in question was effective.

One way of explaining such a disagreement is to say that the observers had different criteria for evaluating available data. Another way of putting it is to say that they were evaluating different things. A teacher speaks to a child for 90 seconds, and one observer rates the teacher high because a clear and full explanation was given in response to the child's question. But another observer rates the teacher low because the teacher's discourse prevented the child from trying out his own answers. To find a way out of this puzzle, one might ask, what *constitutes* good teaching? Giving clear and complete explanations? Or stimulating independent inquiry?

The answer to the question is, of course, "both, and more besides." This answer may be a disappointment to some laymen and administrators who are looking for something simple and straightforward so they can get on with their measuring and cost–accounting procedures. But most teachers are intimately aware that it is just as important to know *when* to give an explanation or stimulate an inquiry as it is to have the *ability* to undertake such performances. Knowing when, which is a matter of timing and judgment, is not itself a performance, nor can it be simply measured by observing a single performance.

To find out about the effectiveness of teaching, we will not get very far by asking, "Does the teacher give clear and complete explanations?"[2] Instead, we must ask, "Is the teacher disposed to provide clear and complete explanations *when they are called for?*" If *this* question is not answered, then it is pointless and even misleading to find out simply *that* a teacher is able to give such explanations. It may be worth remembering that a great many people are capable of providing clear and complete explanations about matters within their own experience. Yet few of them would qualify as good *teachers*. One who *cannot* provide a good explanation *may* not be able to teach effectively, but having the ability to do it is far from a sufficient condition of competence in teaching.

When we try to find out if a person is disposed to give clear, complete

---

[2] Even if this *were* a primary criterion of competent teaching, we should stumble over the fact that the terms "clear" and "complete" cannot objectively be defined, but— if they have any sense at all—must have some reference to the condition of the person who is intended to *receive* the explanation. Hence the attempt to measure *only* the teacher's performance would be frustrated even in this apparently simple case. See Max Black, *Critical Thinking*, 2nd ed. (Englewood Cliffs, N.J.: Prentice-Hall, 1952), pp. 383-384; and John Hospers, "What is Explanation?" in Antony Flew, ed., *Essays in Conceptual Analysis* (London: Macmillan & Co., Ltd., 1956), pp. 102, 103.

explanations when they are called for, we cannot simply record or measure a performance. What we are interested in is a kind of disposition—a characteristic pattern of action that the person is likely to exhibit in a range of situations. To find out if a person has a particular sort of disposition we need not talk about the ineffable; we need, instead, to observe not one but many performances, over an extended period of time, and within a range of somewhat varying circumstances. A disposition, then, is not something that can be directly observed or measured. To ascribe a disposition to someone is to make a judgment about his tendency to behave in certain ways in certain kinds of settings. Such a judgment, based on many observations of a person's past performances, also serves as a prediction of his behavior in the future.

It is only when we have found out something about their attitudes and dispositions that we can make a sensible judgment about teachers' effectiveness. Having a disposition, of course, *implies* having whatever knowledge or skills are needed to *act* on the disposition. For example, to be disposed to provide certain kinds of explanations implies the possession of the *ability* (knowledge and skill) are needed to give those explanations—even though possession of this ability *does not imply* that one will have the disposition in question—that is, to provide explanations at an appropriate time to the appropriate people.[3]

There are many dispositions characteristic of competent teachers: sensitivity to differences among pupils, a sense of humor, fairness in the making of judgments, and clarity in the treatment of complex issues, for example. To be judged "competent," no teacher need possess *every* disposition associated with teaching effectiveness, and most teachers are only relatively effective in some respects and relatively weak in others (hence the terms "effective teacher" and "ineffective teacher," however adequate in everyday discourse, are too oversimplified for purposes of professional evaluation). But the important point is that *however* we judge teaching effectiveness, the objects of our concern are the probable and variable patterns of action called dispositions—or in some cases, traits of personality. We simply would not know what to make of long lists of the performances and utterances that teachers make.

What matters in the evaluation of teachers are their dispositions. Yet the only way to measure or assess a disposition is to record or measure a set of performances. What distinguishes this approach to the evaluation of teaching from the behavioristic orientation of PBTE is the fact that two performances may be utterly *unlike* one another, and yet *both* be exemplifications of the *same* disposition.

---

[3] Lest the importance of this disposition to a teacher be underestimated, recall the times when you were provided with a clear, complete explanation of something for which no such explanation was needed or wanted.

Let us suppose that we are observing a teacher interacting with many different children over several days' or weeks' time. We note that he gives complete explanations at certain times, partial explanations at other times, and no explanation at all at still other times. It may be easy for us to tell whether he *can* provide adequate explanations, but what we want to know is whether he provides them to the right people at the right time (for this is what is necessary to our judgment of his effectiveness as a teacher). The teacher's *varying* performances may *all* serve as evidence of this particular disposition, but in order to find this out, we must know a great deal more about the *context* in which those performances were observed. Thus we need to know the teacher's purpose in teaching the lesson; the background, interests, and abilities of particular pupils; the history of the social climate of this classroom; and other contextual factors. To ignore all this, and simply measure one or even several performances (i.e., the series of utterances that constituted one or more particular explanations) is to miss the whole point of teaching and to risk grievous misunderstanding of what the teacher is trying to do and is capable of doing. And it is just these omissions and risks that are at the heart of performance-based teacher education.

V. The Formulation and Measurement of Objectives in Teacher Education

If we are building a program of teacher education, it is crucially important for us to be as clear as we can about our goals—that is, about what kinds of teachers we want to produce—and to be clear about how to tell if we have been successful—that is, about our measurement techniques. In our efforts to achieve this clarity, we owe a great deal to those who have worked with the concept of behavioral objectives and with the techniques of precise measurement. For if a program has goals that do not indicate what sort of performances are aimed at, or how those performances are to be measured, then it is an unacceptable program.

Yet we have also seen that a program the goals of which consist *only* of lists of performances, and which evaluates success *only* in terms of the achievement of those performances, is also unacceptable. But this does not leave us with a dilemma. If we are clear about the reasons why programs must be condemned both for ignoring behavioral objectives and for being exclusively wedded to them, we will understand what our alternative is.

If we are to prepare people to be effective teachers, we need to know what such teachers would be like. Such a formulation will be cast in ordinary language. We may, for example, speak of teaching teachers to be fair or to be accepting, or to be disposed to convey information only when a pupil is ready to use it, or to tend to criticize in a way that stimulates students to improve their own work. These formulations are necessarily general in form, but *they can effectively guide practice if we can describe what particular instances of them would be like.* There is obviously no single list of performances (or behavioral objectives) that exhausts the meaning of "being fair," or "criticizing in such a way that . . .," but we *can* describe *sample* performances that would be behavioral exemplifications of those dispositions and personality traits. If we can mention clear illustrations of behavior that would satisfy our more generally stated objectives, then it is reasonable to suppose that we know what we are aiming at. And equally important, when a teacher trainee engages in a performance that we had not foreseen or planned on, we will be able to tell whether it satisfies our original aims. Thus formulating objectives in a general way and being able to mention examples of performances that would satisfy those aims not only clarifies their meaning, but also permits flexibility and expansion by allowing for the appearance of the new and unforeseen. In contrast, stating objectives *only* in terms of specific performances—the PBTE approach—locks a program into a rigid, changeless mold.

Instead of allowing our measurement techniques to dictate the form in which we cast our objectives, we can put the horse back in front of the cart, and let our objectives guide the ways in which we go about measuring the extent of our success in achieving them. A teacher who possesses only inert knowledge and isolated skills is not much use to his pupils. If he is to be an effective teacher, he must have the attitudes and dispositions that incline him to *use* his knowledge and skills in helping others to learn. It is these dispositions that must be assessed, and toward which measurement must be directed.

It has already been shown that there is considerably more to measuring the existence and strength of a disposition than there is to measuring a performance. Many teaching performances need to be observed and recorded, and they need to be interpreted in the light of the teacher's intentions, past efforts and expectations, and in the light of the particular children with whom the teacher is working. There is probably no simple way to quantify so complex a measurement, but there is no reason to suppose that the absence of quantification *ipso facto* invalidates the measurement. It is worth remembering that we are not dealing with things as simple as height or weight or cost per pound. We are trying to assess the gradually changing quality of complex human interactions. As in the case of other interactions, like love, humility, and jealously, they do not admit of intelligible quantification. ("How much do you love me?" she asked. "2.63," he solemnly replied.) But they can be carefully described and assessed.

In order to tell whether a teacher trainee has acquired the dispositions that have been judged important for effective teaching, the process of measuring must be built directly into the program itself. And because the trainee's purposes are a part of what is being assessed, his help must be sought in the measurement process. Since the value of his help will be a function of the extent to which *he* is clear about the objectives of the teacher education program, it is doubly necessary for the faculty to be clear about them.

Thus measurement is not a mechanical process, to be undertaken by some "objective" observer outside the teacher education program. Such an observer would be incapable of interpreting the meaning of the events that he witnessed. Instead, measurement in teacher education is a cooperative enterprise, involving students and faculty, and carried on throughout the entire training period. The very act of assessment, then, is likely to have an immediate effect on the performances being assessed. And as those performances change, the assessment, too, will change. If the outcome of so unstable and shifting a situation is that no concrete, standardized, and permanent measurement is ever recorded, there is at least one consolation. The person who is learning to teach is also learning the importance of continuously evaluating his own performance, and he is learning to modify his performance in the light of the evaluation. If these events become incorporated into his developing dispositions, he will be a better teacher for it.

It is to be hoped that the horse will stay in front of the cart. The point of a program of teacher education *is* to prepare teachers, and any time spent on evaluation should contribute to that objective. PBTE turns this relationship on its head and makes the preparation program subordinate to the evaluation procedures. This may be the inevitable result of a dominating concern to effect economies in the education budget. If it is, then a balance in the relation between program objectives and evaluation procedures will have to wait for a time when teacher preparation programs come under the control of the people who teach and learn in them.

14. *Minority Groups and PBTE*

Frederick A. Rodgers

During the past decade there has been a quiet though persistent evolution in teacher education under the rubric of performance-based teacher education. Since about 1970 this evolution has moved at a quickened pace as evidenced by the number of teacher training institutions formulating and initiating performance-based teacher education programs. Likewise, the teacher certification agencies in a growing number of states require teachers to complete their training in a performance-based program as a condition for being certified as a teacher in the public schools. These and related developments in teacher and other professional organizations suggest that PBTE is likely to become and remain a permanent part of the American educational scene.

The support for the growth and development of PBTE has been generated in part by the general trends toward the use of the systems approach in social activity and public demand for accountability in public institutions. Coupled with general dissatisfaction among many professional educators with present approaches to teacher education, the trend toward PBTE has found an acceptance rarely associated with the introduction of new educational approaches. The speed with which PBTE has been accepted outside and within the ranks of professional educators encouraged the adoption of these programs without careful consideration of the possible consequences that might result from such an approach to the education of teachers. Now that PBTE has become entrenched on a large enough scale to expose the intricacies of its approach to training and its effects on the educational process, it is possible to analyze it critically in

This article was prepared especially for this volume.

terms of general and specific learner and instructional demands. With this as background, I will focus on PBTE in terms of learning and instructional demands of minority group students.

In the main PBTE is characterized by at least five essential elements. These elements are:

1. The public statement of specific behavioral objectives in terms of the teaching competencies to be demonstrated.
2. The public statement of criteria and standards employed to assess competencies at prescribed mastery levels.
3. The prime evidence for assessment to be based on the performance of a prospective teacher.
4. The dependence of the individual student program rate on demonstrated competency.
5. The development and evaluation of specific competencies to be facilitated by the instructional program.

Accordingly, PBTE is characterized by the (1) individualization and personalization of instruction, (2) the use of feedback to guide the learning experience of prospective teachers, (3) a systematic program approach, (4) an emphasis on the exit requirements for certifying competence, (5) the modularization of instruction, and (6) holding the student accountable for his performance in a teacher preparation program. Combining the essential elements and the resulting characteristics of PBTE, a picture emerges that can be critically viewed and analyzed to take into account other outcomes expected of the educational enterprise. One such expectation deals with the effective and efficient education of minority group students within a social context that supports and extends a healthy individual emotional outlook and enhances the extension of democratic principles to serve all members of our society. I shall judge PBTE in the spirit of this statement.

Teacher Education and Minority Groups[1]

One of the prime concerns of the American citizenry during the recent past has been the quality of social service being provided members of

---

[1] "Minority" in this paper is used to refer to members of our society who are disadvantaged because they are born into a particular group. The use of this term further implies that common characteristics such as cultural and traditional life styles, poverty, social standing, attitudes and values, prejudice, lack of useful information, and limited exposure negatively affect those so classified in their ability to profit equally (compared to the majority) from their school experience. In some instances the term

minority groups. The social service area that has encouraged not only the most attention and group interaction but also conflict and cooperation has been the delivery of educational services. In the area of educational services, attention has been devoted primarily to the quality of the teacher's relationship with students while conducting and directing the instructional and learning experience of his charges. This has led to an intense examination of the teaching process that is evident in classrooms and how that process might be influenced by the type of training teachers have received. With regard to the preparation of teachers who can work more effectively (achieve measurable results) with minority students, the training emphasis has ranged from exclusive emphasis on the teacher's knowledge of content and unique learning conditions to the attitude and value structure he possesses. Given this continuum, notions concerning the creation or adaptation of teacher education programs to replace teachers slated to work with the minority students have zeroed in on either end though elements of both concerns are always included. However, the predominant characteristic of teacher preparation programs attempting to train teachers to work with minority group students was its basic focus on influencing the attitude and value structure of prospective teachers. This notion serves as the basis for exploring PBTE patterns for training teachers to work with minority group students.

According to the literature, the preparation of teachers for minority students should concentrate on developing a new system of pedagogy geared to the teaching of children from low-income families. This assertion is based on the theory that most teachers have not experienced the daily realities of minority group life and do not appreciate its values or its life styles. Therefore, most teachers are unable to help these children to profit from school experiences. In order to aid prospective teachers in developing an appreciation of other life styles and environmental realities, teacher trainees should be required to familiarize themselves with greater amounts of sociological and anthropological material. Coupled with this new content emphasis, trainees should be exposed to carefully planned community field trips, home visits, and student internship in a variety of realistic situations. Emphasis should be placed on providing trainees with first-hand experience with the daily life conditions of minority group children so that they can gain a better understanding of the motivations and justifications governing the actions of the children they teach and their respective families. In short, teacher preparation for teachers who work with minority group students must deal preponderantly with the affective component of teaching in order to affect positively interpersonal relations that enhance the

---

"minority" will be used in the same sense that "disadvantaged" is employed to identify youth for whom the school experience is not effective, rewarding, or personally satisfying.

learning potential of those taught. Any model for the preparation of teachers for minority group students has to include experiences that enable the prospective teacher to develop a healthy respect for these youth and their life styles. To accomplish this task, teacher education must have as its prime function the changing of teacher attitudes within the context of our democratic value system.

Areas of Concern

When one focuses on the essential elements and the resulting characteristics of PBTE, many areas of concern for the education of youth become apparent. PBTE as a teacher preparation approach has as its prime concern the training of personnel who are competent intellectually, academically, emotionally, and socially to help youth acquire knowledge and attitudes needed to contribute to and compete in our democratic society. In this sense, PBTE—like all teacher–education programs—must prepare teachers who have the skills required to shape the learning behavior of youth consistent with our democratic way of life and the requirements for meeting the basic needs of our society. PBTE has to be judged in relation to its ability to deal with product expectation of all teacher–education programs.

The first concern with PBTE and its effects on the education of minority group students is in the precise definition of teaching roles and behavioral objectives in which teachers are expected to become competent. Research in teacher education has presented us with a confused and sometimes conflicting set of teacher characteristics that are used as the basis for defining a teacher's role. Some of these characteristics focus on the teacher's behavior as a person and as an information processer, while others focus on situational variables and student performance outcomes as the appropriate basis for defining teaching roles. Presently, specific problems that are related to teacher role definition acknowledge the importance of identifying teaching charactertistics by employing different methodological and theoretical approaches. Consequently, there is no way of deciding which approach provides the best analysis of the teaching act that could serve as a basis for describing and defining the role required of teachers instructing minority group students. This situation is understandable when one considers that the ultimate criterion for judging good teaching results from one's value orientation. As long as different value orientations have to be accommodated in the schools, the role definition of good teaching remains an open and public issue.

Unfortunately, the proponents of PBTE have defined too narrowly those who should pass judgment on the nature of good teaching. In the main, proponents of PBTE have based their role definition of good teaching, and the behavior objectives that prospective teachers should demonstrate, on the thinking of a few educators who have spent considerable time and effort experiencing, thinking, researching, and writing in the area of teacher education. There is little evidence that consideration for the concerns and perferences of the clients (children and their parents) have influenced the thrust of PBTE to date. This represents a serious omission because it changes the value placed on the judgments of different interest groups associated with the schools. In this sense, PBTE represents some negation of the gains parents have made in acquiring a voice in the determination of policy affecting the education of their children.

During the 1960s, parents of minority group students argued and fought for the right to help determine the goals of educational practice so critical to the type of school experience their children were to receive. The parents' concerns also covered the nature of the training experience that would be critical to the success of prospective teachers with their children. After many hard-fought battles the concept of parental contribution to the decision-making activity affecting their children's educational experience has been generally accepted as a valuable addition to the wisdom employed to guide school activity. PBTE appears, in fact, to have ignored the principle of parental involvement in decision-making by restricting the range of judgment sources for defining appropriate teacher roles and by specifying behavioral objectives that prospective teachers are to master. This raises critical questions such as "Who shall be judge?" "What is evidence?" "Is the evidence admissible?" "What are appropriate criteria and standards for admissible evidence?" and "What sanctions are to be employed when deviations are noted?" PBTE places entirely too much emphasis on the quantitative judgments of professional educators as opposed to the qualitative judgments of those (parents and students) to be served. Using this as a basis for the preparation of teachers of minority group students sets back the progress that has been made toward expanding the number, quality, and experience of judges such that *the evidence[2] of teaching quality is admissible as valid data for clients to judge the quality of educational experience delivered by the schools.* Without this consideration, PBTE returns to a pattern of professional educators deciding what values are important in teaching behavior. If the right to this kind of decision-making is not granted to representatives of the ultimate recipients of PBTE by its proponents, an unacceptable pattern of educational practice is likely to be perpetuated. Judgments of "good" or "effective" teaching are yet too value-laden to risk the exclusion of those served when teacher educa-

---

[2] A more complete discussion of the nature of evidence in education is now being developed by Robert L. Wolf, a graduate student in CIRCE at the University of Illinois. His insight into this area has aided me greatly in considering this topic.

tion programs are being formulated, implemented, and evaluated. PBTE can continue to ignore this reality and thus sow the seeds for its eventual demise. However, it may do so after causing irreversible damage to those who attempted to follow a trend without a critical analysis of the possible consequences.

The second area of concern with PBTE and minority students deals with the emphasis on individualization, personalization, and modularization of the content and behaviors to be learned and demonstrated with a preset level of acceptable competence. With the present quasi-religious fervor suffusing advocacy of individualized instruction as the predominant instructional mode, I will risk being labeled sacrilegious by asserting that this method is inappropriate for prospective teachers of the minority group students. Since individualization of learning experiences is one of the cornerstones of PBTE, some attention should be directed at analyzing some of the possible consequences resulting from too heavy an emphasis on this mode of instruction. In the main, individualization of instruction in PBTE provides for rates of speed appropriate to the individuals for widely differing backgrounds and purposes, and for instruction that is highly person- and situation-specific. In addition, it allows the student to select, direct, and evaluate parts of his program, to report his own educational opportunity, and to plan ahead for his own growth and development. On the surface, individualization of instruction in PBTE appears to be a mode of pedagogy that encompasses all of the positive aspects of individual learning. A closer look, however, reveals some disturbing realities. Teaching is primarily a group activity because there must be some type of interaction between at least two people. Learning to teach probably requires group interaction to provide a reasonable degree of authenticity and understanding of concepts in teaching that can only be explained and described in a group context. For example, the concept of classroom control cannot be demonstrated by a prospective teacher through a prepared individualized program since a "control" situation is specific and defined by group characteristics involved. In teacher training, a prospective teacher might be able to learn and demonstrate knowledge of *the rules of teaching behavior through an individualized program, but mastery of many teaching concepts require learning in a group context.*

Another problem with the individualization of instruction in PBTE and training teachers to work with minority group students is the requirement that a great deal of attention be paid to affective factors in teaching when working with these kinds of students. Teachers of minority students must be able to relate to them as people worthy of respect, and a quality program of instructional experience is necessary. Evidence suggests that that teachers who are successful in this have mastered the affective areas of the teaching act to an extent that minority group students feel a bond and a respect that enable them to achieve more than would have been the case if the teacher did not have these skills. The mastery of affective skills needed to teach minority students requires learning to take place in a special, situation-specific context. For example, a white middle-class teacher who was socialized completely in all all-white, small-town community from birth to adulthood cannot learn to relate to black children from poor urban areas in a preplanned individualized program of instruction. It is not possible to know beforehand what attitudes a prospective teacher from such a background needs to revise and in what direction. It is probably erroneous to assume that all white teachers from such a background have the same attitudes toward a specific group of black children. Likewise, it is equally erroneous to assume that all white trainees have similar dispositions toward the affective areas of teaching. It is extremely unlikely that concepts describing the affective components of the teaching act can be taught on an individualized basis because of the requirement of group interaction to determine what skills the prospective teacher needs to develop. Since affective factors appear to be critical to the effective teaching of minority students, the emphasis on individualized instruction in PBTE does not appear to offer a reasonable alternative to present teacher–education programs.

The personalization of training suggested by PBTE appears to ask the prospective teacher to choose modes of learning and activities in accord with his personal preference. On the surface, one could conclude that this heightens interest and involvement because of the greater match between the task to be accomplished and use of techniques that are personally satisfying. This approach neglects the use of different methodologies that are unique to the development and understanding of knowledge in specific content areas. This latter notion requires the effective teacher to master a repertoire of methodologies that are appropriate to learning and understanding concepts in a number of different content areas, even if some of the methodologies are not personally satisfying. A professional teacher has the responsibility to learn methods of teaching and learning that transcend personal perferences. If PBTE fails to adhere to this standard of competency, it has precipitated the ultimate barrier to the personalization of teacher development. Skills in teaching are beyond the personal preferences of those who aspire to teach. A teacher's training should open new vistas for prospective teachers by exposing them to new possibilities for enhancing the teaching/learning experience.

Modularization of instruction is another characteristic of PBTE that is not necessarily conducive to training prospective teachers to work with minority students. For PBTE, a module is a set of learning activities (with objectives, prerequisites, pre-assessment, instructional activities, post-assessment, and remediation) intended to facilitate the student's acquisition and demonstration of a particular competency. According to the evidence, modularization of instruction is likely to contribute more to the learning of the person who constructed the module than the person who uses it as a learning device. This conclusion is supported by the findings from tutoring experiences involving disadvantaged students at different age levels. When low-achieving high school disadvantaged students were asked to tutor low-achieving elementary school disadvantaged students in reading, the high school students gained in their own ability to read. In effect, the results indicate that the tutor made greater gains than the individual receiving the instruction in this particular teaching experience. When prospective teachers are asked to acquire and demonstrate knowledge of teaching through the use of modules, there is considerable question as to whether the student gains what the author intended and, as such, learns to perform without mastering the critical assumptions underlying the learning activity. It might be more useful if PBTE would borrow from attempts to provide minority students with an effective educational experience, and have prospective teachers write modules outlining learning activities that will enable one to acquire and demonstrate a particular competency. There would be a greater probability of mastery than would be the case if the same student were asked to study a module constructed by someone else. This seems to be a notion well worth consideration by the proponents of PBTE, especially as it relates to the preparation of teachers for minority students.

Another area of concern for PBTE involves the demonstration of teaching roles. This is a particularly critical consideration because of the apparent focus on the performance of teaching competencies with little emphasis on academic competencies. There is almost universal agreement that many minority group students are extremely deficient in the skills and knowledge necessary to understand new ideas that contribute to personal development through independent learning experiences. Any teacher faced with such children has to be proficient in the methodology of teaching, the skills associated with processing information in a particular content area, and the knowledge of the subject matter serving as the medium of communication. When a teacher attempts to work with minority students, it is absolutely necessary that he be able to explain a concept in a variety of ways utilizing examples and analogies appropriate both to the conceptual development of the content and the experience background of the learner. There is little doubt that in these instances teachers must have academic mastery over the prerequisite skills and content they employ to communicate with minority students.

According to the notions concerning demonstrated teaching competencies expressed in PBTE, there seems too little attention paid to the demonstration of academic competence in content areas intended to be used with minority students. By way of example, it is possible for a prospective teacher in a PBTE program to demonstrate mastery of 10 steps of reading maps and still fail to utilize properly a map in a teaching situation. For instance, to learn to read a map does not necessarily enable a teacher to infer associated factors and other significant relationships. Furthermore, mastering the steps to reading a map does not ensure a teacher's ability to help students to visualize the reality a symbol represents on a particular map. The major point is that competence in a particular skill cannot be demonstrated in a short time span and without considerable effort on the part of the learner to master the skill in question. *Real competence requires a perfect match between talent and the task to be performed and many, many long hours of dedicated practice.* The use of competence as a defining characteristic for outcomes resulting from experiences gained in a PBTE program is either an overstatement of the products or an understatement of its real meaning. The present description of teaching competence employed by PBTE would produce teachers who are ill-prepared to deal with the academic competencies required to teach minority students effectively.

The final area of concern with PBTE and minority groups deals with the motivation necessary to get any student to expend the effort required to learn effectively. Even though the proponents of PBTE do not deal directly with student motivation as a factor in the demonstrated performance of teachers, it is at the foundation of any attempt to teach minority children in particular. According to the rationale of PBTE, it is possible for a prospective teacher to acquire the skills of motivation and to demonstrate his teaching competence in motivating students. Teaching competence in the area of student motivation cannot be demonstrated apart from reference to a particular child in a particular situation. Students are internally motivated to learn all sorts of materials for their own reasons. Some children are motivated to learn by peer approval, teacher approval, personal desires to excel, the need to impress a significant person, or many factors that remain undetectable. The point here is that the teacher cannot demonstrate competence in motivating students in a vacuum. In regard to the relationship between teaching and student motivation, the teacher can be characterized in terms of a good offensive lineman on a football team. The really good offensive lineman avoids direct contact to move the defensive lineman against his direction of movement. His solution is to discern the direction in which the defensive lineman is headed and to provide the necessary force to keep him going a little bit faster and a bit farther than he intended to go. The teacher of minority students must be able to determine the direction chosen by the learners and apply the necessary push to keep him going a little bit faster and a bit farther than they had dreamed or intended. The PBTE pattern does not enable teachers to learn firsthand the critical role that the internal motivations of students play in their own learning. PBTE appears to assume that skills of student motivation can be learned, thus perceiving an affective state as external to the learner. It is questionable that the PBTE pattern can help prospective teachers demonstrate teaching competence in student motivation apart from actual practice with real children.

PBTE is a good idea if its application is limited to a scope commensurate with the areas the approach covers adequately. The major shortcoming of PBTE is revealed when it is pushed as a total program for the education and preparation of teachers. Like all specific cures for specific ills, the misapplication of the remedy is likely to cause patients to fail to seek an appropriate cure that is readily available in other places. PBTE comes dangerously close to being advocated as a cure for all of our educational and instructional ills resulting from the preparation of educational personnel. This is an unfortunate development for all children who will be taught by teachers so narrowly trained, but it is particularly disastrous for minority students who require teaching competence that is more broadly based. The preparation of teachers is still a value-laden activity because there are conflicting notions regarding what constitutes "good" or "effective" teaching. PBTE will not resolve the issues associated with this problem and will probably do a disservice if the approach causes educators to belittle the importance of value conflicts that are reflected in present teacher–education programs. It is entirely possible that the vitality of our democratic society results from our constant search for and use of different perspectives for interpreting the values guiding the selection and presentation of knowledge to youth. To the extent that PBTE fails to honor this tradition, we run the risk of overlooking important new developments that enhance the human condition. That is not an appropriate outcome of any teacher–education program.

15. *A Humanistic Approach to Performance–Based Teacher Education*

Paul Nash

Preface

Last spring (1972) I was invited by the AACTE Committee on Perform-ance-Based Teacher Education to prepare a paper on "the humanistic element in performance-based [teacher] preparation programs." I accepted the assignment and set out to complete the first stage, which was to prepare an outline of my proposed paper for perusal by the PBTE Committee. In preparing this outline, I took a number of questions that the Committee had prepared concerning the humanistic element in PBTE and used them as the main structure of my paper. By taking the essence of each question and turning it into a topic, I obtained my section headings. I then went to the literature on PBTE and combed it for issues, questions, ideas, subtopics, and criticisms that were relevant to my paper and organized this material under the previously assigned section headings. Thus my outline was virtually complete and with little further work I sent it to the PBTE Committee for their response.

The outline was approved, and I was encouraged to proceed to write a first draft of the paper. This I began to do and at first I made reasonable progress. Then my writing was interrupted by a number of other very absorbing activities (a month-long research and lecture trip to England; teaching a summer course on humanistic education at the University of California, Berkeley; traveling across the country; settling in the East again after 15 months in California; and so on). When I picked up the threads

Source. Paul Nash, *A Humanistic Approach to Performance Based Teacher Education* (Washington, D.C.: American Association of Colleges for Teacher Education, 1973). Reprinted by permission of the author and AACTE.

of the paper again, I began to experience severe difficulties with it. By this time I had received a number of reactions from readers of my initial outline. These covered a variety of issues but, although occasionally helpful on specific points, they did not alleviate my general feeling of uneasiness about the paper I was writing.

When I had the paper about two-thirds completed, my dissatisfaction with it became acute. The writing itself was going excruciatingly slowly, I found myself reluctant to find time for it in my schedule and, worst of all, as I reread what I had written, I discovered that often it did not even convince *me*. At this point I forced myself to stop and take stock of what was going on. My reflections over several days led me to a somewhat sobering conclusion. I came to realize that my loss of creative energy, enthusiastic commitment, and effective productivity all stemmed from the same cause: I was writing someone else's paper rather than my own. In a sense I was "performing" for the PBTE Committee. My uncritical acceptance of their questions as the organizing basis for my paper had been a disastrous beginning. From that point, other mistakes followed with sequential inevitability. Even the working title of my paper now appeared, on reflection, to be the wrong way to take hold of the problem.

I was faced with a painful dilemma. I could grind through and complete the paper somehow, knowing that I would not be satisfied with it and that it would not really represent me. Or, I could throw it all out and begin afresh, starting this time from the center of myself, saying what *I* uniquely had to say and relating it to the data and demands of the outside world. The second choice would mean a new investment of my time and energy in a project that I was already beginning to resent in terms of ill-spent effort. But the first choice was even more distasteful, as was the alternative of abandoning the project altogether, which would mean breaking a contract with people who had given time and commitment to it.

So I chose to start again. This time I determined to "perform" only for myself. As I moved into the writing I found that my energy, productivity, and commitment returned as I dealt with topics, ideas, and feelings that meant a great deal to me personally and in which I had a large stake. The organization of the paper now emerged from my own central concerns as these encountered the demands and limits of PBTE. Instead of feeling weak and derivative in my presentation, I gained a strong feeling of being willing to stand firmly behind everything I wrote—without feeling a need to impose my convictions on others.

This paper is the outcome of that second attempt. What had happened was that I had originally trapped myself into taking a nonhumanistic approach to the project of preparing the paper. I am not proud of this lapse, and it involves a considerable risk for me to share this publicly. But I do so because I think my own experience illustrates the central thing

I am trying to say in this paper. That is, *a humanistic approach to education implies that I be centrally and fully present in whatever I undertake*. If we want to nurture people's creative energies, we must try to organize education in such a way that their "performance" will relate to their own innermost yearnings and convictions. PBTE can serve humanistic purposes only if it avoids the kind of external demands for performances that are experienced by the individual as alienating and enervating because of their lack of relation to the deepest parts of himself.

Introduction

In thinking about a humanistic approach to performance-based teacher education, it seems immediately important to become clear about how the word "humanistic" is being used. This raises several problems, since definitions of humanistic tend either to be circular or to lead to an endless regression. Thus, we can say that humanistic is that which fosters humane purposes, but that leads us into a similar definitional process from the word "humane." Or we can say that humanistic is that which concerns the humanness of man. Hence anything that develops a fuller humanness will pass the humanistic test. But what is "human" in this sense? Clearly, we are on the brink of launching into an endless process.

Let me step back and suggest another way. Rather than making a frontal attack on the problem of definition, in an attempt to encapsulate it forever, let me be more indirect and mobile in my approach. This might offer a better chance of making the acquaintance of this large and boundary-shifting concept. One aspect of this approach will be to describe some of my bedfellows—always a self-revealing practice for a lover. The other aspect will be to reveal some of my working assumptions, in particular my assumptions about the nature of the "man" with whose "humanness" I am concerned.

Those who acknowledge themselves as humanistic educators are a diverse group, with overlapping concerns and values that are drawn from a wide range of backgrounds, traditions, disciplines, and fields. They agree in putting man, rather than a doctrine or dogma, at the center of their valuing system.

The humanistic approach to education draws upon many sources, including the humanistic psychology of Rogers and Maslow; the existential psychiatry of May and Frankl; the existential philosophy of Buber and Marcel; the existential theology of Tillich; the propriate psychology of Allport; the work of Assagioli on psychosynthesis; the work of Alschuler on psychological education; the gestalt therapy theory and practice of Perls; the emphasis on individual growth in the progressive tradition of Rousseau, Pestalozzi, and Froebel; some aspects of the pragmatic philosophy of Peirce, James, and Dewey; the utopian and futuristic notions of what man might become in the work of writers from Plato to Michael Young; the work of Simon on value clarification; the work of Newberg and others on affective education; the work of Brown on confluent education; the work of Weinstein on the education of the self; the personalist philosophy of Macmurray; the work of Benne on authority relationships, human relations, and education; the contributions of the human relations movement, as seen in the National Training Laboratories, the Esalen Institute, and other centers; and the radical pedagogy of men like Holt and Dennison. Somewhat more ambiguously located in this picture, and causing uneasiness for some of the people mentioned above, are a number of other sources. These include counter-culture critics like Roszak; disestablishment figures like Illich and Freire; radical sociologists like Friedenberg and Mills; socialist humanists like Fromm; and critics of dehumanization like Marx and Engels.

It would be foolish, of course, to try to put all of these writers into a Procrustean bed. But I must personally acknowledge that I have been significantly jostled by all of them. Let me move, then, from this listing of some of my bedfellows to an announcement about the offspring of our conjugation. I should like to try to advance the discussion of the meaning of "humanistic" by stating my assumptions about the nature of man—the focus of our attempted humanizing.

I see man as a free, unique creature, capable of attaining a self-direction and a creative productivity that stem from his whole person. His freedom implies responsibility and enables him to choose. He is capable, at best, of interdependence and of being an agent of constructive social change. I shall now take this statement of my assumptions and treat the rest of this paper as an extended examination of it. Thus the remainder of my paper will be an attempt to define the notion of humanistic by successive illustrations. Each of the key terms in my statement of assumptions will become a heading under which to examine the problems involved in attempting to make PBTE a more humanistic enterprise.

Freedom

Most humanistic assumptions about the nature of man stem from a basic belief in man as a free creature. This notion of freedom does not imply that human behavior is uncaused, totally random, or uncontrollable, nor does it mean that man is uninfluenced by his environment, his personal history, or his experiences. Rather, it means that he is, in the last analysis, able to make significant personal choices, to frame purposes, to initiate actions, and to take a measure of control over his own life.[1] This philo-

---

[1] For a fuller discussion of the philosophical underpinnings of this position, see Paul Nash, *Authority and Freedom in Education* (New York: Wiley, 1966), Chap. 5.

sophical position is deeply embedded in the western intellectual tradition, but in this century it has been refined by some aspects of pragmatism, with its emphasis on reflective action, learning through experience, and estimating the consequences of different choices. It has also been enriched by existential and phenomenological philosophies, with their focus on concepts like intention, meaning, choice, self–perception, freedom, and responsibility.

A humanistic framework for PBTE would lead us in certain directions and highlight certain problems. The close connection between freedom and purposefulness suggests that the proper education of humans will encourage them to learn to act deliberately and intentionally out of self–framed goals. This attempt to foster purposeful action arising from the integrated experiences of the individual will be threatened by any move to regard human behavior merely as isolated pieces of action with clearly identifiable antecedent stimuli. The humanistic approach will encourage the inclusion in PBTE programs of concern for self–direction, responsibility for one's own learning, involvement in the present learning experience, and the development of qualities like curiosity, wonder, awe, imagination, commitment, openness, and respect for self and others.[2]

Needless to say, in this direction lie some enormous problems of measurement and evaluation. It seems impossible to develop a PBTE program without being able to measure the performances that are deemed desirable. The perennial danger is that whatever cannot be measured will simply be excluded. But, according to humanistic criteria, this would leave out, given our present level of skill in measuring, the most crucial educational values. If the measuring is done by an external evaluator, it may be impossible to distinguish desirable from undesirable behavior. What the humanistic educator wants to develop is "free" (in the sense of intentional, deliberate, integrative, goal-oriented) action. But this may, at any one observed moment, be indistinguishable in its external manifestations from random or manipulated behavior.

Humanistic education gives considerable importance to self–motivation. It is assumed that tasks calling for long lasting commitment, a great range

---

[2] My earlier formulation of desirable emphases in PBTE was incorporated into Stanley Elam's paper in the following form: "1) developing in the student the self-confidence to remain immersed in the learning experience long enough and deeply enough to make the assimilation of that experience personally relevant; 2) encouraging a wide-angled, existentialist vision of his learning experience that will enable him to remain open to unpredicted learning outcomes; . . . 3) developing independent and inter-dependent thinking; 4) helping the student to clarify his preferred learning and teaching styles and allowing him to develop them." Stanley Elam, *Performance-Based Teacher Education: What is the State of the Art?* (Washington, D.C.: AACTE, 1971), p. 19.

of a person's capabilities, or special creativity or initiative, require strong intrinsic motivation for their accomplishment.[3] But where PBTE rests upon one group of people establishing objectives for another group of people to meet, external motivation, in the form of various rewards and punishments, will usually be employed. Thus we risk increasing student passivity and the inability to make strong choices and develop personal goals. We also tend to focus education on those routine and simple tasks whose performance is most amenable to external motivation.

Uniqueness

The humanistic view of men and women regards each one as a unique, unprecedented, unrepeatable creation. Man is, in Martin Buber's words, "the source of all surprise in the universe." Each person contains an essential element of distinctness and hence unpredictability. Although insurance companies can, with highly profitable accuracy, predict the life expectancies of categories of people, their computers cannot tell us the day that you or I will die. Predictions that correctly forecast the behavior of large groups of people are frequently helpless to tell us what any one person in those groups will do. PBTE with a humanistic tone would therefore respect this human uniqueness and unpredictability and be highly conscious of the dangers of crushing some of man's most essentially human qualities under a weight of behavioral objectives.

The practical question is whether it is possible to reconcile a humanistic concern for human uniqueness with the effective use of a performance-based approach. It is not hard to find people who pay lip service to "individual differences." What is enormously difficult is to balance the individual claims of personal morality, choice, responsibility, and self-worth against the social claims of regularity, comparison, ranking, and uniformity There is wide agreement that the educational system is in serious need of greater flexibility, more options and alternatives, and more genuine pluralism.[4] And it may well be that a judicious use of PBTE can help to break open some old rigidities, such as grades, credits, and schedules, and introduce some flexibility and alternatives that will constitute a humanizing influence on teacher education. It also holds promise of enabling teachers to become certified without ever attending an institution, a promise that might have a humanizing effect even before its realization.

However, there are also some hazards in PBTE that threaten human-

---

[3] See Thomas C. Thomas and Dorothy McKinney, *Accountability in Education* (Menlo Park, Calif.: Stanford Research Institue, 1972), pp. 24-26, for a useful discussion of incentives and accountability.

[4] See Thomas and McKinney, op. cit., Part IV, for a clear exposition of alternatives within the system.

istic values. One of these hazards lies in the process of classifying itself. There can be no PBTE without classification of people. But to decide to classify students is a value choice. We are not compelled to classify: we could regard each student as unique and incommensurable. No doubt there are often good reasons—administrative, pedagogical, conceptual— for classifying students. The danger is that the process of classification becomes so attractive and mind-satisfying (not to say soul-satisfying) to the classifier, that he continues the process even when clear justification has ceased and he may convince people (often including himself) that the labels of classification have a permanence and significance that in fact do harm to human potentiality. Research on teacher expectations (the Pygmalion effect) demonstrates with alarming clarity the power of our conceptual classifications to overwhelm our perceptions of persons. The morals are easy to see but hard to apply: never classify people unless there is a clear and defensible justification; classify only as a last resort; do not mistake the label for the person; and change or remove the label as soon as possible.

This leads us to the problem of the persistent tension between the unique, personal meanings that the individual gives to events and the general standards of behavior that society demands of him. A humanistic education would help us to live with this tension without fleeing from one pole or the other. A danger in PBTE is that it may militate against the maintenance of this tension by an inappropriate or unduly exclusive focus on external behavior. The long standing criticism of behavioral objectives, that their use is suitable for only the simplest and crudest educational functions and does not lend itself to complex and subtle functions, is often presented in over-simplistic terms. But the criticism is touching upon something of real significance. Personal perceptions and attitudes are more deeply seated and harder to influence than external behavior. The performance-based approach, with its focus on external behavior, may direct us away from the most important elements in education, which lie in the personal meanings that people give to events. The causes of behavior lie always in these personal meanings rather than in the external appearance of events. But since these meanings are personally unique they are not amenable to general measurement.

A performance-based program that meets humanistic criteria will be one that serves to enhance the unique teaching-learning style of each individual. The alteration of trained behavior among teachers may not be the best way to improve the quality of the teaching-learning process. What most affects students is the interaction around the edges of formal pedagogy, the incidentals of classroom life, the spontaneous responses that come from the depths of the teacher's personality rather than her trained reactions, which she is liable to forget in crises or when she is unselfconscious. A constant danger in the behavioral approach is that of backsliding once the reinforcement is removed. If the "right" way to teach is not congenial to the teacher's unique personality, she will tend to abandon it when she is not being observed or measured.

Overall, what is at issue is the tension or conflict between the claims of society on the individual and the claims of the individual for himself. PBTE serves to remind us that the individual does not live alone, that his actions have consequences for others, that membership in society implies obligations through measurable performance. On the other hand, a humanistic quality is required in PBTE to remind us that the individual is not wholly explained by his group, that he is something more than a member of society, that his person is more precious than his membership label, and that human life is impoverished if demands for performance snuff out or depreciate the individual's unique capacity for joy, zest, curiosity, awe, wonder, or humor. In the face of a largely unpredictable future, it is difficult to justify the sacrifice of these individual human qualities for the sake of higher performance in skills or attributes whose future worth cannot be reliably estimated.

Creativity

The rapid pace of social change makes it increasingly difficult to forecast with confidence what will be "right" behavior in the future. Some central humanistic concerns become of even greater importance in such times of rapid change. I refer to qualities such as a high tolerance for ambiguity, a willingness to postpone closure, an ability to operate effectively within unclear or open structures, and a capacity for using fantasy, metaphor, and symbols in problem solving. These are all qualities that are positively correlated with creativity. In times of uncertainty about the future, the capacity to deal flexibly, creatively, and effectively with unprecedented situations and problems becomes of cardinal importance.

It seems possible that PBTE can bring about some of the structural flexibility that encourages creativity. For example, one can already see promise, in the literature at least, that PBTE can increase the number of routes to certification, break the monopoly of conventional teacher-training institutions, introduce more alternatives and perhaps a genuine pluralism into the system, and be deliberately designed to encourage innovation and experimentation.

But we must recognize that formidable difficulties and serious dangers to the nurture of creativity also accompany PBTE. When we set out to measure performance, it is difficult to avoid notions like right answers, correct behavior, and predicted outcomes. But creativity suffers badly under such conditions, for creative solutions or inventions are necessarily unpredictable and usually unique to a particular problem or condition. It is a formidable task to be ingenious enough to prevent the search for behavioral objectives from leading to convergence of thinking, fixed models of appropriate behavior, and the closing down of alternatives. The humanistic quest is to encourage the development of teachers who are both creative themselves and capable of enhancing the creative energies of their students. We need to build places and atmospheres where we can be awakened by surprise. This will inevitably mean leaving room for the unpredictable to occur.

Moreover, we have much evidence now of the important role of play in the fostering of creativity. A period of free play with materials, tools, concepts, ideas, or whatever, seems to be an essential preliminary to the creative use of them. It also seems to be necessary that this play take place in a low-risk, low-threat atmosphere without regard for goals or objectives. Otherwise, the subsequent ideas or outcomes adhere too closely to convention and precedent and fail to break new ground. Thus, we face a serious dilemma. To the degree that PBTE demands predictable outcomes, fixed goals, and measurable performances, it threatens the nurture of that atmosphere of unpressured, present-oriented playfulness that is a crucial element in the development of creativity.

Productivity

One can hope that PBTE will bring about or encourage the development of a clearer relationship between theory and practice, through emphasizing the need to look at the practical outcomes of theoretical hypotheses. This emphasis on the practical consequences, the tangible payoff, the productive outcomes, can be a very healthy tendency in a field that often operates largely on faith in unexamined tradition. It is important to note, however, that this approach is based upon certain assumptions. These include particularly the notion of productivity as a positive value. It might be widely agreed that we want teachers and students to be "productive." But this idea is so powerful in affecting our behavior that we must look carefully at how the notion of productivity is being used, whether there are numerous meanings of the term, and if so which ones we want to foster and which discourage.

The view that PBTE is merely another example of the invasion of education by business, on a par with the exchange of a guaranteed student performance for a fixed sum of money, is an oversimplification. Nevertheless, the performance that is demanded in PBTE is often spoken of in language that is closely akin to that used to describe attempts to raise industrial productivity or business efficiency. We should be sensitive to the use of the metaphor of industrial productivity and try to estimate its appropriateness to the tasks of teaching and learning.

There are significant dangers, from a humanistic viewpoint, in an uncritical use in PBTE of industrial notions like productivity, efficiency, and cost-effectiveness. An example, perhaps unwitting, of these dangers comes in Weber and Cooper's fictional scenario for a program of competency-based teacher education.[5] In it, they picture a prospective faculty member, Jeff Craig, meeting with a present faculty member, Betty Fry, who is explaining the competency-based program in the university and the way it is evaluated through the use of a cost-effectiveness criterion. In the interview, Jeff asks, "What do you mean by 'cost-effectiveness' data?" Betty replies, "For example, some instructional processes such as computer-assisted instruction are expensive to develop and operate. If relatively few students are choosing this instructional alternative, then we need to know that *in order to decide whether or not it's worth it to continue to offer CAI as an alternative.*"[6]

I do not know whether Weber and Cooper intended to present this as a desirable model of decision–making, and I do not want to saddle them with this responsibility if they did not intend it as such. But the point of the authors' intention is relatively unimportant. What is at issue is that they have shown us an example of the inhumane ways in which a narrow notion of "efficiency" or "productivity" can be used to evaluate programs and make educational decisions. To say that cheap programs are in and expensive programs are out may be sound business practice, but it does not meet the criteria of humanistic education.

What, then, would be a humanistic notion of productivity? It is one in which the productiveness comes from the center of the person. It is creative energy as an expression of individual potency. The humanistic ideal of the productive teacher would be more closely akin to the creative artist than to the assembly-line worker. The kind of productivity I am advocating is a creativeness that stems from inner urgings rather than an activity that responds to an authority, a hypnotist, a jailer, or a controller. Humanistic productivity many be seen as a sort of creative synthesis between accurate perceptions of the world and personal alterations of it. Under PBTE programs we may be in danger of facilitating the education of accurate perceivers who are nevertheless not genuinely productive because they have no idea how to alter their world personally.

There is also the danger that external demands for productivity from teachers may have deleterious effects on their morale if the forms of productivity are unrelated to their inner needs and goals. One consequence of PBTE may be to make teachers feel greater press, anxiety, inadequacy, and guilt, feelings that are dysfunctional in their work with students. At

---

[5] Wilfred A. Weber and James M. Cooper, *Competency-Based Teacher Education: A Scenario* (Washington, D.C.: AACTE, 1972).

[6] Ibid, p. 12 (Italics added).

a time when other forces such as economic uncertainty, emotional insecurity in the face of rapid change, and the threat of unemployment in a contracting field, also press upon teachers, their greatest needs may be for psychological support, time for reflection, and the strengthening of confidence in their own unique productive capacities.

The external evaluation and measurement of someone else's productivity also raises serious questions about the relationship between the subjective and objective domains. We must look carefully at the appropriateness of the degree of objectivity and precision of measurement called for by PBTE. It is true that objectivity and precision are virtues under certain circumstances. But it is important to understand what those circumstances are. Aristotle pointed out 25 centuries ago that the degree of precision of measurement we demand should be related to the nature of the material or task measured. More recently, A. N. Whitehead has warned us against the fallacy of misplaced concreteness. It is no less inappropriate to demand precise measurement of certain subjective states than it is to tolerate imprecise measurement of certain externally observable procedures. Some of the most imporant educational products, such as creative invention, critical thinking, personal goal–setting, choice–making, educability (in the sense that Douglas Heath uses the term), feelings of competence, and so on, may be least amenable to the precise external formulation of behavioral standards.

A more radical criticism of the notion of productivity inherent in PBTE would question the entire value of producing and doing, of being active and useful. There is a strong climate of skepticism, especially among young people, about the superiority of these typically American values. What we need to foster today, according to that un-American critic, Ivan Illich, is "the autonomy of the ludicrous in face of the useful." Disenchantment among many people with some of the more pernicious manifestations of American productivity (from military violence to industrial pollution) has led to a revulsion against producing always more. At the same time there has developed an increasing interest in and respect for oriental and existential values of being, in contrast to western and instrumental values of doing. Marshall McLuhan, with a typical half-truth that is also a helpful provocation, has pronounced that students today are searching for a role, not a goal. By "goal" he seems to mean getting ahead and making it in a conventionally productive sense. By "role" he appears to mean asking oneself existential questions about one's meaning, identity, and place in the world. William Glasser has suggested that the whole notion of "failure" (in the sense of failing to produce what others demand) is an anachronism in a role-oriented society and is appropriate only in a type of goal-oriented society that is already disappearing in the West.

These views, although oversimplifications, serve to remind us that an educational program that focuses on product so exclusively that the nature of the process is ignored, runs grave risk of being dehumanizing for the participants. One reason why humanistic psychology appears more attractive to many young people today than behavioral psychology (which provides some of the intellectual base of PBTE) is that the former is perceived as paying more respect to the quality of the individual's ongoing experience. This may be unique and not behaviorally measurable, but to sacrifice it on the altar of productivity may be to throw away that which is of central human value.

Wholeness

This discussion of being and doing leads us to a consideration of the nature of the being who teaches. In the education of teachers we are, at best, concerned with the quality of the whole persons who are being educated. Harry Broudy has already cogently discussed the organismic nature of human experience and learning.[7] I shall not repeat Broudy's argument but merely mention that I endorse it and say that it lends support to the general position I take here. If we are concerned about the whole quality of a teacher's being, then we will recognize the severely limited nature of the information we gain by measuring his specific attributes or behaviors and will be concerned to protect him from the tyranny of inappropriate measurement.

The problems of measurement place us in a difficult dilemma with respect to PBTE. On the one hand, we know that there is a tendency for educational programs to be dominated by evaluation procedures. Schooling becomes whatever can be measured with available instruments. Hence, if humanistic elements are not measurable they will be excluded. On the other hand, the task of measuring affective, volitional, aesthetic, and other major elements is so difficult that there is constant danger of trivializing the whole educational process in the cause of more efficient testing.

Thus we may well be concerned that PBTE will lead to an atomization of experience, a separation of cognition from affect, of skill from attitude, of fact from value. It is unjustifiable to hold teachers or institutions accountable for the development of teaching skills without also holding them accountable for all the concomitant attitudinal and affective changes that occur in the skill training. To teach skills humanistically is to teach them not as isolated mechanisms but in a gestalt of imagination, purpose, and meaning.

---

[7] Harry S. Broudy, A *Critique of Performance-Based Teacher Education* (Washington, D.C.: AACTE, 1972), pp. 3-5.

Moreover, it appears that PBTE may encourage an emphasis on small, short-term, isolated gains rather than on significant, long-term, integrated growth. There is a crucial need for integration of experience and curriculum, which PBTE may threaten by breaking things down into small, measurable units. Because of the pace of social and technological change, we can imagine future needs in only the most general terms. This renders it unpromising to lay down small, specific goals of behavior that will be appropriate in the future.

We are already seeing one change that bears important implications for the nature of schooling. Advocates of deschooling are not alone in pointing out that changes in educational technology render it much easier than in the past to teach specific skills when they are needed, on the job or in the field. We are developing much greater flexibility in our ability to train people in specific competencies. There is less need to bring people together in schools in order to do this. Indeed, fixed institutions may reduce our flexibility and effectiveness. This development raises important questions about the appropriate function of the school. If isolated work skills can be better taught elsewhere, what is left for schooling? Perhaps the school will become the place to play rather than to work, the place for leisure and the cultivation of man's highest powers, the place for the humane nurture of the whole person.

Responsibility

The concept of responsibility is central to a humanistic view of education. It is, in one sense, the other side of the coin of freedom. PBTE can be seen as serving humanistic purposes in that it attempts to assign responsibility more formally and unambiguously than is usually done in the educational process. However, we must examine more carefully the ways in which responsibility is assigned in order to judge whether the effects are benign or pernicious.

For what are teachers to be held responsible or accountable, and to whom? The lack of clear consensus on the basic skills that should be possessed by the teacher may lead to a demand that he be held accountable for certain student learning outcomes. In this case, the teacher will compare disadvantageously with, for example, the doctor, who is held accountable for prescribing properly but not for whether the patient is cured or not. To hold the teacher accountable not only for what he does but also for what the students learn is to deny certain humanistic assumptions about the freedom of people (in this case students) to respond as they will to others' inputs. Making the teacher accountable for precise student learnings may merely serve to increase the dependency of the student on the teacher.

The degree of accountability that we demand of teachers or educational institutions must also be related to the degree of control they have over their students' lives. How do we know what portion of a student's educational performance or growth to attribute to the teacher, as opposed to peers, parents, television, and other influences? Is making the teacher accountable, even though he is only one among many educational agents, a form of scapegoating? Is it possible that we put our guilt about raising our children onto teachers and make them expiate that guilt through accountability? A humanistic view of responsibility would relate it to power. A teacher should be held responsible only to the degree that he has the power to make the decisions and command the resources that make successful performance possible.

Hence a major humanistic concern about PBTE lies in the field of power, authority, and participation. Who is to make decisions about setting objectives and measuring performance? A humanistic goal is the development of mature men and women who are able to take responsibility for themselves—for their purposes, decisions, actions, and evaluations. If PBTE means that one must be accountable to an external agent, it may militate against the development of this self-responsibility. Respect for persons means that each person affected by a decision should have the opportunity to participate in making the decision. A humanistic program of PBTE will therefore involve widespread student participation in goal setting and evaluating.

We cannot expect students to take responsibility for their own learning if they lack the necessary degree of control over their own lives. But PBTE is concerned with the external control of behavior. When this control is achieved through reward, punishment, manipulation, or coercion, it tends to develop dependence, opposition, sabotage, or passive resistance, rather than self–responsibility. Technocrats will always tend to be tempted by the promise of efficiency and tidiness through rational control over others' behavior and be ready to sacrifice the development of personal responsibility with its unpredictable and varying outcomes. It may be that PBTE as currently conceived contains too many power temptations for technocrats.

Interdependence

The issue of control brings us to the heart of an important potential conflict between humanistic and technocratic values. A humanistic education would foster values like interdependence, collaboration, equality, and dialogue, rather than dependence, competition, hierarchy, and control over others. At the center of a humanistic program would be a concern with the quality of human relationships. One might fear that such humanistic values would be threatened if PBTE engenders competition for higher productivity and "better" behavior.

There are grave difficulties and pitfalls in PBTE when it attempts to achieve humanistic values, since its basic assumptions may nullify its apparent achievements. For example, in the previously mentioned scenario of competency-based teacher education, Weber and Cooper suggest an interview between the prospective faculty member and students in the program. One student points out to the candidate: "One of our *required* objectives regarding classroom management is that we should be able to work with a classroom group in such a way as to achieve group unity and cooperation. All of us *must* show our ability to do this. . . ."[8] But what would be meant by "unity" and "cooperation" under these circumstances? Is it not paradoxical to require such behavior from a student by putting him in a position in which he must compete with his fellow students to demonstrate his competence?

PBTE is in danger of merely perpetuating the thrust of traditional schooling by putting students in the situation where they see others as threats to themselves. Individual performance to meet someone else's requirements fosters the notion of schooling as selection and is divisive of human relationships. The humanistic approach encourages the development of situations in which students regard one another as potential resources. It fosters the notion of schooling as education and attempts to develop fraternal feelings and convictions.

How well this is done depends in part upon the way in which testing and measuring are carried out. We are familiar with many years' criticism of the baleful influence cast on education by testing procedures and the exaggerated faith placed in test results. More recent research on the powerful impact of teachers' expectations on students' performances casts serious doubt on our ability to use testing beneficially. The advent of PBTE raises again the conflict between individual testing and aggregate testing. It seems possible, on humanistic grounds, to justify aggregate testing as sometimes being useful in the advancement of educational research. But I am skeptical of the value of most individual testing and would like to see clearer justification for its practice. Since PBTE must rely on individual testing, it is easier to see how it fosters competitive selection than how it encourages the development of human interdependence.

Social Rehumanization

Perhaps PBTE will lead to a rehumanization of teacher education. It does seem to hold promise of weeding out some anachronistic and tyran-

---

[8] Weber and Cooper, op. cit., p. 3. (Italics added).

nical traditions and opening up some alternatives and options. But if it is to serve humanistic purposes, it must be constantly subjected to critical examination. In particular, we must ask what is happening to the human beings who are experiencing the program. I would hope that this same spirit of criticism would be a quality of the teachers produced by such a program. Thus they would be critical of the status quo wherever it is destructive of humane values. And they would themselves be agents of constructive social change in the world.

Humanistic educators argue passionately for the development of more humane alternatives to the often arid, mechanical, packaged procedures found in schools and colleges. The basic causes of this dehumanization must be sought outside the walls of the school. Yet the reliance of PBTE on individual psychology may divert our attention away from the study of the social, economic, and political contexts of schooling. For example, we must examine the nature of the connections between economic conditions and the demand for accountability itself. It may be that educational institutions are more vulnerable to invasion by business firms and business values at times when they are weakened by economic recession or strong external criticism.[9]

The kind of social rehumanization that seems to be called for by the present situation means that we must look not only at the technology of education but also at its culture. PBTE may result in the reform of educational technology, but its focus on efficiency may lead to a neglect of the culture, which will more than nullify the technological changes. PBTE tends to focus on the surface curriculum. But much of the important learning that goes on in educational institutions occurs through the hidden curriculum—that is, the prevalent network of authority relationships, institutional structures, hierarchical patterns, and power assumptions. To make teachers behave more efficiently in the context of the present authority structure of school and society may be to entrench the very forces that have led to dehumanization. We cannot hope to rehumanize our society by merely tuning up our educational technology. We need teachers who are able to ask radical questions about the educational culture and are equipped with the human qualities and skills to change it.

---

[9] For an excellent historical treatment of this question, see Raymond Callahan, *Education and the Cult of Efficiency* (Chicago: University of Chicago Press, 1962).

16. *Choice versus Performance: An Existential Look at PBTE*

Maxine Greene

When people see themselves as externally controlled, "the marionettes either of psychological mechanisms or of an external history,"[1] they may find it extraordinarily difficult to distinguish between the true and the false. This is because they cannot be sure of what they have been conditioned to believe and what is actually the case. Maurice Merleau-Ponty, discussing the crisis facing the sciences of man, makes clear how important it is for individuals to *see* "the link which binds us to the physical, social, and cultural world . . . to become conscious of it."[2] He has in mind, of course, the phenomenological notion regarding prejudices "established in us by the external environment," prejudices that keep us from recognizing the part we play in constituting our own worlds. He has in mind as well the necessity to become aware of the forces in the environment that play upon us and shape our behavior. He would have us transform what he calls "automatic conditioning" into "conscious conditioning" to the end of becoming present to ourselves.

Given the current reliance upon behavioristic explanations, given the growing insistence that teachers perform "in stated and specified ways,"[3] I find this peculiarly applicable to teacher education today. My concern is with the autonomy and responsibility of the teacher at a time when

---

This paper was prepared especially for this volume.

[1] Maurice Merleau-Ponty, "Phenomenology and the Sciences of Man," in *The Primacy of Perception and Other Essays*, ed. James M. Edie (Evanston, Ill.: Northwestern University Press, 1964), p. 48.

[2] Merleau-Ponty, "Phenomenology and the Sciences of Man," op. cit., p. 49.

[3] Benjamin Rosner, *The Power of Competency-Based Teacher Education: A Report* (Boston: Allyn and Bacon, 1972), p. 51.

his initiatives are being eroded, his right to self-determination overlooked. My concern is with the self-consciousness of the teacher at the moment when, by implication at least, the profession is being blamed for the failures, the manipulativeness, *and* the marginality of the schools. Our condition in teacher education resembles that of the people in Harry Hope's barroom in Eugene O'Neill's *The Iceman Cometh* when Hickey, the salesman, arrives. Hickey, it will be recalled, is the self-appointed destroyer of illusions. He tells the inhabitants of the bar that he means only to save them from pipe dreams: "Just the old dope of honesty is the best policy. . . . Just stop lying about yourself and kidding yourself about tomorrows."[4] Hickey, of course, turns out to be insane; but those offering us analogous "truths" are fearfully sane. They tell us we will stop lying to ourselves only when we being to look at outcomes, when we focus our attention on the measurable—"performance," they say, and "competencies." The teacher is no longer expected to make his own decisions in response to classroom exigencies. He is no longer expected to make practical judgments on the basis of what he knows and believes. His behavior is to be governed by the "protocols and training materials"[5] made available to him by model builders and instructional leaders. No longer able to define himself by means of a "fundamental project"[6] nor to create himself (as John Dewey said) "through choice of action,"[7] he is deprived of influence as a *subject*. How can the teacher educator move the teacher-to-be to choose to learn, if this is so? Does he not become a teacher trainer, conditioning his students to behave in predetermined ways?

It is because of questions like these that I find Merleau-Ponty's summons to self-consciousness so important. It is not simply that consciousness of the "link which binds" saves an individual from victimization and passivity. Awareness of that sort may also free the person for intentional action on his own initiative, because it permits him to authenticate himself as an individual in the face of conditioning forces. As I see it, teaching is by definition intentional: it involves a purposeful engagement in a process of enabling others to learn how to learn. Held accountable rather than responsible, the teacher is told to behave in conformity with predefined rules. He is not free to act as a "norm-regarding" and "norm-creating" person[8] in an open, often unpredictable world. He is likely to become, in consequence, something other than a principled individual; since the one who acts on principle feels himself free to choose reflectively, to ap-

[4] Eugene O'Neill, *The Iceman Cometh* (New York: Vintage Books, 1946), p. 81.

[5] Rosner, op. cit., p. 242.

[6] Jean-Paul Sartre, *Search for a Method* (New York: Knopf, 1963), pp. 91-92.

[7] John Dewey, *Democracy and Education* (New York: Macmillan, 1916), p. 408.

[8] Thomas F. Green, "Teaching, Acting, and Behaving," in *Philosophy and Education*, ed. Israel Scheffler (Boston: Allyn and Bacon, 1966), pp. 128-130.

propriate norms. There can be no free choosing or appropriation when the teacher is certified on the basis of his ability to perform "in stated and specified ways." There can be no choosing or appropriation if the teacher is not encouraged to define real alternatives when it comes to action in the classroom, the kind of action intended to arouse other human beings to critical inquiring, the application of skills, giving reasons, and making sense.

Effectiveness, it appears to me, is in part a function of teacher initiative. The teacher educator cannot but be concerned with the nurture of capacities to create situations in which diverse persons are moved to take cognitive action. There are no blueprints for such situations. There is no "technology" that works in every case. No guarantees of outcome can be given, no assurances of success. It is probably true, as Harry Broudy says, that we are unlikely to get fully professional teachers on every level throughout the schools; it is also true that we do not yet have at hand a "really scientific theory of teaching,"[9] for all the claims of those intent on applying engineering principles to the schools. In spite of this, as Broudy points out, it is desirable to enable each practitioner "to be rational about rules," to rely on interpretive theory, and to understand the usefulness of such theory. In my view, the learning of theory that enables the teacher to treat educational problems in their social and ideational contexts can become a means of attaining the awareness Merleau-Ponty describes. My point is that it becomes meaningless to speak of teacher effectiveness if the teacher is not made responsible for interpreting such contexts and thereby knowingly constituting his world. It becomes equally meaningless to speak of effectiveness if no one attends to the ways in which teachers themselves perceive the act of teaching, if no one engages them in discourse about their intentions, and if no one consults them when decisions of practice are made.

It is necessary to think about the teacher as a person now that the aims of education are again being spelled out in terms of achievement skills, measured by tests that predict success in the existing system "without asking whether the system awards success in an ethically justifiable manner, or whether success itself is an ethically justifiable goal."[10] It is necessary to think seriously about responsibility now that the notion of growth as aim has been set aside again, now that extrinsic measures of adaptation govern ends in view instead of the internal standards of adequacy that Dewey taught some of us to seek. Set aside as well, of course, is Dewey's

---

[9] Harry S. Broudy, *The Real World of the Public Schools* (New York: Harcourt Brace Jovanovich, 1972), p. 55.

[10] Lawrence Kohlberg and Rochelle Mayer, "Development as the Aim of Education," *Harvard Educational Review* (November 1972), p. 481.

view that the principles governing democratic education are moral, not "technical, abstract, narrowly political, or materially utilitarian."[11] Forgotten, it would seem, is the idea that education ought to be oriented to the enrichment of experience or to "a widening and deepening of conscious life—a more intense, disciplined, and expanding realization of meanings."[12] When education is viewed in such a manner, subject and student are both likely to be taken into account, to the end of making educative experiences possible and enabling individuals to effect connections within their experiences and thus to make their own kinds of sense. When education is viewed in such a manner, the teacher's intervention is considered to be thoughtful, deliberate, and significant. The teacher is expected to be *personally* involved. Even then, however, no guarantees are offered. The approach, like all approaches founded in choice of action, is geared to the hypothetical, to always open possibility.

I want to talk about the teacher-to-be with the recognition that the "realization of meanings" and the moral ends of education are no longer of prime concern. I want to talk about the teacher-to-be at a time when he is being asked to become effective in an antiseptic, value-neutral world. In the background of present experiences are the various ways in which the teacher has been scapegoated by popular "romantic" critics who have treated him or her (ordinarily her) as a hypocritical, prissy, narrow-minded Mrs. Grundy, fearful for youthful expressiveness, jealous of creativity, devoted to keeping order, and imposing middle-class properties on the young. In radical or romantic literature, this picture of the teacher has been sharpened by accusations of racism; and this has led to the sometimes contemptuous demands that he or she be held accountable for teaching the skills simple prejudice prevented him or her from teaching before the ill will was exposed. In addition, it will be remembered, the teacher has been widely charged with imposing social controls on the powerless young, in spite of his or her presumed inadequacy. Carl Bereiter, for example, subsuming value teaching under what he scornfully calls "humanist commitment," asserts that teachers only do damage when they concern themselves with values and attitudes. In any case, he points out, such a commitment has a negative effect on teachers' training functions. He recommends, therefore, that the teacher be restricted to training in "well-defined, clearly teachable skills" and that children be left free the rest of the time "to do what they want."[13] Bereiter is but one of many radical critics whose position has fed into and finally merged with that of the apostles of efficiency.

---

[11] John Dewey, *Freedom and Culture* (New York: Capricorn Books, 1963), p. 162.

[12] Dewey, *Democracy and Education*, op. cit., p. 417.

[13] Carl Bereiter, "A Time to Experiment with Alternatives to Education," in *Farewell to Schools???* eds. Daniel U. Levine and Robert J. Havighurst (Worthington, Ohio: Charles A. Jones Publishing Co., 1971), p. 22.

There are good historic reasons for the emergence of the apostles of efficiency, notably those now proselytizing for performance-based teacher education, modularization, power in competence, outputs, "management by objectives," "accountability emphases," and the rest. The teacher-to-be may be enabled to conceptualize the influences of a corporate society and the engineering mentality. Looking back in time, he may assess the effects of the "cult of efficiency" in the early years of the century in relation to scientific management and "reform."[14] Engaging in informed dialogue with the educational and cultural past, he should be enabled to break with what is given where social reality is concerned and clarify his own relationship to the business society, to the obligations it imposes on him, and to the "waste"[15] for which it has been responsible. Only as he examines it within his own systems of relevance is he likely to become conscious of what it signifies for his own life projects, his teaching in the world.

But even that is not enough for the teacher-to-be in search of heightened consciousness. There have been the multiple critiques of public education throughout the century, culminating in the strange concatenation of social protest and romanticism in the 1960s. It is clear enough by now that the old legends regarding the school could not be maintained once poor people and minority groups propelled themselves to center stage to proclaim how the schools had failed. Few thoughtful people can any longer take refuge in the belief that the public school has the power to equalize, insure social harmony, popularize knowledge, and inculcate righteousness. Few thoughtful teachers can think of themselves as redeemers any longer, people chosen to liberate and to save. They have been compelled to count the numbers of children who have been "selected out," forgotten, and demeaned. This recognition has played a part and must play a part in teacher education, now that the teacher-to-be can no longer be promised a type of nobility, a special dignity as bearer of the American Dream. It seems eminently clear to me that if there *is* to be a dignity in public school teaching, individual teachers must be freed to create it themselves.

This was made peculiarly difficult by the romantics' onslaught and by the emerging vision of the teacher as agent of an unjust, stratified society. Not only is the teacher made to bear the onus for imposing false consciousness on the young, for inducting them into consumerism and "the vast, vulgar, and meretricious beauty"[16] now identified with the American

---

[14] Raymond E. Callahan, *Education and the Cult of Efficiency* (Chicago: The University of Chicago Press, 1962).

[15] Dewey, "The School and Society," in *Dewey on Education*, ed. Martin S. Dworkin (New York: Bureau of Publications, Teachers College, Columbia University, 1959), pp. 70-73.

[16] F. Scott Fitzgerald, *The Great Gatsby* (New York: Charles Scribner's Sons, 1953), p. 99.

Dream. He is described, implicitly and explicitly, by Marxist critics as a legitimator of technocracy, the stratification system, and "the hierarchical division of labor."[17] On the one hand, he is repeatedly exposed as incompetent and a failure; on the other hand, he is blamed for the evils of the "I.Q. ideology" and a socialization process that demeans. How is he to respond as an individual to charges of incapacity from some quarters, charges of manipulativeness from others? How is he to respond to the claim that teachers simply fail to do what everyone assumes they know how to do, no matter what predicaments and inequities exist in the community, no matter how confused are prevailing norms and cues?

It seems to me that teacher educators and their students ought to understand that the preoccupation with performance and competencies signifies a resurgence of the "cult of efficiency," now intensified by financial pressures in communities and a general awe in the face of management expertise. They ought also to see that the implicit attack on teacher self-determination in the literature of PBTE has found a legitimation in the romantic exposés and the revisionist histories that present school teachers as primary agents of social control.[18] This is not to affirm that teacher education, as we have known it, is effective; nor is it to say that today's practicing teachers are to be considered professional or even "competent." With the plight of the teacher-to-be as a person in mind, I am proposing that the rationales of PBTE be understood as part of the same "external environment" that establishes prejudices respecting what is real and true. Here, too, the individual must take action against a conditioning process, unless he is willing to be a clerk, someone guided by programmers and their extrinsic rules. If he is to articulate his life as a subject, he must pose questions with regard to what is happening; he must reject value neutrality and pose moral questions with regard to performance emphases, with regard to PBTE. In the official report of the Committee on National Program Priorities in Teacher Education,[19] there is much discussion of controlling evolutionary change and testing national alternatives. But nowhere is there an examination of the moral dimensions of what is being proposed, of the goods and bads of particular objectives, nor of the predicaments of individual teachers certified in terms of competencies the experts have defined. I cannot help seeing those who wrote the report as "marionettes" in Merleau-Ponty's sense. Treating experience as a series of

---

[17] Samuel Bowles and Herbert Gintis, "I.Q. in the U.S. Class Structure," *Social Policy* (November/December 1972 January/February 1973), pp. 65-96.

[18] See, for example, Colin Greer, *The Great School Legend* (New York: Basic Books, 1972); Clarence J. Karier, Paul Violas, and Joel Spring, *Roots of Crisis* (Chicago: Rand McNally, 1973); Michael B. Katz, *Class, Bureaucracy, and the Schools: The Illusion of Educational Change in America* (New York: Praeger, 1971).

[19] Rosner, *The Power of Competency-Based Teacher Education*, op. cit.

psychological events, treating teaching as a sequence of discrete behaviors, they may well be confusing behavioral descriptions with life as it is lived by teachers and by those who are expected to learn. My concern is with calling the attention of teachers and teachers-to-be to their own biographies, their own life-worlds,—and to the ways in which they themselves bring meaning into being. Teacher educators who ignore this necessity —this philosophical necessity—become mere training agents, acting in the name of abstract systems, "protocol and training materials," impersonal structures of thought. ("Performance must be analyzed," writes Alan Purves, "so that the performer can be trained, and the performer must learn about both form and content. Performance in education deals with people teaching or learning something. The disciplines tell us about the something; pedagogy and psychology tell us about teaching and learning; both must help the student become a performing teacher."[20])

There is a kind of irony in the fact that the PBTE proposals are being offered at a moment of what has been called "retreat from education." They are being offered at a time of growing realization that there is, as Christopher Jencks and his associates have pointed out, little correlation between the skills learned in schools and later economic success.[21] Although I question Jencks's statement that school reform has been demonstrated to be irrelevant, I welcome the possibility of conceptualizing education as an end in itself rather than as a means of advancing economically, even to the point of economic equality. In addition, I welcome the opportunity to clarify the place of social inequities and injustices when it comes to the inhibition of learning. Like Jencks, I believe that such inequities and injustices will have to be dealt with politically, that no increase in teacher competence or improvement in performance is likely to insure that people will live better, more fulfilling lives.

Obviously, this does not mean that teachers should not be brought to as high a level of effectiveness as possible. Nor does it mean that behavioral research should not be utilized, nor that we ought to pay no heed to objectives, to our ends in view. It does, however, suggest that the preoccupation with the merely measurable is unwarranted. It suggests that an exclusively skill-oriented mode of education can no longer be justified from the point of view of outcomes. In fact, when we do consider the injustices prevailing in our society, the indifference to inequalities, and the acquiescence to amorality, that type of education seems totally unjustified.

What is required, as Jencks and others have suggested, is an approach to education that is oriented to a variety of possibilities for a variety of

---

[20] Rosner, op. cit., p. 237.

[21] Christopher Jencks, et al., *Inequality: A Reassessment of the Effect of Family and Schooling in America* (New York: Basic Books, 1972).

human beings. What is also required, I believe, is an approach oriented to justice as well. Justice, as Lawrence Kohlberg says, may be conceived as a reason for action, a reason that "is called respect for persons."[22] Conceived as fairness, it is the principle that, other things being equal, all individuals' claims should be considered in social situations. John Rawls supplements this by adding that the claims of the "least advantaged" should be considered "in particular."[23] Conceived as relevance, justice is the principle that persons should be treated differently only when there are relevant grounds for treating them differently (and undeserved disabilities might be relevant grounds). The main point is, however, that to act justly is to act on principle. If a person is to act on principle, he has to feel himself to be autonomous. It is difficult to imagine teachers being moved to take ethically principled positions in places where they are evaluated in terms of discrete outcomes from a value-neutral point of view. It is difficult to imagine, in schools where objectives are spelled out solely in terms of achivement skills, where the notion of development as objective is belittled, where the governing criteria have vaguely to do with adaptation and efficiency and "success."

This brings me back then to my main argument, which has to do with the dangers of automatism and the importance of self-consciousness. There are many people in this society who believe that submission to systems, to bureaucracies is the greatest danger facing us today. They suspect but too seldom articulate the possibility that the way to combat mindlessness, mechanism, and submission is by being present as a person, prepared to take the risks of one's own freedom and the freedom of others. To be present in this fashion is not simply an affair of affect or a way of feeling. It involves a kind of wide-awakeness that must be deliberately achieved through engagement in the knowing called *praxis.* This mode of knowing can be carried on with respect to all the situations in which the teacher finds himself: the educational situations in which he is directly involved and the cultural situations, including the moral dilemmas, the injustices, the tensions among disparate groups, the cover-ups and the denials, the gropings for autonomy, and the definitions of possibility. By *praxis* I mean a type of cognitive action that involves problem-posing as well as problem-solving and, in Paulo Freire's words, "action and reflection . . . upon the world in order to transform it."[24] As Jean-Paul Sarte says, *praxis* is a pur-

---

[22] Lawrence Kohlberg, "Education for Justice," in *Moral Education: Five Lectures* (Cambridge: Harvard University Press, 1970), p. 70.

[23] John Rawls, *A Theory of Justice* (Cambridge: Harvard University Press, 1971), pp. 14-15.

[24] Paulo Freire, *Pedagogy of the Oppressed* (New York: Herder and Herder, 1970), p. 66.

poseful human activity that involves a going beyond or a refusal of some given reality in the name of a reality to be produced.

I am suggesting that, if teachers are to be effective in the contemporary school, they must create themselves as principled subjects responsible enough to be consulted by those engaged in certifying and evaluating what they do. They must identify themselves as persons concerned with articulating their own existential and professional purposes so that they can arouse others to articulate *their* life purposes and, in doing so, bring their reality closer to what they want it to be. Without empirical support, I believe that young people are likely to be stirred to learn when they are challenged by teachers who are themselves able to think about what they are doing and to engage in dialogue with the young. For teachers to be competent in this fashion, they must be enabled to understand—no matter how long they have tried not to think about them (or have been discouraged from thinking about them)—their own projects and their own realities. This means breaking with the world-as-taken-for-granted, no matter how comfortable that world may be. It means taking a fresh look at what may be so familiar it has receded into the dull background—a fresh look at preconceptions, disillusionments, accommodations; a new vantage point on the tensions and paradoxes inescapable in teaching; a new perspective on the constraints in the institution, on the educative and miseducative forces in the world. I know no other way to avoid submergence in reality and "automatic conditioning." I know no other way to avoid the *ennui* that accompanies an automatic life, a life of frustrations and routines.

There is no guarantee that teaching will be more effective if the teacher is enabled to attain self-consciouness. But I believe the individual practitioner will have a better chance of becoming a subject and a competent professional if he is liberated to take this kind of cognitive action on his own initiative. He will have a better chance of creating a significant role for himself if he is willing to take a fresh look at the context, at the impinging world. I believe that marginality can be refused and a new dignity created if teachers are equipped to transform the jobs for which they are preparing into projects through which they define themselves, if they are aroused to commit themselves to principles and to act on principle, if they are freed to choose themselves with regard to the injustices they perceive. There is much to be done in the way of liberating persons to transform the reality of the everyday, much to be done in the way of helping them pose questions with regard to what is oppressive, mindless, and wrong. But these things can only be done by human beings who are given regard and held responsible, who participate in the creation of the norms by which they are judged. They can only be done by human beings who open themselves to the demands of *praxis,* who see horizons always stretching further and enticing them to extend themselves further. Such human beings will reach out for new perspectives, new disciplinary vantage points, in order to see more, in order to understand. But they must be set free to break with the given, to move beyond performance—to surpass and to transform.

17. *PBTE: A Question of Values*

Arthur G. Wirth

The educational techniques of PBTE derive from the very fabric of the technological age. They will not disappear, and it would be immoral not to use them if they are helpful in dealing with some of the intractable problems we confront in education today. The important task is to learn to judge them in terms of their consequences for the human beings involved.

I became engaged in wrestling with value choices in teacher education while participating in a small, alternative teacher education project at Washington University in the academic years 1970-72. This was about the time that the performance movement achieved prominence. Our attention inevitably was drawn to it while we tried to clarify the values we wanted to represent in our own program. In a hundred-page report, "An Inquiry-Personal Commitment Model of Teacher Education: The Hawthorne Teacher Education Project (H-TEP)," I described what happened during a trial of the plan with a group of seniors at the Hawthorne School. The report also included a comparison of the value orientation of our program with several other teacher–education models, including PBTE.[1]

Since that was the actual process which led me to reflect on PBTE, I shall attempt a brief sketch of several of the value preferences in our program as a base for some comments on competency–based teacher educa-

This article was prepared especially for this volume.

[1] Arthur G. Wirth, "An Inquiry-Personal Commitment Model of Teacher Education: The Hawthorne Education Project (H-TEP)," Washington University, 1973, unpublished.

tion. I do this with full recognition that an attempt to summarize a lengthy report in a few paragraphs is bound to produce distortions.

I. An Inquiry-Personal Commitment Model

In the fall of 1970 a committee was formed in the Graduate Institute of Education at Washington University with the charge of planning a pilot alternative teacher–education program. We rather quickly agreed on the general goals we wanted to pursue. We decided that what was needed in the schools was not teachers who wanted to be told how to do the right thing, but teachers who could see the school as a place to raise inquires from which they could learn and grow—teachers who had learned to come at problems through productive colleagueship rather than dependence on executive authority. In short, we wanted teachers who could "think their way into teaching." Our operational plans were based on the assumption that essential to effective learning at all levels of the educational process —from the efforts of the young child to those of the teacher and research scholar—are inquiry and personal commitment. We described our concept of *inquiry* as a process that moves in cycles from experience to conceptualization, from conceptualization to practice, and from practice to an evaluation that produces the data necessary for the step back to experience, thus repeating the cycle. *Personal commitment*, we said, develops in the process of making personal choices with which one identifies. The student who engages in the process of inquiry develops personal strategies for acquiring knowledge and using it in practice.

We wanted the inquiry dimension to include more than question-raising, goal-setting, and hypothesis-trying by individuals. We wanted prospective teachers to be working with senior professional colleagues who were research oriented and who worked from a variety of theory-practice models that could be applied to teaching-learning activities. During the first, or junior year, the teacher trainees would be paired with faculty members and some advanced graduate students and formed into "communities of inquiry." Much of their study and work would go on outside of regular university classes. They would do extensive observations and help as teacher-aides. They would engage in simulation techniques using microteaching, training tapes, and role-playing. They might teach short units from various curriculum materials. They would identify what else they needed to learn.

The following year the prospective teachers would be located in an off-campus teaching-learning center, The Hawthorne Elementary School, in a suburb experiencing racial integration. In place of the standard campus courses, the students, in collaboration with university faculty and Hawthorne teachers, would plan a variety of workshops, mini-courses, and other experiences to help move them toward readiness to teach. Out of their interactions with research-oriented professors and the teachers, they would begin to formulate their own hunches and plans for teaching.

It is clear that we saw inquiry and personal commitment as closely related. The person-commitment concept grew out of the work of committee member Richard DeCharms, who developed the "origin-pawn" theory as applied to teacher training. People who act as pawns feel that events in their inner and outer lives are determined by forces beyond their control. By contrast, persons who act as origins feel that have the capacity to give direction to events in their inner and outer environments. Origin type persons are reality–oriented. They are capable of taking personal responsibility for defining realistic goals, for taking appropriate action, and for assuming the consequences.[2]

Enough has been said, perhaps, to indicate that the origin-pawn concept was relevant to our goal of preparing teachers who could "think their way into teaching rather than being dependent on the prescriptions of authority figures."

Finally, we assumed that teacher education programs could not escape the philosophical or ideological value questions. These are explicit or implicit in all teacher education rationales including the inquiry-origin and PBTE models. If we are interested in helping people to make knowledgeable choices, all of the facts should be in the open. The inquiry-origin approach contained a commitment to develop attitudes and procedures toward persons that might free them from the manipulative tendencies that grip so many in educational or work situations today. We were on the side of critics who assume that insights are available to help us break the numbing effects of bureaucratic prescriptions and move toward humanization of institutions. More specifically, we were interested in countering the technocratic-efficiency image of twentieth–century schools that Ellwood Cubberly described and commended in 1916.

> Our schools . . . are, in a sense, factories in which the raw products (children) are to be shaped and fashioned into products to meet the various demands of life. The specifications for manufacturing come from the demands of twentieth-century civilization. . . . This demands good tools, specialized machinery, continuous measurement of production according to specifications, the elimination of waste in manufacturing, and a large variety in the output.[3]

---

[2] Richard DeCharms, "Personal Causation Training in the Schools," *Journal of Applied Psychology*, Vol. 2 (1972), pp. 95-113 and *Personal Causation* (New York: Academic Press, 1968).

[3] Ellwood Cubberly, *Public School Administration* (Boston: Houghton Mifflin, 1916), p. 338.

As we saw it the pressures today are even greater to place schools at the service of social efficiency ends. There are, however, ample reasons for becoming disenchanted with the school model that intrigued Cubberly. The factory school model is designed to treat children as products, and teachers as functionaries trained to process the products according to programs designed by outside programmers. Traumatic events of the last 10 years have demonstrated that endless efforts to increase the efficiency of institutions by mechanistic, cost-accounting means may lead to apathy or irrational violence. Sooner or later, human beings will resist being treated as nothing but mechanical parts of institutional machines.

In order to reveal, in shortest order, the chief value choice at issue between the inquiry-origin rationale and some competency-based proposals, it may be useful to refer to Martin Buber's analysis of the two basic types of relationship available to men in modern mass societies: I-Thou and I-It patterns of relations. In Buber's view, we relate to our world in three spheres of relations: our life with nature, our life with men, and our life with "intellectual essences."[4] We are interested here only with the relations of men to each other.

In the I-It pattern men relate with only parts of themselves. There is no real meeting of persons. In I-It, the emphasis is on efforts to manipulate and control—to serve the efficiency needs of organizations or societies. In I-Thou relationships, men are present to each other with the wholeness of their persons. I-Thou is marked by presentness, mutuality, directness, openness and by the possibility of dialogue in which people get through to each other. It must be made clear though that there is no pure I-It or I-Thou. I-It relations are necessary because the work of the world must be done. To survive we must have skills to control and use things and social institutions. The great danger at present, according to Buber, is that massive, impersonal institutions exert pressures to force us to live more and more in the I-It. It is the predominance of I-It relations that is the real evil in contemporary life. "Without 'It' man cannot live; but he who lives with 'It' alone is not a man, 'for all real living is meeting.' "[5] The great task of our time, said Buber, is "to become persons again."

I risk this ridiculously simplified reference to Buber's philosophy in the hope that his poetic terminology will yield a stark portrayal of the bedrock issue that must be faced in efforts to renew all institutions today, including teacher education.

---

[4] Martin Buber, *I and Thou*, 2nd ed. (New York: Charles Scribner's Sons, 1958), pp. 101 ff.

[5] Maurice Friedman, *Martin Buber: The Life of Dialogue* (New York: Harper Torch Books, 1921), p. 58.

There were flaws, of course, in the Hawthorne Project (H-TEP) but I believe that a closer look at it would support the proposition that it was a program designed to strengthen I-Thou possibilities. We tried to move in the direction of openness of communication so that people could relate in a community of trust. We tried to create some conditions in which people could feel themselves as originators of their own efforts to learn, rather than being manipulated solely by "right answer" requirements of the system.

II.　PBTE vis-à-vis H-TEP

How do competency-based models fare in light of Buber's values? After studying some of the growing mass of literature on the subject, the answer is by no means clear. PBTE is no single thing at this stage. Its proponents do not rally around a single detailed program, therefore, generalizations are risky.

Some proponents conjecture that PBTE could open new possibilities for individualizing and personalizing learning and teaching. Thus one finds statements like the following in *The Report* of The Committee on National Program Priorities in Teacher Education.

> (1) The Operational Plan provides a teaching/learning facility which derives its focus from carefully defined and publicly displayed sets of performance criteria. . . . *In its fullest operation* the teaching/learning facility is extensive enough, both in quantity and in variety to provide for a vast array of individual differences in goals (the kind of teacher I want to be), sequence (I'm really more interested right now in creativity, whatever the content area), instructional mode (I'm on the independent study kick right now), rate (political activities are taking much of my time this month) and personal involvement (I have this one instructor who helps me make sense of all of this). Without this variety potential a model is static and modeling impossible.[6]

> (2) The models . . . are designed to enable students to choose frequently among sequence alternatives. Minimal sequence requirements are established; beyond that, personal choice dictates the student's next topic for study. Not only can a student pursue topics of personal interest, he can delay other topics until he feels he is ready; or until he can pursue such a topic in close association with related topics; students enjoy the benefits of many possible variations. . . .

---

[6] Benjamin Rosner, ed., *The Power of Competency-Based Teacher Education: A Report of the Committee on National Program Priorities in Teacher Education* (Boston: Allyn and Bacon, 1972), p. 53.

Within the experimental models, each learner has an opportunity to determine to a considerable extent the kind of teacher he wishes to become. His area of specialization, his level of competence (aide, teacher, master teacher) and the manner in which his professional program is related to his education in the arts and sciences are determined by the individual learner in cooperation with his advisors. We have recognized that no one learning theory describes all teaching or all teachers. The models permit individual students to determine the theory or theories they wish to use to design their teaching styles. This will result in teachers who differ substantially from each other but understand the bases on which they make their individual decisions.[7]

If performance-based planners could give assurance that their aims would be controlled by such possibilities for personalizing learning, there would be considerable congruence with inquiry-personal commitment values. Competency-based instruments and material would be welcomed as potentially valuable tools for learning and practice. Why, then, not simply be grateful for the new and helpful instrumentalities? The reason is because there are grounds for doubt.

My first source of doubt is philosophical. Many of the PBTE advocates seem to operate from the reductionist assumption that what is measurable within the systems frame of reference contains all that is necessary for sorting teachers into various categories of worth. This runs counter to the view I proceed from—that human beings are much more complex than the sum of their measured behaviors. Martin Buber's analysis of relationships points to the degree of difference. The I-It concern with use and efficiency is necessary but the I-Thou dimension is what makes men distinctively human. The great need of our time is to resist the encroachment of I-It tendencies—even while we seek to improve skills necessary for contemporary life.

A second cause of concern centers on a more pragmatic matter. I question the wisdom of committing major resources for PBTE in view of the fact that there is precious little evidence from field tests about the workability of PBTE techniques. I refer, for example, to the comments of one of the writers of the report, *The Power of Competency-Based Instruction.* In the course of arguing the case for competency-based teacher certification, he makes the following striking observation.

A number of problems are inherent in implementing an output referenced personnel development program. The most obvious one . . . [is] the necessity of being clear about the educational outcomes that

---

[7] Ibid., p. 71.

we want from our schools, the difficulty in measuring such outcomes, and the fact that the discipline is not at all clear as to the factors that contribute to the development of particular learning outcomes in particular kinds of children. . . . [T]he fact of the matter is that at this point in time there is no firm evidence as to the knowledge or skill base needed to effect desired educational outcomes.[8]

I respect this author's candor but draw conclusions different from the PBTE advocates who seem to look at such facts and reason as follows: We lack clarity about educational goals stated in behavioral terms, and performance-based skills to achieve them. Since these are needed, the thing to do is to proceed as if they will become available—and they will. That logic is not convincing to me. The same facts lead me to question the propriety of committing huge sums for implementing *any* program that is at such a stage of development. Responsible evaluations of PBTE efforts would also include provisions for spotting deleterious side effects —effects that might be a threat to humanizing I-Thou values. We have had too many sad experiences when powerful technologies have been set loose without adequately questioning the consequences.

One also finds in *The Power of Competency–Based Teacher Education* examples of shifts in the style of thinking that develop when proponents start spelling out practical procedures for the near future, for example, the next five years. The fine hopes for realizing the personalizing of learning are not available for now, so other courses of action are plotted. The main trend seems to move in the direction of developing standardized tests for monitoring the "performance" of teachers.

A five-year development plan, for example, projects the goal of developing, field-testing, packaging, and distributing 1000 units of instructional material over the five-year period. It is then pointed out that no factor is more important to the success of competency-based teacher education than the method of assessing the mastery of concepts and skills. "The preparation of instruments to define performance criteria is the sine qua non of competency-based certification. The committee cannot emphasize too strongly the needed development of measures of teacher performance in the classroom.[9]

Another writer looks ahead a bit further to the time when instruments for measuring teacher performance will have been created. He comments on the consequence of such a development: "The *form* of legal and extra-legal certification manipulates the form of training. If certification is based on profiles of specific competencies, teacher–education programs will pro-

---

[8] Ibid., pp. 120, 122.
[9] Ibid., p. 30.

vide training addressed to these competencies."[10] A short summation would seem to be, "He who controls the tests controls the programs."

Although a consensus about PBTE development has not yet emerged, it is worthwhile to note one more proposal presented in one of the report's working papers. Here, the call is made for "A National Model For Reform In Teacher Education."

> The central theme of the Model is the potential of systems design in education, and the National Model is based on a systems design. A system which establishes controls by providing a knowledge about the nature of change and its impact on learners delivers a continual flow of information useful in determining the future course of the various alternatives. Through the operating systems design, the National Model for teacher education serves as a major research instrumentality—to direct continuing reform in teacher education. Reform in teacher education will result from the National Model through the dissemination of both its products and processes (use of systems management, procedures for training faculty, etc.).[11]

I am willing to concede goodwill on the part of the authors of these statements. I am willing to admit the possibility of paranoid tendencies in the present writer. But I do get a clear impression that the "National Model for Reform in Teacher Education" does not seem to be taking us either toward Martin Buber's I-Thou values or toward the values of the inquiry-personal commitment rationale. We might even anticipate a strong acceleration in the direction of "I-It." If the actual trend moves toward the establishment of monolithic testing procedures that purport to define teaching, then I would agree with Martin Levit's conclusion that "the generally defining characteristics of the present accountability movement should be rejected as unfit for human beings."[12]

We are in a period of social change and discontent that will require us to explore radically different possibilities for learning. The selection, training, and work roles of teachers will change in the process. The techniques of programming, testing, and measuring from the new technology will have important roles to play. They are potentially valuable tools—

---

[10] Ibid., p. 101.

[11] Ibid., p. 250.

[12] Martin Levit, "The Ideology of Accountability in Schooling," in Robert L. Leight, ed., *Philosophers Speak on Accountability in Education* (Danville, Ill.: The Interstate Printers and Publishers, 1973), p. 37. Reprinted in this volume. (My position on PBTE has been influenced generally from the reading of Professor Levit's insightful paper.)

to reject them out of hand when they may enable us to accomplish things that so far have eluded us would, again, be self-defeating and immoral.

The folly is to get ourselves into the trap of assuming that because competency-based techniques are efficient for securing a variety of specific learnings, we should submit ourselves to them as the all-encompassing model for learning and teaching. To do that is to impose on ourselves a falsely mechanical image of human learning. It is an image that is over-simplified and false to the complexities that in fact do exist. One must expect to pay a heavy price for self-delusion.

From the value perspective of the inquiry-personal commitment model the competency-based rationale reverses the priorities we should pursue. Our rationale assumed that students and teachers in schools should be given tools and a climate of learning that could increase their capacities to gain control over their goals and to create means to realize them. Its aim was to reduce the depersonalizing, alienating tendencies of techno-cratic organization. Our philosophical bias led us to give priorities to values such as self-direction, personal responsibility, critical reflection, authenticity in relations, caring, and human relations skills.

An exclusively defined competency-based model of teacher education, like all others, has its ideological implications. Its tendency is to approve the efficient functioning of present institutional arrangements. The cost-accounting techniques, though well intentioned, tend to lead us to think of children as products to be processed and to define teachers as the pro-cessors. Competency-oriented planners stress that their model can be adopted to encompass goals beyond skill and knowledge acquisition. That may be, although the burden of proof remains on them. The very logic of the model, which is rooted in the measure of specifics, wobbles when stretched to encompass broader goals such as creativity in the arts or in-sightful discussion of social issues. Until demonstrations are developed to the contrary, the basic "package" style of the movement appears to lend itself to treating teachers as pawns. The goals to be pursued and measured are given to teachers by outside planners. Their attention and energies are co-opted by goals of prepackaged programs. Until it is made very clear that safeguards have been built in against such tendencies, Martin Levit's warning is worth noting.

Accountability programs are geared to the production of functionaries within a technological society rather than to the development of inde-pendent people who are social critics and constructors. The prospect is intensified development of modularized man, increasingly condi-tioned to being conditioned and to have "the changing times and new social needs" replace bits and pieces of himself with other skills and beliefs and values, but lacking in the virtues necessary to help control his society and his commitments. The approach is likely to intensify some of the worst features of American life—competition for personal gain; domination of efficiency over moral and rational values; confusion of fad and technology with science.[13]

The debate on the performance idea has just begun. I have limited my remarks to a critique based on the values of the inquiry-origin model. My plea is to avoid true believer endorsement. The need to identify all consequences, unfortunate as well as fortunate, is very great.

There are several significant reasons for trying to restrain the PBTE movement. While I am a critic of PBTE, I am confident that teachers and researchers with opportunities to become involved in the design of pilot projects will discover aspects of the techniques that could be useful for humane teaching. It would be a shame to be denied the chance to find out what these might be because over-eager zealots bring discredit on the whole idea by premature and exaggerated claims that are unwarranted. It was the unseemly rush to production and the "big sell" that led to the downfall of the performance–contract operatives in places like Texarkana and Gary. The record is quite clear now that in Texarkana, for instance, at the time the contractors were giving assurance to people in the community about the marvelous results they could secure for the children, that, in fact, these programs were nonexistent.[14] Albert Shanker's trenchant comments on this deception makes the point quite clear.

> What is rather surprising . . . is the government's willingness to buy programs which were not only completely untested previously but, in many cases, not even developed. In many places if the students had been a little bit brighter there would have been no work for them the next morning, because the people were busy writing up the program which was "guaranteed" the year before—a nonexistent program. In other fields society feels a responsibility. In the field of medicine, for example, we do not allow any company or any doctor without any prior testing or without any evidence to go around selling medicines and advertising that they are the answer to some incurable disease. In other fields we call this quackery, and we throw people into jail. In education we give them government grants and a lot of publicity.[15]

---

[13] Ibid., p. 45.

[14] James A. Mecklenberger, *Performance Contracting* (Worthington, Ohio: Charles A. Jones Publishing Co., 1972). See Chap. VI, "Implementation of the Texarkana Project."

[15] *AFT—Quest Consortium Yearbook* (Washington, D.C.: American Federation of Teachers (April 2-6, 1972), p. 156.

I am not close enough to the evidence to say whether "oversell" is involved in PBTE operations. There is a lot of able thinking going on in the preparation of programs and protocol materials. I admit to uneasiness, however, when an AACTE Report (September 1972) indicates that 14 states already have specified requirements for some form of PBTE. I am especially uneasy when I recall the comments of the PBTE advocate who noted that "the fact of the matter is that at this point in time there is no firm evidence as to the knowledge or skill base needed to effect desired outcomes."[16] Nor are my doubts allayed by the observation of the director of a New York study who recommends PBTE reforms in teacher education: "Every state that is exploring performance-based certification notes the extreme complexity associated with the type of activity. Trying to code in behavioral terms the professional competencies expected of successful teachers is a prodigious task."[17]

The last comment about "trying to code in behavioral terms the professional competencies expected of successful teachers" points to another cause for concern. PBTE planners often talk about consulting with teachers in developing the new scheme but, in practice, as politicians get intrigued with making teachers accountable, they tend to rush into legislation with precious little, if any, involvement of teachers. It is no wonder that teacher morale suffers. Teachers resent being treated as pawns when outside system analysts confront them with new unproven instrumentalities by which they will be judged.

June Wells, a teacher from Colorado, has voiced eloquently the outrage that teachers felt when they are brought under "the system" in this manner.

> We have an accountability law that has been enacted by the legislature in effect now and we are busy writing behavioral objectives, spending many, many hours which could be spent in preparation and planning for creative teaching directly in the classroom. Beginning next year we have the monster of the whole thing, PBES, Planned Budgeting and Evaluation System, which will assign an accountability code number to every subject we teach and every dollar spent. They tell us that by accounting for the time we spend on each subject, we can tell how much is spent and can relate back the amount of achievement that comes out of it. . . .
>
> Charges by accountability advocates that the teaching profession has refused to be accountable are pious pouts. I won't listen to them

---

[16] Rosner, op. cit., pp. 120, 122.

[17] Mario Fantini, "The Reform of Teacher Education: A Proposal for New York State," *Phi Delta Kappan* (April 1972).

another minute. Since teachers have been systematically deprived of any participation in decision-making, I don't think we can be held accountable for the mess we are in.[18]

In closing, I wish to raise one more question about the performance movement. If it succeeds, what will be the place of the intellectual-theoretical study of education in teacher education programs? On this point, PBTE advocates speak with different voices. Some give assurance that the theoretical study of education will be included. Yet reports of colleagues inform me that in some places the competency planners are impatient about including study of the theoretical foundations of education. Such study results in no measurable payoff. It diverts energy and resources from the enormous task of teaching the myriad of specific competencies teachers must master to produce measurable results with their pupils—results by which their own worth will be measured.

On the other hand the concept of an inquiry-origin teacher education program assumes that teachers, nourished by training in "communities of inquiry," should be more than efficient practitioners. They should be professionals competent to take part in the search for more humane and effective modes of education to help the young to live in an era of revolutionary change. They need to have made thoughtful inquiries into the relations between schools and patterns of culture. They need a historical sense of the forces and ideals in American life that have made for transitions and change in education. They need insight into the issues in psychological and philosophical theory that undergird professional and public debates over education. Without these, they will be passive bystanders, subject to the manipulations of succeeding waves of planners.

---

[18] *AFT—Quest Consortium Yearbook,* op. cit., p. 126.

18. *Performance–Based Teacher Education and the Teaching of English*

Walter H. Clark, Jr.

I.

As one who teaches writing and literature to students preparing to teach, I should like to speak to the matter of performance-based teacher education. How is this program to be described? Stanley Elam, in a paper commissioned by the AACTE Committee on Performance-Based Teacher Education, offers us a set of criteria.[1] He says there appears to be general agreement that a teacher education program is performance-based if:

1. Competencies (knowledge, skills, behavior) to be demonstrated by the person completing the preparation program are:
   a. Derived from explicit conceptions of teacher roles.
   b. Stated so as to make possible an assessment of a student's behavior in relation to specific competencies.
   c. Made public in advance.
2. Criteria for assessing competencies.
   a. Are based upon and are in harmony with specified competencies.
   b. Make explicit expected levels of mastery under specified conditions.
   c. Are made public in advance.
3. Assessment of the student's competence:
   a. Uses his performance as a primary source of evidence.

This article was prepared especially for this volume.

[1] Copies of this paper, unpublished at the time of this writing, may be obtained from AACTE Performance-Based Teacher Education Project, One Dupont Circle, Suite 610, Washington, D.C. 20036.

b. Takes into account evidence of the student's knowledge relevant to planning for, analyzing, interpreting, or evaluating situations or behavior.

4. The student's (i.e., prospective teacher's) rate of progress through the program is determined by demonstrated competence rather than by time or course completion.

5. The instructional program intended to facilitate the development and evaluation of the student's achievement of competency is specified.

Let us examine these criteria one by one. "*The competencies, or abilities, to be demonstrated by the person completing the preparation program are to be made public in advance.*" This is a criterion that can hardly be faulted. The very notion of a teacher who deliberately conceals from his student what it is he wants him to learn is repugnant. We should like to be able to say to any person preparing to teach; "These are the things we want you to be able to do. When you are able to do these things you will know that we think you are ready to go out and teach." To this extent the criterion sets forth a standard to which all can subscribe. Unfortunately, it does not always seem possible to be as specific as we should like about the competencies expected of prospective teachers. On the one hand, there are competencies of such exceedingly general a nature that they cannot readily be broken down into specific skills or behaviors. Sometimes it is hard even to put into words exactly what these competencies are. They are like the special abilities of a really good chess player that set him apart from other chess players who appear to be his equals in knowledge and skill. There are other things important to teaching success that we sometimes state as if they were competencies, but they are not. It might be, for example, that we should want a teacher to be able to get his students to write *easily*. To be able to get one's students to write easily is, I suppose, neither a knowledge, a skill, nor a behavior. Although stated as if it were a competence—it is more properly described as a goal (as, for example, winning chess games is not a capacity but a goal), and no combination of knowledge, skill, or behavior can be equated with the achievement of such a goal. We can make the goal public in advance, but it is not possible, it seems to me, to tell the prospective teacher exactly what it is that he should do to assure success in getting his students to write easily.

At the other extreme of specificity are a broad range of skills, knowledge, and behaviors that *can* be made public in advance and that may be very useful to a prospective teacher; they may indeed be necessary to his later success. The fact that they are necessary, of course, does not mean that they are sufficient. While it is a good general principle for any teacher of teachers to be as open as he can be at the start about what he wants the prospective teacher to learn, I think it is misleading to suppose that one can lay out all the required competencies in advance with the specificity of an engineer designing a factory production line.

"Competencies to be demonstrated by the person preparing to teach are to be stated so as to make possible assessment of a student's behavior in relation to specific competencies." If this means simply that teachers of teachers should strive to conform their testing procedures as closely as possible to what they are trying to teach it would seem unobjectionable. Teachers should always be on the lookout for situations where they teach one thing but test for something else. If, however, the criterion implies that the instruction of prospective teachers is to be shaped by the need for maximum reliability in testing, then I wish to enter a *caveat*. First, teaching is not scientific experiment, though it may draw upon the results of scientific experiment. It is a practical art, in much the same sense as medicine, which also draws upon the results of scientific experiment. In neither education nor medicine does the desire for a precise quantifiable measurement of success play the dominant role that the need for quantifiable results plays in shaping scientific experiment.

Second, it is necessary to point out that reliability in testing does not entail validity. The fact that one has a reliable test that enables one to make fine quantifiable distinctions between students with respect to knowledge and skill behavior does not guarantee that the action or state that the behavior is supposed to exemplify has in fact been demonstrated. We are all aware that two similar behaviors may constitute the executive aspects of two entirely different actions. And two similar behaviors may proceed from quite different levels of knowledge and skill in the students manifesting them. More important, two prospective teachers may demonstrate equal levels of teaching competency by quite different behavior. The point at issue is the degree to which competency can be tied to behavior. Of course, Behaviorism ducks the problem of reliability versus validity by refusing to face up to the concept of action—or rather by redefining it in terms of its public, executive aspect. By defining action in terms of those aspects that are susceptible to reliable testing, the problem of validity is simply swept away. We can admire the simplicity of this reductionist approach, but we are in no way compelled to accept it. All teachers, it is true, have a legitimate interest in testing students to discover whether educational aims have been achieved. The teaching act, however, has priority over the testing act, and where there is conflict between the two, the methods and aims of teaching should not be distorted in the interests of reliable testing.

"*Competencies to be demonstrated by the person completing the preparation program are to be derived from explicit conceptions of teacher roles.*" I must confess to some puzzlement at the way in which this criterion is formulated. I take it that the institutional position of the teacher is to be defined in terms of his function. If this be so, there are two sorts of remarks that might be made. On the one hand we can point out that the training of prospective teachers relies to a considerable extent upon *implicit* conceptions of teacher roles. What this means in terms of teaching English is that the student absorbs attitudes, techniques, and styles in content-centered courses. Most of us, I think, would admit to the influence of one or several former teachers upon the ways in which we go about teaching as well as upon our conceptions of what we are trying to accomplish. No doubt these have been considerably modified by experiences in our own classrooms and discussion with peers, but nevertheless there is an important sense in which we have learned things by example; things it might not always be possible to specify in writing or even to convey by means of demonstration classes.

On the other hand we might say that we expect *additional* competencies of the prospective teacher beyond knowledge, skills, and behaviors. Let me cite an example. A good teacher, like a good moral agent, should be able to act in accordance with general principles, and indeed, to derive his own general principles. To act in accordance with a general principle or to derive a general principle is not a skill, though it may require that one have command of a skill in order to put a principle into effect. To act in accordance with a general principle or to derive a general principle is not a form of knowledge, though to do so may presuppose knowledge. Nor does it seem that action in accordance with a principle or derivation of a principle can be reduced to behavioral terms, though action in accordance with a principle often issues forth in the form of behavior. Principled action is of a higher order than skill. A skill is an activity that can be described or defined in terms of rules. To the extent that this is the case, it is capable of being broken down into a series of discrete steps. The person learning a skill can be talked through it if he is willing to act in accordance with the set of rules that specifies this series of discrete steps. While it may be necessary for a practitioner to exercise judgment in the performance of a skill, judgment is not of its essence. Indeed, the object of a person acquiring a skill is very often to reduce much of the activity to the status of habit, thus decreasing the role of judgment.

The point I am trying to make about learning to act in accordance with general principles and to derive general principles might be best made in terms of an analogy. Imagine that we are training infantry officers. Here, too, we may speak of competencies (knowledge, skills, behaviors) to be demonstrated by the person completing the preparation program. Yet some of the most important things that we would want the infantry officer to learn are best described as arts rather than skills. To be sure, we want him to be able to maneuver men and this ability can be trained into him. It can be taught as a skill. He may acquire it in a series of steps by following a set of discrete imperatives as issued by a commanding officer, or contained in a manual. More important, however, we should want him to be able to achieve certain tactical objectives in battle with his unit, or if he is a higher level officer, to identify and achieve strategic ends. In teaching tactics, we may offer the student officer a set of tactical principles to be born in mind when planning an attack on a military objective. (Take advantage of cover! Achieve surprise!) What we are unable to do here is to provide him with a set of rules or perhaps even of principles for telling which tactical principle applies in a particular situation or which has precedence in case of conflict. It is for this reason that so much of the tactical education of an infantry officer involves simulated combat conditions where he is invited to make decisions subject to critique. What happens is that he is invited to choose a principle or principles from among many and to act upon them. Then, listening to the critique, he is encouraged to re-examine his entire set of general principles and either to reaffirm the principle acted upon or to choose another principle. He is learning how to act in accordance with a principle, and it is unlikely that he can learn to do this without examining the set of his own specific successes and mistakes. Insofar as he achieves greater and greater success in this process, he is not only learning how to act in accordance with principles, but he is most likely learning how to develop his own higher order of principles for choosing amongst lower–order principles. The point I wish to make is that the competencies involved cannot be described solely in terms of knowledge, skills, or behavior; and that this competency is crucial to his profession. I argue, by analogy, that the preparation of teachers of writing and literature requires a concern for similar competencies. Even if he is unable to state very clearly *why* he is teaching writing or reading to high school English students, the high school English teacher is faced with a variety of possible ways of achieving these ends, just as the infantry officer is faced with a variety of possible ways of achieving a tactical goal. Our task as teachers of teachers, then, is not so much one of teaching high school English teachers how to achieve a particular role, as it is one of making them good inventors of ways of achieving goals (and, if possible, good assessors of goals). This means that we have to be concerned with their ability to act in accordance with general principles and to derive general principles relevant to the achieving of certain goals in the classroom. The competencies involved are crucial, yet they are not public in the way that competencies involving knowledge or skill are. There is no way in which these competencies can reliably be tied to behavior, since we must always admit the possibility that an action in accordance with general principles may achieve the end in view yet differ radically from accepted practice. It is this which teachers of military tactics have in mind when they admit of the possibility that a student may provide a solution to a problem that differs from the "book" solution.

"The student's rate of progress through the program is determined by demonstrated competence rather than by time or by course completion." This is the most unobjectionable of all the proposals attached to this program. It seems to me that anything we can do to allow students to proceed through any educational program whatsoever at the rate that is most natural to them is justifiable so long as it does not wreak violence on other aspects of the educational program. It does seem as if we ought to be able to do more here if we exercise more ingenuity.

II.

I should now like to step back from consideration of the criteria for success in performance-based teacher education to a vantage point from which it may be possible to offer comments of a more sweeping nature. Often, when we are search for the underlying philosophical position that vivifies a particular educational program, we discover that it is best conveyed by a metaphor in terms of which we can identify the teacher's position *vis-à-vis* the student. Often, too, the metaphor will contain implicit hints as to a philosophical position on the nature of mind and the process of its maturation, as well as an outline of a theory of learning. Two of the classical educational philosophies are associated with the following metaphors: (1) that the teacher is a potter and (2) that the teacher is a gardener.

The metaphor of the teacher as potter emphasizes the active role of the teacher and the passive role of the student. The potter can inform the clay with any of a multitudinous variety of shapes, but once it has been fired, it is "finished" and cannot be changed. In this metaphor the firing, or teaching process, assumes a crucial importance and the teacher undertakes an awesome responsibility. Nor does the clay have anything to recommend it to our attention except insofar as it is given shape by the potter. When we consider how unsatisfactory is the role that this metaphor assigns the student we may be reminded parenthetically of medieval paintings that portray infants as having the same proportion of head to torso as adults, or of the doctrine of infant damnation. These give evidence of the extent to which earlier times saw (literally as well as metaphorically) children as little adults. From the standpoint of the present day, these examples join the metaphor of the teacher as potter to support the view that the men of former days did not examine very closely the question of the nature of childhood.

The second metaphor is more congenial to our times. To be sure it assigns a superior position to the teacher, since the gardener is seen as controlling his plants. However, it finds a more active role for the student than that of the potter's clay, and it allows for the concept of maturation. A plant will grow whether the gardener tends it or not. The processes controlling maturation are built into it, and it will come to fruit in any case. Much learning, we know, takes place in the absence of teaching. Many public goals of the educational establishment (and other goals too) are achieved by the individual through his own efforts or by osmosis, quite outside the institutional framework. What role is assigned the teacher by this metaphor? First, he can nurture those processes already present. He can cooperate with nature. Second, he can, within certain limits, shape the student. The gardener who would espalier a pear tree is in a somewhat similar position to the potter who would shape clay. But the range of the gardner's freedom to do so is sharply circumscribed by the nature of his material. He is more attentive to it, more cognizant of its recalcitrance and of its capacities. The difference between the metaphor of the potter and the metaphor of the gardener is paralleled by the difference between Lockean and Kantian theories of mind. The passivity of the clay is matched by the passivity of the *tabula rasa*. The relative (but not absolute) activity and independence of the plant is matched by the Kantian view of the mind as an entity that not only is acted upon by the world, but which reaches out actively, which apperceives. The metaphor of the gardener assigns yet a third possible role to the teacher. He can prune, stunt, or kill the tree. This is simply to point out the negative powers implied by the concept of nurturance.

These rather extended remarks are by way of introduction to a consideration of metaphor with respect to performance-based teaching. What metaphor or metaphors might lie at the root of the proposals put forth in this program? How do they compare with those of the potter and the gardener for richness, and what might they have to say about the nature of mind and the nature of learning? When we consider these questions the first thing we realize is that the program for performance-based teaching requires us to take three positions into account. Whereas the metaphors of gardener and potter apply to teacher and student, performance-based teaching requires us to take into account the teacher of teachers, the prospective teacher, and the student. We may well ask whether and to what degree the program takes the student into account, and to what degree the learning experience of the student will be influenced by the nature of what goes on between the teacher of teachers and the prospective teacher. These are questions to which we must return.

In trying to discover or invent an appropriate metaphor for performance-based teaching, we may be guided partly by an examination of the style of diction that exponents of the programs employ, but perhaps even more by an examination of what appears to be the single key term by which the program identifies itself. Thus we may note the use of such terms in Elam's criteria as, "explicit," "specific," "public," and "behavior," all of which, however, are encompassed in the word "performance." Why is it, for example, that proponents of this program choose not to call it "Action-Based Teacher Education," or "Activity-Based Teacher Education"? The reasons are significant, and they are best illustrated in an examination of the concepts of performance and action. The important fact is that the two concepts overlap. If anything is an action, it contains an aspect that may be described as performance. If anything is a performance we may assume (correctly or incorrectly) that it is an aspect of an action, but we do not trouble ourselves as to its intentional or cognitive aspects. To undertake to shape a person's action involves us in a concern for the intendedness and "mindedness" of his behavior. To undertake to shape a person's performance does not. It is simply to manifest concern for behavior—a public version of what Gilbert Ryle calls "the upshot." The teacher is not to be prevented from talking about "intentions" if this should prove to be a useful way of shaping behavior, but neither is he required to concern himself with them. All that matters is that the student manifest the behavior. The difference between action and performance is made more clear when we reflect that mental activity may lead to an upshot (the solving of a problem, for example) for which there is no behavioral equivalent (i.e., there can be act without behavior). If, then, we define actions as acts that *do* have behavioral aspects, it is clear that they are not to be defined *simply* in terms of behavior or performance.[2]

The analysis carried out above suggests the need for a metaphor that will emphasize the public and executive aspect of action quite divorced from any aspect that might include plan or intention. It occurs to me that the metaphor most appropriate to this situation is that of production. The teacher of teachers is a manager and the prospective teacher is a worker whose production is to be seen in terms of the manifestation of certain behaviors (i.e. skill behaviors, knowledge behaviors). The metaphor points to certain areas of educational concern, to wit: (1) A concern for clarity in the statement of educational aims. Educational aims are to be stated in terms of desired production. (2) A concern for the measurement of efficiency. It will be possible to measure the efficiency of both managers and workers in terms of production. Failure on the part of workers

---

[2] For a careful analysis of the concept of performance, see F. E. Sparshott, *The Concept of Criticism* (Oxford: Clarendon Press, 1967), Chap. 9.

to meet production goals (i.e. to manifest behaviors) will indicate inefficiency on the part of one or both—although it will presumably not be immediately evident which. (3) A concern for efficiency of production. The existence of public production goals will mean that the prospective teacher can leave the educational factory as soon as he has met them, thus circumventing the inherent inefficiencies of the chronological lockstep. Furthermore, it will be relatively easy to promote efficiency by the reward system. Prospective teachers who produce rapidly will save tuition. Teachers of teachers may have bonus clauses written into their contracts. Thus teachers and students will be encouraged to cooperate, a desirable state of affairs.

If we compare the production metaphor to the potter and gardener metaphors we realize that there is a sense in which it is more modest. The relation between the manager and the worker is a contract one, and rather narrowly restricted. The production metaphor is not one to encourage broad generalizations. At the same time, the outcome of the educational enterprise is seen to be curiously dissociated from the learner. In the case of the potter and gardener metaphors, the student is seen as essentially changed by the educational process. His being is altered. The student in the production metaphor is simply seen to have satisfied certain production standards. Nothing is implied as to his essential being. This is of course appropriate to a philosophy that is fundamentally positivistic.

Can the production metaphor serve as a vehicle for criticism of performance-based teaching? I think so. If we regard the teacher of teachers as a manager and the prospective teacher as a worker, it makes sense to ask where the student fits in. Our first temptation might be to treat the student as analogous to the auto body coming down the assembly line, upon which the worker will perform certain operations. But examination of the metaphor of the teacher as potter will show why this analogy is unsatisfactory. Like the metaphor of the student as clay, that of the student as auto body represents him in much too passive a role, one which neither present-day psychology nor educational practice will accept. If the metaphor of the teacher of teachers as manager and the prospective teacher as worker is to have an application for the relationship between the prospective teacher and his student, it must be by transposition. The prospective teacher must assume a position similar to that of a manager with respect to his own students whom he will see as workers. The point of my criticism arises from an examination of how it is that managers learn their jobs, in contrast to how it is that workers on a production line learn theirs. Presumably, the skills required of a worker on the line are described in a manual or are outlined for him by his foreman. Presumably, his particular part in the operation has been rationalized by some engineer and has been ultimately fitted into the overall production aims of the business by a manager. If we turn to the actualities of how it is that managers learn to manage, a sharp contrast emerges. The case study method, for example, now used so widely in graduate schools of business administration, has a remarkable similarity to the kind of tactical sandbox exercise already described with respect to infantry officers. In each case the emphasis is on the derivation and application of principles. In neither case could the instructors be described merely as inculcating skills (in the sense that I have used the word) or behaviors, since the goals in question admit of approach through a variety of means. Now, if the disparity between the activities and preparation of managers and that of workers be admitted, it remains only to point to the following paradox. The prospective teacher is a worker when he is being taught to teach and a manager when he himself is a teacher. But the kind of activity that he engages in as a worker is quite different from that which he engages in as a manager. But the best way to prepare someone to manage is to get them to do the sorts of things in their preparation period that they will be called upon to do in the actual situation. If the metaphor be accepted for purposes of investigation, and also the translation: teacher of teachers/prospective teacher// prospective teacher/student, as manager to worker, then the objection can be made that performance-based teacher education has the disadvantage that it proposes to turn out managers who have been trained to do the sorts of things that workers do, rather than the sorts of things that managers do.

The paradox outlined above would seem to lead us to one of two conclusions. Either the metaphor of production does not do justice to the program of performance-based teaching, or else it points to a flaw in the program. I hold the latter view. It does seem that doing management is a different sort of thing from working on the production line. A manager acts in complex ways. He does not simply behave. Nor does the figure of the production line worker do justice to the learner's role. I reject the notion that learning can be *reduced* to a matter of performance. At whatever level education is taking place, the teacher must be concerned that the student learn to perform in "minded" and "intended" ways. This means that the teacher must always be concerned to know what the student is trying to do, and what he thinks he is doing. The teacher must place the student's performance (behavior) in the context of action. The teacher must also open himself to questions from the student as to the ends that the teacher is trying to achieve, and as to the efficacy of the methods by which he is trying to achieve them. Here at least the manager should be ready to share the managerial tasks of setting goals and planning means to achieve them with the worker. In such cases, it will not make sense to speak of the student as merely "performing."

III.

In conclusion let me make a few general remarks. Insofar as performance-based teacher education urges us to define clearly what it is that we want the students to do and then to judge both our activities and their activities in terms of the achievements of these goals, it cannot be faulted. Indeed, such considerations should continually be present in the teacher's mind. However, should our concern with reliability of testing and with the specific and public nature of methods and goals lead to a narrowing of these same methods and goals, then, and to such extent, performance-based teacher education constitutes a threat. The process of education is not a matter of putting out a product—although some would profess to see it that way. Beyond its more pragmatic aspects, it is more like a form of contemplation. It is one of the primary ways in which we see and form our world. It is not an exclusively practical enterprise. It contains aspects of mystery and uncertainty, like its fellows, religion and medicine. If we refuse to accept the responsibility that goes with the realization that the questions of what we should teach and how we should teach indirectly raise the central questions of who we are and where we are going, then we will have missed a great opportunity to define ourselves. To reduce the teaching of English to the acquisition on the student's part of certain knowledge, skills, and behavior is not only to oversimplify a complicated problem, it is to do a disservice to the prospective teacher in the complexity of his humanity, as well as to ourselves and, regrettably and ultimately, to the students he will meet in primary and high school classes.

19. Do Behavioral Objectives and Accountability Have a Place in Art Education?

Elliot W. Eisner

In the past few years, "behavioral objectives" and "accountability" have become familiar terms to American art educators. When first introduced into the discourse of the field, these terms filled many people with anxiety and some with anger. Now it seems more people in the field are, if not eagerly embracing them and the conception of education they implicitly suggest, apparently resigned to the belief that "the Establishment" has won the battle and as good professionals they should try to live with them. Indeed, in a newsletter issued by the NAEA, readers were told that rather than acting like Chicken Little we should make the most of the new demands issued by both state departments of education and local school districts to formulate behavioral objectives and to be accountable for the teaching of art. We were told that about 50% of the states have adopted accountability procedures and require the formulation of behaviorally defined objectives so that teachers can be evaluated by the progress their students make. The trend, it appears, is gaining momentum and the wisest course of action if you can't beat 'em, is to join 'em.[1]

Although bandwagons have their luster, they also have their liabilities. One might find that after having jumped aboard, one has indeed been taken for a ride. Furthermore, professional responsibility requires, I believe,

Source. This article was first published in *Art Education*, Vol. 26, No. 5 (May 1973), pp. 2-5, and it is reprinted here with the permission of the author and *Art Education*.

[1] A good indication of this trend can be found in the topics that have been used this year and last for workshops and institutes sponsored by the National Art Education Association. A significant number deal with the use of objectives and evaluation in art education.

not simply embracing edicts on educational matters issued by state legislators but criticizing and appraising the edicts in order to predict their possible consequences in light of the educational values one cherishes. I will
try, therefore, in this paper to identify the issues in which behavioral objectives and accountability are embedded and to describe the historical context in which they have emerged in the field of education. It is by understanding their evolution and by clarifying their meaning and uses that we
can best determine the place of behavioral objectives and accountability
in the field of art education.

In the most fundamental sense the recommendation by curriculum theorists and educational evaluators to formulate behavioral objectives derives
from the belief that educational goals must be operationalized in empirical, that is, observational terms in order to be meaningful. It is argued
that the purpose of education is to change student behavior and that those
changes should be described in words that point to the things that students will be able to do after having engaged in a set of learning experiences that they could not do before having had those experiences. Statments of educational goals that describe mental events, feelings, attitudes,
or values that one cannot observe in manifest behavior are not considered
adequate as statements of behavioral objectives. Thus, a teacher of art who
said that he would like to have his students become more aesthetically
sensitive or more perceptive would need to rephrase his statement so that
it referred to what a more aesthetically sensitive or perceptive student
would do.

This conception of the correct way to formulate educational goals has
of course consequences other than those of operationalizing goal statements. To produce operational goal statements—description of specific
student behavior—a teacher or curriculum developer almost always has to
specify such behaviors for small units of material or skills to be learned,
since the larger the unit, the more difficult it is to describe behaviors that
are not vague or ambiguous in character. This prescription for precision
tends to encourage teachers to think of their educational programs in
chunks, each chunk having a set of behavioral objectives that are to be
mastered before proceeding to the next chunk.

It is further argued by those who advocate the use of behavioral objectives in curriculum planning that the formulation of such objectives not
only makes the goals clear for the student and the teacher, but that behaviorally stated objectives make it easier to select curriculum content and
to evaluate student performance. It is not an exaggeration to say that curricular theorists who advocate the use of behavioral objectives believe that
their formation is the most crucial step in curricular planning. In this regard, Ralph Tyler has written: "By defining these desired educational
results (educational objectives) as clearly as possible the curriculum-maker

has the most useful set of criteria for selecting content, for suggesting learning activities, for deciding on the kind of teaching procedures to follow, in fact to carry on all the further steps in curriculum planning. We are devoting much time to the setting up and formulations of objectives because they are the most critical criteria for guiding all the other activities of the curriculum-maker."[2]

But enough of beliefs about the uses of behavioral objectives today. When did they first emerge as a concern in the field of education? And, more importantly, *why* did they emerge as a concern? By understanding the tradition in which they are embedded, I believe we will be better able to understand the values that lie behind them.

Interest in the use of behavioral objectives in the United States first developed near the turn of the twentieth century. One of the reasons for using objectives in educational planning at that time was due to the desire to make educational practice more rigorous and more effective and to become better able to manage it scientifically. The scientific management movement that Frederick Taylor initiated in the late 1890s was admired by school administrators who, because of criticisms of inefficiency by the popular press, were attracted to the scientific procedures that Taylor and his colleagues were using to make the steel industry more productive.[3] These developments, which heralded the beginning of time and motion study and the use of quality control procedures, employed techniques of high-level specification, not only for describing goals but for prescribing the ways in which the goals were to be attained. The scientific manager was to lay down to the worker what he should accomplish at a given hour or day and the specific ways in which he was to accomplish it. Furthermore, the manager was to inspect the work at regular intervals to make sure that the prescribed method was being employed and that the products produced were of high and even quality.

These procedures were adapted by school administrators who tended to conceive of the school as a kind of factory, the children as the raw material, and the teachers as workers who were to process the raw material (the children) according to the specifications of the consumers (the society). It was all very neat. It was, as Callahan describes it in his history of this movement, a "cult of efficiency." Callahan writes, "The tragedy [of the efficiency movement] itself was fourfold: that educational questions were subordinated to business considerations; that administrators

---

[2] Ralph W. Tyler, *Basic Principles of Curriculum and Instruction* (Chicago: University of Chicago Press, 1950), p. 40.

[3] For a critical review of this movement in American education see Raymond Callahan, *Education and the Cult of Efficiency* (Chicago: University of Chicago Press, 1962).

were produced who were not, in any true sense, educators; that a scientific label was put on some very unscientific and dubious methods and practices; and that an anti-intellectual climate, already prevalent, was strengthened. As the business-industrial values and procedures spread into the thinking and acting of educators, countless educational decisions were made on economic or on non-educational grounds."[4] In spite of its tragic consequences, the professors of education sanctified the basic procedures and became preoccupied with ways of making it more refined and theoretically respectable. One such professor was Franklin Bobbitt, a professor of educational administration who worked at the University of Chicago from about 1913 through the 1920s. Bobbitt was one of the earliest curriculum theorists in the country, and in his book, *How To Make A Curriculum*[5] published in 1924, he outlines his basic assumptions about the process of developing a curriculum. Bobbitt writes, "The central theory [of curriculum] is simple. Human life, however varied, consists in the performance of specific activities. Education that prepares for life is one that prepares definitely and adequately for these specific activities. However numerous and diverse they may be for any social class, they can be discovered. This requires only that one go out into the world of affairs and discover the particulars of which these affairs consist. These will show the abilities, attitudes, habits, appreciations and forms of knowledge that men need. These will be the objectives of the curriculum. They will be numerous, definite and particularized. The curriculum will then be that series of experiences which children and youth must have by way of attaining those objectives."[6]

The "cult of efficiency" or the engineering movement in education that was salient during the 'teens and 20s was counteracted by those in the progressive movement whose conception of the child, of the teacher's role, and of the conditions that educate were essentially biological rather than industrial in character. The progressives rejected the prespecification of ends and the preoccupation with order. Furthermore, they were much more interested in the process of education than with its products. The children did not help either. Rather than being placid, inert matter that could be pressed into predetermined shapes, the children were spontaneous, unpredictable, ornery, sporadic, and did not fit the pattern of expectations and assumptions that the scientific managers held. The progressive movement both in education and in politics embraced a spirit and viewed human life in ways fundamentally different from those who sought to give education a managerial, "scientific" tone.

---

[4] Ibid., pp. 246-247.
[5] Franklin Bobbitt, *How to Make a Curriculum* (Boston: Houghton Mifflin, 1924).
[6] Ibid., p. 42.

As we all know, progressive education, too, was not without its critics. One of its major failings according to critics like Albert Lynd, Arthur Bestor, and James Koerner was that progressivism was chaotic. Progressive educators who tried to unlock the creative spirit of childhood ended up by being laissez-faire, mindless, and without purpose or direction. The corrective for this state of educational affairs came in the early 1950s with attempts to rationalize curriculum planning by once again formulating educational objectives that would restore a sense of order and purpose to schooling. During the 1950s, Ralph Tyler published his influential monograph, *Basic Principles of Curriculum and Instruction* in which educational objectives played an essential role, and it was in this period also that Bloom's *Taxonomy of Educational Objectives*[7] appeared.

Now each of these men, Tyler and Bloom, has rather generous views of education and talk about the importance of understanding and appreciation as educational goals. They were, and are now, concerned with educational objectives of a wide and general variety. But in the late 1950s a subtle but important shift from *educational* objectives, to *instructional* objectives, to finally *behavioral* objectives took place. This shift was due, in my view, to the entry into the educational field of people whose background and training was in military and industrial psychology. Once again there was a return to an industrial model with the consequence of confusing education with training. This military or industrial approach to teaching and learning is manifested in the prescriptions that are made to teachers and students preparing to become teachers to formulate specific behavioral objectives for each learning activity they formulate for students. Those making such recommendations apparently do not realize the enormity of such an exercise. An elementary school teacher working in a self-contained classroom who divided his class into three groups in an attempt to even partially deal with individual differences, who taught six subjects each day, and who had a different learning activity in each subject taught per day would need to formulate 90 behavioral objectives each week; 300 each month, and 3240 each academic year. Some educators have recognized the difficulty—dare I say the impossibility—of such a feat and have tried to resolve it by establishing a bank of objectives. It is now possible for teachers to *buy* their objectives from such a bank and thus avoid the task of formulating them for themselves!

The major issue amid all of the prescriptions concerning behavioral objectives is not an issue that rests merely upon determining the best techniques in curriculum development or teaching or evaluation. The major issue is one of educational values. Under the rug of technique lies an image

---

[7] Benjamin Bloom, et al., *Taxonomy of Educational Objectives: The Cognitive Domain* (New York: Longmans Green, 1956).

of man. The specificationists and behavioral engineers simply hold a view of education that differs in fundamental ways from those who think of teaching and learning as organic in character and who see discovery and surprise as central values to be sought for in educational practice.

Now where in all of this theory and history do I stand? What is my view of the place of objectives and accountability in art education?

First, I accept the idea that behavioral objectives can be useful in art education. What I object to is the failure to recognize their limitations and the consequential overemphasis of their importance. The major problem regarding objectives is to find out where they are useful, when they are useful, and for what purposes. I reject the views of enthusiasts who claim that the formulation of specific objectives is the single most important step in educational planning, and I reject those arguments that claim that any attempt to describe or predict what children are to learn is educationally misguided.

Does this position make me a middle-of-the-roader, an eclectic who sits on the fence? Am I a man without a country? I think not. What I have tried to do in my work[8,9,10] is to explicate the concept, "educational objectives," and to distinguish between three types of educational objectives in order to loosen and liberalize the ways in which teachers and curriculum developers can think about what they do in curriculum planning.

I said that I had distinguished between three types of educational objectives: What are they? The first type, that type called behavioral or instructional objectives, we are all familiar with. It is a statement that describes the specific behavior a student will be expected to perform in a particular content or material. For Ralph Tyler, the behavioral objective has three characteristics. First, it is a description of the student's behavior; it is not a description of what the teacher is to do. Second, the statement should contain not only a description of behavior, it should also identify the content in which the behavior is to be displayed. Third, the objective should be sufficiently specific so that it is possible to recognize the behavior if the student is able to display it. An example of a Tyler–type objective in art would be the following. The student will be able to use a potter's wheel and to construct the bowl at least five inches high having walls no thicker than ¾ of an inch. Robert Mager, whose brief book, *Preparing*

8 Elliot W. Eisner, "Educational Objectives: Help or Hindrance?," *School Review*, Vol. 75, No. 3 (Autumn 1967), pp. 250-266.

9 Elliot W. Eisner, "Instructional and Expressive Objectives: Their Formulation and Use in Curriculum," in W. James Popham, ed., *Instructional Objectives*, AERA Monograph Series on Curriculum Evaluation (Chicago: Rand McNally, 1969).

10 Elliot W. Eisner, "Emerging Models for Educational Evaluation," *School Review*, Vol. 80, No. 4 (August 1972), pp. 573-590.

Instructional Objectives,[11] has had such an impact in the field, goes further than Tyler in setting the conditions necessary for having behavioral objectives. Mager says that a "true" behavioral objective will contain a description of the conditions within which the student is to work, the operations he is to perform, and the criteria that will be used to determine whether or not he has been successful. For Mager, a behavioral objective should be stated like this: "Given a list of ten names of artists who worked during the 19th century, the student would be able to select the three out of the ten who were Impressionists within a two minute period."

Robert Gagne, an educational psychologist who, like Robert Mager, had a background in military and industrial psychology, is even more specific than Mager in stating that, "possibly the most fundamental reason of all for the central importance of defining educational objectives is that such definition makes possible the basic distinction between content and method. It is the defining of objectives that brings an essential clarity into the area of curriculum design and enables both educational planners and researchers to bring their practical knowledge to bear on the matter. As an example of the kind of clarification which results by defining content as 'descriptions of the expected capabilities of students,' the following may be noted. Once objectives have been defined, there is no step in curriculum design that can legitimately be entitled 'selecting content'."[12] What is important to note with respect to all three conceptions of objectives, but especially Mager's and Gagne's, is that the instructional or behavioral objective is designed to predict what the student will be able to do at the end of instruction. Effective teaching is therefore conceived of as enabling the young to achieve these expectations. Ideally at some period during the course or year, the student's behavior and the description used in the objectives will be isomorphic: there will be a perfect match between the two. If the teacher is teaching math and he operationalizes his objectives in an examination that is given to all students in his class, and if he has been effective, then all the students' answers will be alike. There will be no variance in performance. If a teacher is teaching spelling and he has been effective as a teacher of spelling, when a test is given to the class, then all of the students' answers will be spelled the same way—the correct way. The last thing a teacher of spelling wants is creative spellers!

Does the same situation hold for the teaching of art? Although a math or spelling teacher might often, but surely not always, want similarity of

---

[11] Robert Mager, *Preparing Instructional Objectives* (Palo Alto, Calif.: Feron Publishers, 1962).

[12] Robert Gagne, "Curriculum Research and the Promotion of Learning," in Ralph Tyler, Robert Gagne, and Michael Scriven, eds., *Perspectives of Curriculum Evaluation*, AERA Monograph 1 (Chicago: Rand McNally, 1967), pp. 21-22.

performance among students, the times in art when this is desired are limited. Few art teachers nowadays are interested in a class producing 35 yellow ducks. Yet, there are some tasks or skills on which a teacher of art might want uniform behavior from the students: the way one should stack a kiln, for example, or exercises dealing with certain procedures in weaving or techniques in painting. But these behaviors in art, when sought, are not the core of art education; they are its means. They are the means that one uses to get to what is really important, personal, and idiosyncratic in art.

With this in mind, I conceptualized a second type of objective, one that I call the *expressive objective* to complement—not replace—the instructional or behavioral objective.[13] The expressive objective is an outcome realized by the student after having engaged in an activity that was intended to generate a personal, idiosyncratic response. If we think for a moment about instructional objectives and instructional activities, we will see that the instructional activity is designed to yield predictable outcomes, outcomes that instructional objectives describe. The instructional objective is prescriptive, and the instructional activity is a prescription of what it will take to achieve it. The expressive activity is not prescriptive; it is evocative. It does not seek to anticipate what kind of particular response or product the student will produce. Instead, it aims at constructing an encounter, creating a setting, or forming a situation that will stimulate diverse and largely unanticipated responses and solutions from students. What students learn from such encounters become—post-facto—the expressive objective.

Some people say that if a teacher does not have objectives, he does not have any criteria for judging a student's development or his work. I think this objection results from confusing criteria with objectives. Critics of art, literature, music, dance, and poetry do not assign painters, writers, composers, dancers, and poets behavioral objectives. Yet critics lose no time evaluating their work. One does not have to have an objective in order to evaluate or appraise the quality of experience or of art. One can and does look backwards, as it were, not to see if artists realized specific objectives that were assigned in advance, but rather to determine what they did achieve. Indeed, art at its best enables both critics and artists to expand their criteria regarding the nature and quality of art. Some of the greatest art forms man has produced have been iconoclastic. They fit none of the criteria that existed at the time they were created. Dewey, writing in *Art As Experience* in 1934, had some relevant remarks in regard to relationship of criteria to standards. "If there are no standards for works of art and hence none for criticism (in the sense in which there are standards of

---

[13] Elliot W. Eisner, "Instructional and Expressive Objectives: Their Formulation and Use in Curriculum," op. cit.

measurement), there are nevertheless criteria in judgment, so that criticism does not fall in the field of mere impressionism. The discussion of form in relation to matter, of the meaning of medium in art, of the nature of the expressive object, has been an attempt on the part of the writer to discover some of these criteria. But such criteria are not rules or prescriptions. They are the result of an endeavor to find out what a work of art is as an experience: the kind of experience which constitutes it."[14]

The expressive objective is complementary to the instructional objective. The two are different in kind and rest on different educational assumptions. But the assumptions are not mutually exclusive. Within the same art program they can coexist.

But neither the prescriptiveness of instructional objectives nor the evocativeness of expressive objectives accounts for all that we attempt to do in art education. Think for a moment about the architect's task. The task that an architect encounters, like the task industrial designers encounter, can seldom be characterized by either instructional objectives or expressive objectives. The architect is most often assigned a problem that comes to him complete with high–level design constraints. His task is to take this problem and, within the constrains that accompany it, arrive at one or more solutions that provide a satisfying resolution. The architect or designer is not assigned both the problem and the solution and then merely functions as a technician or a draftsman. The client does not have a solution to give, although he believes he can recognize a good one if he sees it. The architect's objective is to conceive of ways in which the problem can be solved and to select the best solutions.[15]

This type of objective is significantly different from either the instructional objective or the expressive objective. In the instructional objective the teacher or test-maker knows in advance what the behavior, solution, or product is to be. In the expressive objective, not only is the answer not anticipated, the problem itself is not specified. A studio workshop that provides a setting for students to work in exploratory ways is one exemplification of such a situation. However, designers and architects and students in art classes are given problems that have high–level constraints, problems that are strictly set but which allow for an infinite number of possible solutions. I call objectives of this type "Type 3 Objectives" simply because I have not thought of a better name as yet.

When I was a student at the Institute of Design in Chicago, a school that was started by Maholy-Nagy and others who worked in the Bauhaus

---

[14] John Dewey, *Art as Experience* (New York: Minton, Balch and Company, 1934), p. 309.

[15] For an elaboration of this type of objective, see my article "Emerging Models of Educational Evaluation," *School Review,* op. cit.

in Germany before the Nazis closed it, we were given tasks that were based upon what I have called Type 3 Objectives. One such task was to take two sheets of manila paper, 9″ × 18″ in dimension, and to construct a structure using no other materials that would hold two bricks at least 12 inches off a table. Although the problem is a tough one, it can be solved, and the variety of solutions that students came up with were fascinating. The fact that some of the solutions were new to the instructor was not a problem. On the contrary, it was a delight, and it was apparent to all that some solutions were better than others.

Examples of Type 3 Objectives in art education are the following: build a clay structure using repetitive form that will convey a sense of loftiness to the viewer. Using water colors, acrylic, or tempera paints, create a surface that visually vibrates. Using a loom and wool thread, create a rug when laid on the floor looks as if it is convex. Using a piece of 24-inch wire, design a form that can be used to carry six empty milk bottles to the grocery.

In each of these examples, the design constraints are given, but the forms the solutions can take are, in principle, infinite. I believe that it is not only possible, but in general desirable to design art programs in such a way that each of these types of objectives is provided for. Given the distinctions between these three types of objectives, theoretical and empirical studies can be undertaken to find out if in fact they are used in art classes, to find out what emphasis on one rather than on another type means for effecting the character of the art curriculum, and to find out under what conditions each type is most appropriately used.

I have conceptualized expressive and Type 3 Objectives not only because they invite interesting research and stimulate more diversified curriculum development, but in order to counteract a tendency that I believe is growing in American education. That tendency is to view the school as a factory and the teacher as a worker concerned with producing products. The production or industrial model, as I have called it in previous writing, is strong in this country, and it manifests itself most often in the accountability movement. Those who view the school as producing products believe that the public school should know what it is getting for its investment. The school should pay off, and teachers should be held accountable for results. Furthermore, they argue that results should be demonstrable in the present and not at some unforseeable future. To know that results have been achieved, objectives must be stated in specific behavioral terms.

Now to a degree, the factory metaphor is useful; almost any root metaphor is useful for illuminating some aspect of schooling. Yet behavioral objectives enthusiasts believe the formation of behavioral objectives is the only way to properly design a curriculum and to evaluate its results. Those in state legislatures responsible for allocating large scale funds find this approach attractive since for many it fits their experience in business and industry and because it takes the complexity out of education. But the denial of complexity is the beginning of tyranny, in education as well as in politics. We can, I believe, convert our schools and programs of art education from institutions and programs concerned with education to ones concerned with training. But if we do this, it should be by choice, not by fuzzy thinking or by an unwillingness to recognize the scope and complexity of education.

We should be careful not to utilize doctrine or language that gives implicit and at times explicit endorsement to practices that are at the least questionable, which are clearly oversimplifications of what art education might be, and which can in fact be deleterious to students and teachers alike. When such unexamined and uncriticized doctrine is used in the education of students preparing to become teachers of art, it is yet another way of polluting the stream at its source.

What then am I suggesting? Am I suggesting that we should have no objectives, behavioral or otherwise, in art education? I am not. I am suggesting that we should act as responsible professionals in this field. We should not try to reduce a potentially rich, even noble, field within education for the sake of oversimplified administrative edicts. I am suggesting that because of such edicts the parameters of our educational responsibilities have expanded. We need to help those who have come out of military training programs and industrial management understand that being accountable is not the same as becoming an accountant and that education is not the same as training. In other words, we need to help them understand the nature of education and through such an understanding to appreciate the range, playfulness, and potential of the educational enterprise. If we can do this, rather than jumping on bandwagons, we will not only make a contribution to our own students, we will make a contribution to students and teachers throughout the country.

Editor

Ralph A. *Smith* did his undergraduate and graduate work at Columbia University and is currently a member of the Bureau of Educational Research and Department of Educational Policy Studies at the University of Illinois at Urbana-Champaign. His writings have appeared in such volumes as *The Teacher's Handbook, Accountability for Educational Results, Readings in the Humanities, Organizations and Human Behavior, Foundation Studies in Education, Challenges from the Future* (Japan), *and Papers on Educational Reform, Vol. IV.* Dr. Smith is also the editor of the *Journal of Aesthetic Education* and has recently edited *Aesthetic Concepts and Education* (1970) and *Aesthetics and Problems of Education* (1971).

Contributors

Michael W. Apple is an Associate Professor in the Department of Curriculum and Instruction at The University of Wisconsin, Madison. He has written numerous articles and monographs on such topics as ideology and curriculum thought, the hidden curriculum, and student rights. His most recent publications include *Educational Evaluation: Analysis and Responsibility* and the forthcoming *Schooling and the Rights of Children*.

Donald Arnstine is Professor of Education at the University of California, Davis. He has written several articles on the topic of teacher education, as well as a monograph for the ERIC Clearinghouse on Teacher Education. He has served as President of the Philosophy of Education Society and the John Dewey Society, and has taught at the University of Missouri-Kansas City, the University of Wisconsin, and Boston University. He is also the author of *Philosophy of Education: Learning and Schooling*.

J. Myron Atkin is Dean of the College of Education at the University of Illinois at Urbana-Champaign. He was co-director of the Elementary School Science Project, a course content improvement project supported by the National Science Foundation. The author of numerous articles and monographs, his current interests focus on governmental strategies for educational change, particularly actions that foster teacher-based initiatives. In recent years he has become known as a major critic of industrial models of education.

Harry S. Broudy is Emeritus Professor of Philosophy of Education at the University of Illinois at Urbana-Champaign. He is the author of several important volumes, including *Building a Philosophy of Education*, *Paradox and Promise*, *Democracy and Excellence in American Secondary Education* (with B. Othanel Smith and Joe R. Burnett), *Exemplars of Teaching Method* (with John Palmer), *Enlightened Cherishing: An Essay on Aesthetic Education*, and, most recently, *The Real World of the Public Schools*.

Walter H. Clark, Jr. teaches in the English Department at the University of Michigan. His major interests are in the theory of criticism and philosophy of aesthetic education, and he has written numerous articles and reviews in these areas, including chapters in Jane Roland Martin, ed., *Readings in the Philosophy of Curriculum*; and R. A. Smith, ed., *Aesthetic Concepts and Education*.

Elliot W. Eisner is Professor of Education and Art at Stanford University. Active in both the fields of curriculum theory and art education, he has edited *Readings in Art Education* (with David W. Ecker) and *Confronting Curriculum Reform*, and he is the author of *Educating Artistic Vision*. He has received the O. Johnson Memorial Award from the American Educational Research Association and was a Guggenheim Fellow during 1969-70.

Maxine Greene is Professor of English and Educational Philosophy at Teachers College, Columbia University, where she has taught since 1965. Editor of the *Teachers College Record* from 1965 to 1970, she is a past president of both the Philosophy of Education Society and the American Educational Studies Association, and has held official positions with the John Dewey Society and the American Educational Research Association. A multidisciplinary person, she has written *The Public School and the Private Vision, Existential Encounters for Teachers,* and *Teacher as Stranger.*

Ernest R. House is a member of the Center for Instructional Research and Curriculum Evaluation (CIRE) at the University of Illinois at Urbana-Champaign. In 1967, Professor House directed an evaluation of the state-wide gifted program in Illinois, the findings of which have been used both as a model for many later evaluation projects and as a basis for designing the federal gifted program. In addition to numerous articles, papers, and evaluation reports that he has written, he has edited *School Evaluation: The Politics and Process.*

Mauritz Johnson has been engaged in teacher education since 1953, when he joined the faculty of State University of New York at Albany. Between 1960 and 1968 he was on the faculty of Cornell University serving as director of the Ford Foundation-supported junior high school teacher education project and later as field services coordinator, department head, and dean of the School of Education. Subsequently, he returned to SUNY at Albany, where he is currently a professor in the Department of Curriculum and Instruction. He is the coauthor of *Junior High School Guidance* and *The Teacher in Curriculum Making,* and author of *American Secondary Schools.*

Martin Levit is Professor of Education and Philosophy at the University of Missouri-Kansas City. He has taught at several universities in this country and in Europe and is a past president of the Philosophy of Education Society. He has written numerous articles on the philosophical and social foundations of education, and has authored *The Role of the School in American Society* (with V. T. Thayer). He is also the editor of two volumes, *Curriculum,* and *Philosophy of Science and Problems of Education,* from the Philosophy of Education series.

Paul Nash is Professor of Education in the Department of Humanistic and Behavioral Foundations of Education at Boston University. He has taught at several universities in this country and abroad and is a past president of both the History of Education Society and the American Educational Studies Association. He has written *Authority and Freedom in Education* and edited *The Educated Man, History and Education, Culture and the State: Matthew Arnold and Continental Education,* and *Models of Man.*

Frederick C. Neff is a professor in the Division of Theoretical and Behavioral Foundations of Education at Wayne State University. He has been visiting professor at several universities in this country and Canada and has written *Philosophy and American Education, The Dewey Tradition and the American*

Scene, and numerous articles for educational journals. In 1973 he received the Distinguished Achievement Award for Excellence in Educational Journalism, presented by the Educational Press Association of America.

Hugh G. Petrie is Associate Professor of the Philosophy of Education at the University of Illinois at Urbana-Champaign. His major interests lie in the methodology and philosophy of educational research. In particular he has written on the relation of theory to observation and the thesis that one's acceptance of a theory implicitly structures the facts that can be observed under that theory. Other related interests include work in the epistemology of interdisciplinary inquiry and the problems of intelligence testing in education. He is also working on feedback models of learning and action.

Frederick A. Rodgers is Associate Professor of Elementary and Early Childhood Education at the University of Illinois at Urbana-Champaign. He has been involved in numerous professional activities, including, while at New York University, the directorship of the Teacher Corps and the NYU–College of the Virgin Islands Teacher Education Project; membership for three years in the Leadership Training Institute for the Development of Protocol and Training Materials for Teacher Education; and director of the University of Illinois Alternate Teacher Education Program. His research interests include teacher education, social studies, policy in curriculum development, and research and development problems of schools.

Philip G. Smith is chairman, Department of History and Philosophy of Education, Indiana University. He is a member of the American Philosophical Association, the American Educational Research Association, and a past president of the Philosophy of Education Society. He has written numerous articles and books in the field of education, including *Philosophical Mindedness in Educational Administration, Reflective Thinking: The Method of Education,* and *Philosophy of Education.*

Leonard J. Waks received his Ph.D. in philosophy from the University of Wisconsin. He has taught philosophy at Purdue and Stanford, and is currently Associate Professor of Education at Temple University. His interests include educational planning and evaluation and innovative curricula, and he has published several articles on these topics. He is also a member of the board of editors of *Studies in Philosophy and Education.*

Arthur G. Wirth is Professor of History and Philosophy of Education at Washington University. A writer and editor, he has authored *John Dewey as Educator* and *Education in the Technological Society,* and he has edited the John Dewey Society Lecture Series and the Society's Monographs in Educational Theory. In 1973 he was honored by the Research Division of the American Federation of Teachers for his report "An Inquiry-Personal Commitment Model of Teacher Education," discussed in his essay in this volume.